The Distressed Hotel Blueprint

A Comprehensive Guide to Navigating Distressed Hotel Assets

Guidance Hotel Solutions
Stephen Nalley and Kent Hricko

About the Authors

Stephen Nalley is an accomplished real estate executive, entrepreneur, veteran, and author with over 20 years of experience in the hospitality and real estate industry. As the Founder and CEO of Black Briar Advisors, a full-service real estate investment company specializing in the acquisition, repositioning, and turnaround of distressed real estate assets, Stephen has participated in the ownership of over 100 hotel and resort assets and has managed over $2 billion worth of distressed real estate assets. His expertise extends to transforming underperforming properties into thriving ventures, earning him a reputation as a leader in the industry.

Before embarking on his professional career, Stephen served in the United States Army as a Light Infantry Squad Leader with the elite 10th Mountain Division and the 2145th in the US Army Reserves. His military experience instilled in him a sense of discipline, resilience, and strategic thinking, which have been instrumental in his success in the real estate sector. Stephen holds a Bachelor of Science Degree in Healthcare Administration from the University of North Florida, an MBA and Doctorate in Business Administration from the University of Atlanta, and a Law Degree from the University of Washington School of Law. He is also a Certified Hotel Administrator through the American Hotel & Lodging Association and is an active member of the Forbes Business Council, as well as a writer for the Entrepreneur Leadership Network.

As an author, Stephen wrote the best-selling book "The Ultimate Guide to Managing Distressed Hotel Assets," which has become a valuable resource for investors, asset managers, and industry professionals seeking to navigate the complexities of distressed real estate assets.

Kent Hricko is a seasoned real estate executive with over 20 years of experience and a proven track record in the hospitality sector, having transacted over $2 billion worth of real estate deals. Kent began his career at CNL Hospitality Corp as a financial analyst, gaining valuable experience in the underwriting of hospitality assets. He later joined Ocean Waters Development, where he oversaw investment activities, including acquisitions, dispositions, and financing, completing over 120 individual real estate transactions valued at more than $750 million and an additional $500 million in financings.

In 2012, Kent joined Marcus & Millichap, where he led the Orlando hotel brokerage division. By 2019, he co-founded Guidance Hotel Group with Grizzard Commercial Real Estate, focusing on providing industry-leading marketing, technology, and experience in the strategic acquisition and disposition of hotel assets. His extensive experience has made him a trusted advisor in the hotel brokerage space, helping clients grow wealth through targeted investment strategies.

Together, Stephen Nalley and Kent Hricko bring decades of hands-on experience, knowledge, and a deep understanding of the challenges and opportunities within the distressed hotel sector. They first met at a hospitality conference over a decade ago, where they discovered their shared passion for revitalizing distressed assets and commitment to excellence in hotel asset management. Their partnership, combining Stephen's expertise in asset management and repositioning distressed properties with Kent's vast experience in hotel investment, brokerage, and finance, led to the formation of Global Hotel Solutions.

As managing partners of Global Hotel Solutions, they have guided numerous hotels through the intricate process of turnaround, repositioning, and eventual profitability. Their combined experience and insights have shaped "The Distressed Hotel Blueprint: A Comprehensive Guide to Navigating Distressed Hotel Assets," a book that serves as a definitive guide for anyone seeking to navigate the challenges of distressed hotel management, offering practical strategies, case studies, and actionable steps drawn from their real-world experience in the hospitality industry.

Preface

"The Distressed Hotel Blueprint: A Comprehensive Guide to Navigating Distressed Hotel Assets" was created to serve as a definitive guide for hotel owners, operators, investors, and industry professionals facing the daunting challenge of managing distressed hotel properties. In an ever-evolving hospitality landscape, distress is a reality that many hotel assets face due to economic downturns, mismanagement, or shifts in market dynamics. This book aims to demystify the complexities of distress, offering actionable insights, proven strategies, and real-world case studies to help you navigate this journey with confidence and clarity.

Our goal is to equip you with the knowledge and tools necessary to transform a distressed hotel into a thriving, profitable asset. We recognize that each hotel's situation is unique, and that's why this guide covers every aspect of the turnaround process, from identifying the early signs of distress to executing a successful recovery plan and ensuring long-term profitability.

Here's a comprehensive overview of what you can expect from the 11 chapters of this book and the key takeaways you'll gain along the way:

Chapter 1: Understanding Distressed Hotels lays the foundation by introducing the concept of distressed hotels. You'll learn how to identify the common causes and signs of distress, understand the impact on stakeholders, and recognize the opportunities that distressed assets can offer. This chapter provides a clear understanding of what it means for a hotel to be distressed, allowing you to assess whether an asset is truly in need of turnaround or simply requires strategic adjustments.

Chapter 2: Analyzing Distressed Hotels focuses on conducting a detailed analysis of distressed properties. You'll gain insights into operational, financial, and market analyses, enabling you to pinpoint the root causes of distress. This chapter emphasizes the importance of thorough due diligence and offers guidance on how to evaluate a hotel's financial health, operational efficiency, and market position, ensuring you have a complete understanding of the asset's challenges and opportunities.

Chapter 3: Creating a Turnaround Plan for Distressed Hotels guides you through the process of developing a comprehensive turnaround plan. This chapter covers establishing clear goals, implementing operational improvements, and developing a financial restructuring plan. It offers actionable strategies for engaging stakeholders and building a roadmap for recovery, ensuring you have a structured approach to revitalizing your distressed property.

Chapter 4: Repositioning Distressed Hotels explores the strategies for repositioning a distressed hotel to attract a new target market and improve profitability. You'll learn how to identify repositioning opportunities, develop a compelling brand identity, plan renovations, and align operations with the new vision. This chapter provides practical tips on how to effectively execute a repositioning plan that resonates with your desired audience.

Chapter 5: Bank Workouts for Distressed Hotels delves into the process of collaborating with lenders to resolve financial distress. You'll understand the different types of bank workouts, learn how to negotiate with lenders, and explore alternatives to bank workouts. This chapter offers valuable insights into managing lender relationships and navigating the complexities of financial restructuring, helping you find a path forward when faced with financial challenges.

Chapter 6: Financing Options for Distressed Hotels presents a range of financing options available to support turnaround efforts, including traditional loans, government programs, private equity, mezzanine financing, and crowdfunding. This chapter provides guidance on selecting the right financing option based on your hotel's needs, and shares practical tips on how to secure funding for renovations and improvements, ensuring you have the capital necessary for a successful turnaround.

Chapter 7: Disposition and Sale of Distressed Hotels provides a comprehensive guide to selling or disposing of a distressed hotel. You'll learn how to prepare the hotel for sale, market the asset effectively, negotiate offers, and close the sale successfully. This chapter also covers the lessons learned from hotel dispositions, offering insights into how to maximize value and manage the complexities of a sale process.

Chapter 8: Bankruptcy for Distressed Hotels offers a detailed exploration of the bankruptcy process and provides strategies for navigating bankruptcy proceedings. You'll understand the differences between Chapter 11 and Chapter 7 bankruptcy, learn how to operate a hotel during bankruptcy, and discover ways to emerge from bankruptcy stronger. This chapter equips you with the knowledge to make informed decisions should your hotel face this challenging scenario.

Chapter 9: Receivership for Distressed Hotels explains the receivership process and its implications for distressed hotels. You'll gain insights into how to operate a hotel under receivership, work with professional advisors, and develop exit strategies. This chapter offers practical guidance on navigating the legal complexities of receivership, ensuring you can manage the process effectively and maintain operational stability.

Chapter 10: Asset Management of Distressed Hotels emphasizes the importance of effective asset management in ensuring long-term success. You'll learn about implementing revenue management strategies, controlling costs, planning capital improvements, and monitoring performance. This chapter provides actionable steps for maximizing the value of your hotel asset, ensuring you're equipped to drive profitability and maintain operational excellence.

Chapter 11: Building a Sustainable Future for Distressed Hotels brings together all the insights from previous chapters to help you develop a sustainable growth strategy. You'll learn how to foster a culture of continuous improvement, implement risk management practices, and prepare for market changes. This chapter provides a blueprint for achieving long-term success and stability, ensuring that your hotel not only recovers but thrives in a competitive market.

Throughout this book, you'll find case studies and real-life examples that illustrate the principles and strategies discussed, offering practical insights into how others have successfully turned around distressed hotel assets. These examples serve as inspiration and guidance, demonstrating that even the most challenging situations can be overcome with the right approach and mindset.

As you journey through "The Distressed Hotel Blueprint," you'll gain a deep understanding of the complexities involved in managing distressed hotel assets, along with actionable strategies for overcoming obstacles and seizing opportunities. Whether you're an experienced hotel owner, a new investor, or a hospitality professional, this book will provide you with the knowledge, tools, and confidence to navigate the challenges of distressed hotels and transform them into thriving, profitable ventures.

We invite you to use this guide as your roadmap to success, drawing from the insights and strategies presented to build a brighter, more sustainable future for your hotel assets.

Table of Contents

Page Left Blank Intentionally

Chapter 1
Understanding Distressed Hotels

Understanding distressed hotels is the first step toward successfully navigating the complex process of revitalizing a struggling property. Distressed hotels face significant operational, financial, or market challenges that threaten their profitability and long-term sustainability. These challenges can stem from a variety of factors, including declining revenues, rising expenses, mismanagement, changes in market conditions, or excessive debt burdens. When left unaddressed, these issues can escalate, turning a once-thriving hotel into a distressed asset. This chapter aims to provide a comprehensive understanding of what constitutes a distressed hotel, helping you recognize the early warning signs, identify the root causes of distress, and distinguish between temporary setbacks and long-term failures.

A distressed hotel isn't always obvious at first glance. While some hotels may show visible signs of neglect, such as poor maintenance, low occupancy, or outdated amenities, others may suffer from less apparent issues, such as financial mismanagement, poor marketing strategies, or an inability to adapt to changing guest preferences. Understanding the full scope of what makes a hotel distressed requires a deeper analysis of its financial health, operational efficiency, market positioning, and the external factors that influence its performance.

The causes of distress are often multifaceted, with economic downturns, shifts in market demand, intense competition, and ineffective management practices all playing a role. For example, a hotel located in a once-thriving business district may experience a sudden drop in demand due to a recession or changes in corporate travel trends. Alternatively, poor management decisions, such as overleveraging debt or neglecting essential maintenance, can lead to a downward spiral that's difficult to reverse. By exploring these various factors, this chapter will help you gain insight into the common pitfalls that lead to distress and how to recognize them before they become insurmountable challenges.

Recognizing the difference between short-term distress and long-term failure is crucial for developing an effective turnaround strategy. Not all hotels facing temporary setbacks, such as seasonal dips in occupancy or fluctuations in local demand, are destined for failure. However, hotels experiencing chronic issues, such as sustained financial losses, declining market share, or an inability to meet debt obligations, may be at risk of long-term failure. By understanding the characteristics that define each scenario, you can make informed decisions about the level of intervention required to restore a hotel to profitability.

In this chapter, we will also explore real-life examples of distressed hotels, offering valuable insights into how different factors contribute to their struggles. These case studies will highlight the impact of external market conditions, poor management decisions, and operational inefficiencies on a hotel's performance, demonstrating the complexities of distress in the hospitality industry. By learning from these examples, you will be better equipped to recognize the warning signs and develop strategies to prevent similar challenges from arising in your own hotel operations.

Ultimately, understanding distressed hotels is about more than identifying problems; it's about recognizing the opportunities that exist within these challenges. By gaining a clear understanding of what constitutes a distressed hotel, why distress occurs, and how to identify the signs early, you will be well-prepared to navigate the process of revitalizing a struggling property. This knowledge will serve as the foundation for developing targeted solutions and implementing effective strategies to restore profitability, enhance guest experiences, and position the hotel for long-term success.

Defining a Distressed Hotel

A distressed hotel is a property that is struggling to maintain profitability, often facing significant operational, financial, or market-related challenges. These challenges can manifest in various ways, such as declining occupancy rates, deteriorating guest experiences, financial losses, or a failure to keep up with market trends. Understanding what constitutes a distressed hotel is crucial for identifying early warning signs, addressing the root causes of distress, and developing a comprehensive turnaround plan.

What is a Distressed Hotel?

A distressed hotel is characterized by its inability to operate profitably, often resulting from a combination of internal inefficiencies and external pressures. Such hotels may suffer from dwindling revenues, excessive operational costs, outdated amenities, or an unsustainable debt load. This distress can emerge due to various reasons, including poor management practices, market shifts, economic downturns, or intense competition. Distressed hotels often struggle to cover their operating expenses, service debt obligations, or generate positive cash flow, making it challenging to sustain long-term viability.

It's important to recognize that not all distressed hotels are on the brink of closure. Some may experience temporary setbacks due to seasonal fluctuations or unexpected market changes, while others may face deeper, systemic issues that require significant intervention. The key to defining a distressed hotel lies in assessing its overall financial health, operational efficiency, and ability to adapt to market conditions.

Practical Example: A hotel situated in a once-busy business district began experiencing distress when several major corporations relocated, reducing demand for business travel accommodations. As a result, the hotel's occupancy rates dropped, and its revenue declined, making it difficult to cover operational costs and debt payments. This situation exemplifies how external factors, such as changes in the local economy, can lead to distress.

Common Signs and Symptoms of Distress

Identifying the signs and symptoms of distress early is essential for preventing long-term failure and implementing effective turnaround strategies.

Common indicators of a distressed hotel include:

- Declining Occupancy Rates: One of the most visible signs of distress is a consistent decline in occupancy rates, which can signal a lack of demand, poor marketing, or operational inefficiencies.

- Reduced Average Daily Rate (ADR) and Revenue per Available Room (RevPAR): Distressed hotels often struggle to maintain competitive pricing, leading to reduced ADR and RevPAR. This decline indicates the hotel's inability to attract guests at profitable rates.

- Negative Guest Feedback: Frequent complaints, negative reviews, or declining guest satisfaction scores are red flags indicating operational or service-related issues. These can damage the hotel's reputation and further exacerbate distress.

- High Employee Turnover: High turnover rates suggest problems with management, employee dissatisfaction, or inadequate training, all of which contribute to operational inefficiencies and declining service quality.

- Cash Flow Problems: Difficulty meeting financial obligations, such as paying vendors, servicing debt, or covering payroll, is a clear sign of financial distress.

- Deferred Maintenance: Neglected maintenance or outdated facilities can indicate that a hotel lacks the financial resources to invest in necessary improvements, leading to further declines in guest satisfaction.

Actionable Step: Regularly monitor key performance indicators (KPIs) such as occupancy rates, ADR, RevPAR, and guest satisfaction scores to identify potential signs of distress early. Implement a system for tracking guest feedback and reviews to quickly address any issues that may arise.

Differences Between Short-Term Distress and Long-Term Failure

It's crucial to differentiate between short-term distress and long-term failure to determine the appropriate course of action. Short-term distress may be caused by temporary factors, such as seasonal fluctuations, one-time operational setbacks, or market disruptions. In these cases, the hotel may recover once the external pressures subside or operational inefficiencies are addressed.

Short-Term Distress Characteristics:

- Temporary drops in occupancy due to seasonality or events

- Minor cash flow issues resulting from unexpected expenses

- Operational inefficiencies that can be quickly corrected

Long-Term Failure Characteristics:

- Chronic financial losses over multiple quarters

- Inability to service debt or meet financial obligations

- Deteriorating guest experiences and reputation

- Structural or systemic issues, such as outdated facilities or ineffective management

Practical Example: A beachfront hotel experienced short-term distress due to a hurricane, which led to a temporary decline in tourist arrivals. However, the hotel quickly recovered after implementing a targeted marketing campaign to attract guests once the weather improved. In contrast, a city-center hotel faced long-term failure due to ongoing mismanagement, outdated amenities, and a lack of competitive positioning, resulting in sustained financial losses over several years.

Actionable Step: Conduct regular financial and operational assessments to determine whether distress is temporary or indicative of deeper, long-term issues. For short-term distress, implement quick fixes, such as targeted marketing campaigns or operational adjustments. For long-term failure,

develop a comprehensive turnaround strategy that addresses systemic challenges.
Real-Life Examples of Distressed Hotels

To understand the complexities of distress, it's helpful to examine real-life examples that highlight how different factors contribute to a hotel's struggles.

Case Study 1: Luxury Hotel Facing Financial Mismanagement

A luxury hotel located in a prime tourist destination struggled with financial distress despite high occupancy rates. Upon investigation, it was discovered that the hotel's operational costs were excessively high due to poor financial management practices, such as overstaffing, inefficient procurement processes, and unnecessary expenses on luxury amenities. By conducting a thorough financial audit and implementing cost-saving measures, such as renegotiating vendor contracts and optimizing staffing levels, the hotel successfully reduced its operating expenses and returned to profitability.

Case Study 2: Mid-Tier Hotel Impacted by Market Conditions

A mid-tier hotel in a suburban area experienced declining occupancy rates due to increased competition from nearby branded hotels. The hotel's management failed to adapt to changing market conditions, resulting in outdated marketing strategies and a lack of differentiation. As a result, the hotel lost market share and struggled to remain profitable. A market repositioning strategy, including renovations, targeted marketing, and the introduction of unique amenities, helped the hotel regain its competitive edge and improve its financial performance.

Actionable Step: Analyze case studies of distressed hotels to identify common themes and challenges. Apply the lessons learned to your own hotel operations to avoid similar pitfalls and implement effective turnaround strategies.

The Impact of Market Conditions on Distress

Market conditions play a significant role in influencing hotel distress. Economic downturns, changes in travel trends, increased competition, or shifts in demand can all contribute to a hotel's challenges.

Economic Downturns: Recessions or economic slowdowns can lead to reduced discretionary spending, causing a decline in leisure travel and business bookings. This decrease in demand can severely impact hotels, especially those that rely heavily on corporate or high-spending leisure travelers.

Changing Travel Trends: Shifts in traveler preferences, such as the rise of alternative accommodations like Airbnb or increased demand for eco-friendly lodging, can affect a hotel's ability to attract guests. Hotels that fail to adapt to these trends may experience declining occupancy rates and revenues.

Increased Competition: The entry of new hotels or

branded properties into the market can create intense competition, making it difficult for independent or outdated hotels to compete effectively.

Actionable Step: Stay informed about market trends, economic forecasts, and competitor activity to anticipate potential challenges. Adjust your hotel's marketing, pricing, and service strategies to remain competitive and adapt to changing market conditions.

The Role of Management in Hotel Distress

Management plays a critical role in either preventing or exacerbating hotel distress. Effective management can identify issues early, implement corrective measures, and guide the hotel toward recovery. Conversely, poor management practices can lead to financial mismanagement, operational inefficiencies, and a decline in guest satisfaction, contributing to distress.

Common Management Pitfalls:

- Ineffective Leadership: Lack of experience, vision, or strategic planning can result in poor decision-making and an inability to respond to market changes.

- Poor Financial Oversight: Failing to monitor expenses, manage budgets, or control cash flow can lead to financial instability and debt accumulation.

- Neglecting Guest Experience: Ignoring guest feedback, cutting corners on service quality, or failing to invest in property upgrades can damage the hotel's reputation and drive away repeat business.

Case Study: A boutique hotel faced declining occupancy rates and revenue due to ineffective management practices, including inconsistent service quality, poor marketing strategies, and a lack of financial oversight. After hiring an experienced general manager who implemented a comprehensive turnaround plan focusing on staff training, cost control, and targeted marketing, the hotel improved guest satisfaction, regained market share, and returned to profitability.

Actionable Step: Evaluate your management team's strengths and weaknesses, and provide training or mentorship where needed. Consider hiring experienced professionals with a track record of turning around distressed hotels to guide your property through the recovery process.

Defining a distressed hotel involves recognizing the complex factors that contribute to financial instability, operational inefficiencies, and declining guest experiences. By understanding the common signs and symptoms of distress, differentiating between short-term setbacks and long-term failure, and analyzing real-life examples, hotel owners and managers can identify distress early and implement effective strategies to address the root causes. Recognizing the impact of market conditions and the critical role of management in either exacerbating or alleviating distress is essential for developing a comprehensive turnaround plan. Armed with this knowledge, you will be better equipped to navigate the challenges of distressed hotels and create a path to recovery and long-term success.

Causes of Distress

Understanding the causes of distress in the hotel industry is essential for identifying solutions that can prevent or reverse the decline of a property. Distress often arises from a combination of external economic factors, internal operational challenges, and ineffective management practices. In this section, we will explore the key causes of distress, using in-depth analysis, practical examples, case studies, and actionable steps to highlight how hotels can avoid or address these challenges.

1. Economic Downturns and Market Shifts

One of the most significant external factors that contribute to hotel distress is an economic downturn or sudden market shift. Economic recessions, regional crises, or changes in travel trends can lead to a dramatic decline in hotel bookings and revenues, pushing properties into distress.

Impact of Economic Downturns:

- During a recession, both business and leisure travelers cut back on expenses, leading to reduced demand for hotel rooms. Corporate travel budgets are often the first to be slashed, and families may postpone vacations.
- International events, such as pandemics, political instability, or natural disasters, can

severely impact tourism and business travel, resulting in occupancy declines.

Practical Example: The COVID-19 pandemic caused a sudden and unprecedented drop in hotel demand worldwide, leading to widespread distress. Many hotels faced months of low or no occupancy, forcing them to cut costs, furlough staff, or temporarily close.

Actionable Step: To mitigate the impact of economic downturns, diversify your hotel's target markets to reduce reliance on a single segment. Consider marketing to local travelers, offering staycation packages, or adjusting pricing strategies to attract new guests during periods of low demand.

2. Mismanagement and Operational Inefficiencies

Ineffective management practices and operational inefficiencies can quickly push a hotel into distress. These internal factors often stem from poor decision-making, lack of experience, or inadequate oversight, leading to high operating costs, declining service quality, and a negative guest experience.

Signs of Mismanagement and Inefficiencies:

- High employee turnover due to poor leadership or inadequate training

- Excessive labor costs resulting from overstaffing or inefficient scheduling
- Inconsistent service quality, leading to negative guest reviews

- Failure to implement cost-saving measures, such as energy-efficient practices or inventory management

Case Study: A mid-range hotel located near a convention center experienced distress due to mismanagement. The general manager lacked experience in revenue management and failed to adjust pricing strategies during low-demand periods, resulting in consistently low occupancy rates. Additionally, the hotel's housekeeping department was overstaffed, leading to unnecessary labor expenses. After conducting an operational audit and hiring an experienced hotel manager, the hotel implemented efficient staffing schedules, adjusted pricing strategies, and improved guest service, resulting in a significant turnaround.

Actionable Step: Conduct regular operational audits to identify inefficiencies in staffing, service delivery, and resource allocation. Invest in training programs for managers and staff to ensure that your team has the skills and knowledge to operate efficiently.

3. Poor Marketing and Branding Strategies

Marketing and branding play a crucial role in attracting guests and building a hotel's reputation. However, many distressed hotels suffer from outdated marketing strategies, inconsistent branding, or a failure to adapt to changing market trends.

Consequences of Poor Marketing:

- Inadequate online presence, leading to reduced

visibility and fewer direct bookings

- Outdated branding that fails to resonate with target guests

- Failure to engage with guests on social media or respond to online reviews

- Ineffective promotions or pricing strategies that do not attract the desired market segments

Practical Example: A boutique hotel in a popular tourist destination struggled with low occupancy rates despite its prime location. Upon analysis, it was discovered that the hotel's website was outdated, lacked mobile responsiveness, and failed to highlight the unique features of the property. By investing in a modern website, optimizing for search engines, and launching targeted social media campaigns, the hotel increased its direct bookings by 40% within six months.

Actionable Step: Conduct a marketing audit to evaluate your hotel's online presence, branding, and messaging. Ensure that your website is user-friendly, mobile-responsive, and optimized for search engines. Regularly engage with guests on social media, respond to reviews, and promote your hotel's unique selling points.

4. High Levels of Debt and Financial Mismanagement

Financial distress often results from high levels of debt, poor financial planning, or mismanagement of cash flow. Hotels with excessive debt burdens may struggle to meet loan payments, especially during periods of low occupancy or reduced revenue.

Signs of Financial Mismanagement:

- Inability to service debt or meet financial obligations

- High-interest expenses that eat into profit margins

- Inadequate cash flow management, leading to delays in paying vendors or employees

- Overleveraging during property acquisitions or renovations

Case Study: A luxury hotel in a metropolitan area took on substantial debt to finance a major renovation, expecting increased revenue to cover the loan payments. However, the hotel faced a drop in demand due to a market downturn, making it impossible to meet its debt obligations. The hotel's management worked with financial advisors to restructure the debt, negotiated with lenders for more favorable terms, and implemented cost-saving measures, ultimately preventing bankruptcy.

Actionable Step: Regularly review your hotel's financial statements, debt obligations, and cash flow to identify potential issues early. Avoid overleveraging and maintain a cash reserve to navigate periods of reduced revenue. Work with financial experts to develop a debt management strategy that aligns with your hotel's revenue projections.

5. Competition and Changing Guest Preferences

The hospitality industry is highly competitive, and hotels must adapt to changing guest preferences to remain relevant. Failure to differentiate your property, keep up with amenities offered by competitors, or address evolving traveler expectations can lead to distress.

Common Challenges from Competition:

- New hotels entering the market with modern amenities and technology

- The rise of alternative accommodations, such as Airbnb, attracting budget-conscious or experience-focused travelers

- Guests demanding personalized experiences, sustainability, or wellness amenities

Practical Example: A well-established hotel in a busy downtown area began losing market share to newer properties with modern amenities and tech-savvy guest experiences. Recognizing the shift in guest preferences, the hotel invested in smart room technology, upgraded its fitness center, and introduced eco-friendly initiatives. These changes helped the hotel regain its competitive edge and attract a new segment of environmentally conscious travelers.

Actionable Step: Regularly conduct competitor analysis to identify trends and gaps in your offerings. Stay updated on traveler preferences through market research and guest feedback, and be willing to invest in upgrades or changes that align with current demand.

Case Study: A Luxury Hotel that Fell into Distress Due to Poor Financial Management

Background: A luxury hotel located in an upscale urban neighborhood enjoyed years of success, with high occupancy rates and strong revenue. However, financial mismanagement led to a rapid decline in performance. The hotel's management had taken on significant debt to finance an expansion project, expecting increased revenues to offset the cost. Unfortunately, an economic downturn led to reduced demand, and the hotel struggled to meet its debt obligations.

Challenges Faced:

- High debt payments and interest expenses put pressure on cash flow.

- Operational inefficiencies, such as overstaffing and excessive spending on amenities, increased costs.

- The hotel's marketing efforts were outdated, failing to attract new guests or maintain loyalty among existing ones.

Actionable Steps Taken:

- Debt Restructuring: The hotel's management worked with financial advisors to negotiate with lenders, securing more favorable terms and reducing monthly payments.

- Operational Audit: An operational audit revealed areas of inefficiency, leading to a reduction in unnecessary expenses and optimization of staffing levels.

- Targeted Marketing Campaign: The hotel rebranded itself as an exclusive urban retreat, focusing on personalized experiences and luxury amenities. A new website, social media engagement, and partnerships with local influencers helped attract a high-end clientele.

Outcome: Within 18 months, the hotel achieved a 25% increase in occupancy rates, reduced operational costs by 15%, and successfully regained profitability.

Hotels can fall into distress due to a variety of causes, including economic downturns, mismanagement, poor marketing strategies, financial mismanagement, and increased competition. Recognizing and addressing these challenges early can prevent long-term damage and create opportunities for recovery and growth. By conducting regular audits, staying attuned to market trends, maintaining sound financial practices, and adapting to changing guest preferences, hotel owners and managers can proactively address the causes of distress and develop strategies to achieve profitability and long-term success. The case study of the luxury hotel illustrates how even high-end properties can face distress due to financial mismanagement, but with the right actions and strategies, a successful turnaround is possible.

Identifying Distressed Hotels in the Market

Recognizing distressed hotels in the market is a crucial step for investors, operators, and stakeholders who seek to either rescue a struggling asset or capitalize on an opportunity to acquire a property with turnaround potential. Identifying these distressed assets involves analyzing key financial indicators, spotting operational red flags, utilizing industry reports, leveraging technology, and working closely with brokers and industry contacts. This section provides an in-depth analysis of how to identify distressed hotels, supported by practical examples, actionable steps, and a case study of an investor who successfully identified a distressed hotel opportunity.

Key Financial Indicators of Distress

Financial indicators are often the first and most reliable signs of a distressed hotel. By examining key metrics, investors and stakeholders can identify properties that may be struggling to maintain profitability. The most important financial indicators to monitor include:

- Occupancy Rates: A consistently low occupancy rate suggests that a hotel is not attracting enough guests, indicating potential distress. While seasonal fluctuations are normal, a year-over-year decline in occupancy can be a red flag.

- Practical Example: A hotel with an average occupancy rate of 40% in a market where competitors maintain 70% occupancy is likely experiencing distress. This discrepancy suggests issues with marketing, pricing, or operational inefficiencies.

- Average Daily Rate (ADR): The ADR reflects the average revenue earned per occupied room. A declining ADR could indicate that a hotel is struggling to maintain its pricing power, often due to increased competition, poor marketing, or a lack of value perceived by guests.

- Actionable Step: Compare the hotel's ADR to the market average or competitors in the same area. If the hotel's ADR is significantly lower, it may be an indicator of distress.

- Revenue per Available Room (RevPAR): RevPAR combines occupancy rates and ADR to provide a comprehensive view of a hotel's revenue performance. A declining RevPAR indicates that a hotel is facing both demand and pricing challenges.

- Case Study Example: A hotel in a popular tourist destination experienced a drop in RevPAR over several consecutive quarters. Further investigation revealed that the property had not invested in renovations for over a decade, leading to declining guest satisfaction and a reduced ability to charge competitive rates.

Actionable Step: Regularly monitor occupancy rates, ADR, and RevPAR through industry reports or hotel benchmarking platforms to identify potential distressed assets in the market.

Operational Red Flags

While financial indicators provide valuable insights, operational issues often contribute to a hotel's distress. Common operational red flags include:

- Negative Guest Reviews: A high volume of negative reviews on platforms like TripAdvisor, Google, or Yelp indicates service quality issues, poor maintenance, or outdated amenities. Consistent complaints about cleanliness, staff behavior, or outdated facilities suggest deeper operational problems.

- Practical Example: A hotel received numerous complaints about unclean rooms and unresponsive staff, resulting in a decline in guest satisfaction scores. These reviews signaled operational inefficiencies that contributed to the property's distress.

- High Employee Turnover: Frequent staff turnover can indicate management issues, poor working conditions, or inadequate training. High turnover often leads to service disruptions, inconsistency, and a decline in guest experiences, which further exacerbates the hotel's distress.

- Deferred Maintenance: Signs of deferred maintenance, such as worn-out carpets, malfunctioning elevators, or outdated furnishings, suggest that the hotel may be struggling financially. Deferred maintenance can lead to safety hazards, lower guest satisfaction, and decreased property value.

Actionable Step: Monitor online review platforms, conduct mystery shopping, or visit the property to identify operational red flags that indicate distress. Pay attention to recurring issues mentioned by guests or signs of neglected maintenance.

Identifying Distressed Assets Through Industry Reports

Industry reports offer valuable data on market performance, trends, and individual hotel performance. These reports can help identify distressed assets by providing insights into occupancy rates, ADR, RevPAR, and overall market conditions. Key sources for industry reports include:

- STR Reports (Smith Travel Research): STR provides data on market trends, hotel performance metrics, and competitive benchmarking. Comparing a hotel's performance against market averages can reveal signs of distress.
- Practical Example: An investor used STR data to identify a hotel with declining occupancy rates despite being located in a market

experiencing growth. This discrepancy indicated that the property was underperforming compared to its competitors, making it a potential distressed asset.

- CBRE Hotel Research: CBRE offers comprehensive reports on hotel trends, market forecasts, and investment opportunities. Their reports can help identify regions or properties experiencing financial challenges.

- HVS Market Intelligence Reports: HVS provides detailed analysis of hotel markets, including occupancy trends, ADR, and RevPAR data. These reports can highlight properties that are struggling to keep up with market trends.

Actionable Step: Subscribe to industry reports from STR, CBRE, and HVS to stay informed about market trends and identify distressed hotels. Use these reports to compare individual property performance against market averages.

Using Technology and Data Analytics to Detect Distress

Advancements in technology and data analytics have made it easier to identify distressed hotels. By leveraging data analytics tools, investors and operators can analyze large volumes of data to uncover patterns and trends that indicate distress.

- Revenue Management Systems (RMS): RMS tools, such as Duetto or IDeaS, provide insights into pricing strategies, booking patterns, and demand fluctuations. By analyzing data from these systems, you can identify hotels that consistently offer deep discounts or have low booking volumes, which may indicate distress.

- Social Media Monitoring: Tools like Brandwatch or Sprout Social allow you to track guest sentiment, reviews, and online mentions of a hotel. Consistent negative sentiment or a lack of engagement can signal operational challenges or distress.

- AI and Machine Learning: AI-driven platforms can analyze multiple data points, such as occupancy rates, guest reviews, and pricing trends, to identify distressed hotels. These tools can predict future performance and highlight properties at risk of distress.

Case Study Example: An investor used data analytics to identify a hotel with declining ADR and negative guest sentiment on social media. The analysis revealed that the hotel was offering deep discounts during peak seasons, suggesting distress. The investor purchased the property at a discounted price and implemented a targeted turnaround strategy, resulting in a significant increase in profitability.

Actionable Step: Invest in data analytics tools to monitor hotel performance, guest sentiment, and pricing trends. Use technology to identify properties that are underperforming or exhibiting signs of distress.

Working with Brokers and Industry Contacts

Networking with experienced hotel brokers, consultants, and industry contacts is an effective way to identify distressed hotel opportunities. These professionals have access to insider information, off-market deals, and firsthand knowledge of properties that may not be publicly listed.

- Hotel Brokers: Brokers specializing in distressed hotel assets can provide valuable insights into properties that are struggling financially or operationally. They often have access to listings before they reach the open market.

- Industry Associations: Joining organizations such as the American Hotel & Lodging Association (AH&LA) or Hospitality Financial and Technology Professionals (HFTP) can help you connect with industry experts who may be aware of distressed hotel opportunities.

- Networking Events: Attending hotel investment conferences, such as the Americas Lodging Investment Summit (ALIS) or the Hotel Investment Conference Europe (HICE), can provide opportunities to meet brokers, investors, and operators who have firsthand knowledge of distressed assets.

Actionable Step: Build relationships with hotel brokers, consultants, and industry contacts to gain access to distressed hotel opportunities. Attend industry events and join associations to expand your network and stay informed about market trends.

Case Study: How an Investor Identified a Distressed Hotel Opportunity

Background: An investor was looking for a hotel acquisition opportunity in a competitive market. By leveraging multiple data sources, including STR reports, social media analytics, and broker contacts, the investor identified a four-star hotel that had been struggling with declining occupancy rates, negative guest reviews, and deferred maintenance.

Steps Taken:

- The investor analyzed the hotel's financials and discovered that its RevPAR was significantly lower than the market average, indicating distress.

- Using social media monitoring tools, the investor identified recurring guest complaints about outdated facilities and inconsistent service, confirming operational challenges.

- By networking with a hotel broker, the investor learned that the property owner was eager to sell due to mounting financial pressure.

Outcome: The investor acquired the hotel at a substantial discount and implemented a comprehensive turnaround strategy, including renovations, staff training, and targeted marketing campaigns. Within two years, the hotel's RevPAR increased by 35%, and guest satisfaction scores improved dramatically.

Identifying distressed hotels in the market requires a comprehensive approach that includes analyzing key financial indicators, recognizing operational red flags, utilizing industry reports, leveraging technology, and building relationships with brokers and industry contacts. By employing these strategies, investors and operators can uncover opportunities to acquire, manage, or turn around distressed hotel assets. The actionable steps, practical examples, and case study provided in this section offer valuable insights into how to effectively identify distressed hotels and capitalize on opportunities for growth and profitability.

Impact of Distressed Hotels on the Market and Stakeholders

Distressed hotels can have far-reaching effects that extend beyond their own operations, impacting local economies, surrounding properties, investors, lenders, and brand reputation. Understanding these impacts is crucial for stakeholders, as it allows them to address challenges proactively and develop strategies to mitigate negative consequences. This section provides an in-depth analysis of how distressed hotels influence various aspects of the market and offers actionable steps for minimizing their impact.

Effects on Local Economies and Employment

Hotels are often a significant source of employment and economic activity in local communities, especially in tourist destinations. When a hotel becomes distressed, the resulting decrease in revenue, occupancy, and operations can have severe repercussions on the local economy.

Job Losses: Distressed hotels often respond to financial challenges by cutting staff, reducing wages, or limiting work hours, leading to job losses and reduced income for local employees. This can be particularly damaging in regions that rely heavily on tourism, where hotel jobs may be a primary source of employment.

Reduced Local Spending: A distressed hotel typically attracts fewer guests, which translates to reduced spending on local services, attractions, and businesses, such as restaurants, shops, and entertainment venues. As guest spending declines, these businesses may experience financial strain, resulting in a broader economic downturn for the community.

Decline in Tax Revenue: Hotels generate tax revenue through occupancy taxes, sales taxes, and other local levies. When a hotel is in distress, the decrease in bookings and revenue leads to a decline in tax contributions, which can affect public services and infrastructure development in the area.

Practical Example: A large convention hotel in a mid-sized city experienced financial distress and was forced to cut staff and close several of its restaurants. The reduction in guests led to a drop in sales for nearby businesses, and the city experienced a decline in tax revenue, impacting funding for public services such as road maintenance and park upkeep.

Actionable Step: Hotels can mitigate their impact on local economies by collaborating with local businesses and government agencies to create special packages, promotions, or events that attract visitors. This partnership can help boost occupancy rates, generate additional revenue, and maintain employment levels during periods of distress.

The Ripple Effect on Surrounding Properties

Distressed hotels can create a ripple effect on surrounding properties, influencing the perception of an entire area or destination. When a hotel is visibly neglected or exhibits signs of financial distress, it can negatively impact nearby hotels, businesses, and real estate values.

Decreased Property Values: A distressed hotel can lead to a decline in the value of nearby properties, as potential buyers may view the area as less desirable. This can affect both commercial and residential real estate, leading to decreased investment and development in the region.

Reduced Occupancy Rates for Neighboring Hotels: Guests may be deterred from staying in an area if they perceive it as rundown or unappealing due to the presence of a distressed hotel. This can result in decreased occupancy rates for other hotels in the vicinity, even if they are not experiencing distress themselves.

Negative Perception of the Area: The presence of a

distressed hotel can create a perception that the destination is declining, leading to a decrease in tourist interest. This can harm the broader hospitality industry and impact other businesses that rely on tourism, such as restaurants, attractions, and transportation services.

Practical Example: A once-popular beachfront area experienced a decline in tourism after a major hotel fell into distress and was visibly neglected. The hotel's deteriorating condition deterred tourists from visiting, causing occupancy rates at neighboring hotels to drop by 20%, and local businesses reported a significant decrease in sales.

Actionable Step: Local tourism boards, hotel associations, and property owners should work together to address the issue of distressed hotels, offering support, marketing initiatives, or investment incentives to help these properties recover. This collaborative approach can help maintain the attractiveness of the area and prevent a decline in demand.

Impact on Investors and Lenders

Investors and lenders are directly affected when a hotel becomes distressed, as their financial interests are tied to the property's success. Distressed hotels may struggle to meet debt obligations, generate returns, or maintain the value of investments, leading to potential financial losses.

Loss of Investment Value: Distressed hotels often experience a decline in property value, which can result in significant losses for investors. The inability to generate sufficient revenue or sell the property at a favorable price can lead to reduced returns on investment.

Increased Risk of Loan Defaults: Lenders face the risk of loan defaults when a hotel is unable to service its debt due to financial distress. This can result in foreclosure, legal proceedings, and additional costs for lenders, who may need to take over the property or sell it at a loss.

Limited Access to Financing: Distressed hotels may find it challenging to secure additional financing, as lenders and investors may view them as high-risk. This lack of access to capital can hinder the property's ability to invest in renovations, marketing, or operational improvements, further exacerbating distress.

Practical Example: An investor who acquired a hotel at the peak of the market experienced significant losses when the property became distressed due to the economic downturn. Unable to service the debt, the investor was forced to negotiate with the lender to restructure the loan, resulting in reduced returns and financial strain.

Actionable Step: Investors and lenders should conduct thorough due diligence and risk assessments before investing in or financing a hotel. Regularly monitor the property's financial performance and be proactive in addressing any signs of distress to minimize potential losses.

Brand Reputation and Guest Perception

Distressed hotels often suffer from negative guest experiences, which can damage the property's brand reputation and deter future bookings. A tarnished reputation can be challenging to recover from, even if the hotel manages to overcome its financial distress.

Negative Guest Reviews: Guests who encounter issues such as poor service, unclean rooms, or outdated amenities are likely to leave negative reviews on platforms like TripAdvisor or Google. These reviews can significantly impact a hotel's reputation, leading to a decline in bookings and revenue.

Loss of Trust in the Brand: Guests may lose trust in a hotel brand if they perceive it as unreliable or poorly managed. This loss of trust can extend to other properties within the same brand or chain, affecting their performance as well.

Impact on Franchise or Management Agreements: Distressed hotels that are part of a franchise or management agreement may face penalties, termination, or reputational damage, impacting the broader brand's image and profitability.

Practical Example: A distressed hotel belonging to a well-known brand received numerous negative reviews due to poor maintenance and service quality. As a result, the hotel's occupancy rates plummeted, and other hotels within the brand's portfolio experienced a decline in bookings due to the negative association.

Actionable Step: Regularly monitor guest feedback and reviews to identify areas for improvement. Invest in staff training, maintenance, and service quality to enhance the guest experience and protect the hotel's reputation.

Case Study: How a Distressed Hotel Negatively Affected a Local Tourism Economy

Background: A large resort hotel in a popular tourist destination became distressed due to mismanagement, financial missteps, and a decline in guest satisfaction. The hotel's occupancy rates dropped significantly, and it struggled to maintain its facilities, leading to visible signs of neglect.

Impact: The hotel's decline had a ripple effect on the local tourism economy. Nearby hotels experienced reduced occupancy rates, local businesses saw a decline in sales, and the destination's reputation suffered as negative guest reviews spread. Tour operators and travel agencies began to avoid the area, further reducing visitor numbers.

Outcome: The local tourism board, along with the hotel's management, initiated a recovery plan that included renovations, marketing campaigns, and partnerships with nearby attractions. These efforts helped restore the hotel's reputation and contributed to the overall recovery of the local tourism economy. Strategies for Mitigating the Impact on Stakeholders

Mitigating the impact of a distressed hotel on stakeholders requires a proactive approach that addresses the root causes of distress and implements strategies for recovery.

- Collaboration and Partnerships: Engage with local businesses, tourism boards, and industry associations to create joint marketing campaigns, events, or packages that attract guests and stimulate demand.

- Investment in Renovations and Upgrades: Allocate resources to improve the hotel's facilities, service quality, and guest experience. Investing in renovations can help attract more guests, increase revenue, and restore the property's reputation.

- Transparent Communication: Communicate openly with stakeholders, including investors, lenders, employees, and guests, about the hotel's situation and the steps being taken to address distress. Transparency helps build trust and confidence in the recovery process.

- Engage Professional Management: Consider hiring experienced hotel management companies or turnaround specialists to address operational inefficiencies, improve financial performance, and implement a strategic recovery plan.

Actionable Step: Develop a crisis management plan that outlines strategies for addressing distress and communicating with stakeholders. Regularly review and update the plan to ensure it remains relevant and effective.

Distressed hotels can have a profound impact on the market, local economies, surrounding properties, investors, and brand reputation. Understanding these effects and implementing proactive strategies can help mitigate negative consequences and create opportunities for recovery and growth. By collaborating with stakeholders, investing in improvements, and maintaining transparent communication, distressed hotels can navigate challenges and emerge stronger, benefiting both the property and the broader community.

The Opportunities in Distressed Hotels

Investing in distressed hotels can present lucrative opportunities for savvy investors, operators, and developers. Despite the challenges associated with these properties, they often offer the potential for substantial returns when the right strategies are applied. This section explores why investors are drawn to distressed hotels, how to identify turnaround opportunities, assess profitability, evaluate risks and rewards, and provides a real-life case study demonstrating a successful acquisition and turnaround of a distressed property.

Why Investors Seek Out Distressed Hotels

Distressed hotels are attractive to investors for several reasons. One of the most compelling motivations is the opportunity to acquire assets at significantly discounted prices, often well below market value. This lower entry cost can create opportunities for substantial returns on investment when the property is successfully turned around.

1. Acquiring Assets Below Market Value: Distressed hotels are often sold at a fraction of their original value due to financial pressure, operational inefficiencies, or mismanagement. Investors can purchase these assets at a discount, allowing for a greater margin of profit when the property is revitalized.

- Practical Example: During an economic downturn, an investor acquired a 150-room hotel in a prime urban location for 50% below its original market value. After investing in renovations and implementing an effective turnaround strategy, the hotel's value increased by over 80% within two years.

2. Potential for High Returns: Distressed hotels, when successfully managed, have the potential to yield higher returns compared to stabilized properties. Once the property is improved, investors can benefit from increased cash flow, higher occupancy rates, and rising property values.

3. Market Resilience and Recovery: The hospitality industry is cyclical, and downturns are often followed by periods of recovery and growth. Investors who acquire distressed hotels during a market downturn can capitalize on the subsequent upswing as travel demand returns.

4. Opportunity for Repositioning and Value Creation: Distressed hotels often suffer from outdated branding, poor management, or lack of market relevance.

Investors can reposition the property to target a different market segment, upgrade amenities, or implement innovative marketing strategies, significantly enhancing the property's value.

Actionable Step: Conduct market research to identify regions or cities experiencing economic challenges, as these areas are more likely to have distressed hotels available for acquisition at discounted prices.
How to Identify Opportunities for Turnaround

Identifying distressed hotels with turnaround potential requires a strategic and analytical approach. Not all distressed properties are suitable for investment, so it's crucial to identify hotels with characteristics that indicate the potential for successful revitalization.

1. Analyze the Location: A distressed hotel located in a desirable or high-demand location is more likely to succeed after a turnaround. Properties near airports, business districts, tourist attractions, or convention centers have a better chance of attracting guests once improvements are made.

2. Evaluate the Property's Physical Condition: Identify hotels with cosmetic or operational issues rather than structural problems, as these can be addressed more cost-effectively. Properties requiring minor renovations, upgraded amenities, or improved maintenance present excellent opportunities for turnaround.

- Practical Example: An investor identified a beachfront hotel with peeling paint and outdated decor but discovered that the building's structure and utilities were in good condition. This made the property a prime candidate for a turnaround.

3. Review Financial Performance: Examine the hotel's financial statements, occupancy rates, ADR, and RevPAR. If the property's performance has declined due to mismanagement, outdated branding, or operational inefficiencies rather than market-related issues, it may have significant turnaround potential.

4. Assess Competitor Performance: Compare the distressed hotel to similar properties in the area. If neighboring hotels are performing well, this suggests that demand exists and the distressed property can improve with the right management and marketing strategies.

Actionable Step: Conduct a comprehensive analysis of the property's location, physical condition, financial performance, and market potential to identify whether it's a viable candidate for turnaround. Assessing the Potential for Profitability

Once an opportunity is identified, investors must assess the potential for profitability to determine if the investment is worth pursuing. This assessment involves a thorough evaluation of the costs, revenue potential, and overall return on investment (ROI).

1. Estimate Renovation and Improvement Costs: Calculate the total investment required to bring the property up to competitive standards. Include costs for renovations, marketing, staffing, technology

upgrades, and operational improvements. A realistic estimate ensures that the investment does not exceed the potential return.

2. Project Revenue Growth: Forecast future revenue based on market demand, projected occupancy rates, ADR, and RevPAR. Use data from competing hotels and historical trends to develop realistic revenue projections.

- Practical Example: After acquiring a distressed hotel, an investor projected that renovations and a targeted marketing campaign would increase occupancy from 40% to 75% within 18 months. This projection helped the investor secure financing and develop a timeline for profitability.

3. Calculate the Break-Even Point: Determine how long it will take for the property to generate enough revenue to cover the initial investment and ongoing expenses. A shorter break-even period indicates a higher likelihood of profitability.

4. Consider Exit Strategies: Identify potential exit strategies, such as selling the property, refinancing, or retaining ownership for long-term cash flow. Understanding how and when to exit the investment helps maximize profitability.

Actionable Step: Create a detailed financial model that outlines renovation costs, projected revenue, operating expenses, and ROI. Use this model to assess the potential profitability and inform decision-making.

Evaluating the Risks and Rewards

Investing in distressed hotels carries inherent risks, but these can be managed with careful planning and analysis. Understanding the risks and rewards allows investors to make informed decisions and implement strategies to mitigate potential challenges.

1. Financial Risks: The most significant risk is the potential for cost overruns during renovations, which can erode profitability. Conduct thorough due diligence to identify hidden issues, and build a contingency fund to cover unexpected expenses.

2. Market Risks: Changes in market conditions, such as a downturn in tourism or increased competition, can impact the hotel's ability to achieve projected revenue. Regularly monitor market trends and adjust strategies to adapt to evolving conditions.

3. Operational Risks: Operational challenges, such as staffing shortages or supply chain disruptions, can affect the hotel's turnaround efforts. Implement effective training programs, hire experienced management teams, and establish relationships with reliable vendors.

Rewards: The rewards of investing in distressed hotels can be substantial, including high ROI, increased property value, and long-term cash flow. Investors who successfully turn around a distressed property can enjoy significant financial gains and the satisfaction of revitalizing a struggling asset.

Actionable Step: Conduct a comprehensive risk assessment before investing in a distressed hotel. Develop risk mitigation strategies, such as contingency funding, flexible marketing plans, and experienced management teams, to enhance the likelihood of success.

Case Study: A Successful Acquisition and Turnaround of a Distressed Property

Background: An investor acquired a 200-room hotel in a popular tourist destination that had been in decline for several years. The property suffered from poor management, outdated facilities, and a lack of marketing, resulting in low occupancy rates and negative guest reviews.

Steps Taken:

- Acquisition: The investor purchased the hotel at a 60% discount due to its distressed condition, recognizing its prime location and potential for turnaround.

- Renovations: The investor allocated funds for renovations, including modernizing guest rooms, upgrading common areas, and enhancing amenities such as a rooftop bar and fitness center.

- Rebranding and Marketing: The hotel was rebranded as a boutique luxury destination, targeting upscale travelers. A comprehensive digital marketing campaign, including a new website, social media engagement, and partnerships with travel influencers, helped attract guests.

- Operational Improvements: The investor hired an experienced management team to implement efficient operational processes, improve staff training, and enhance guest service.

Outcome: Within two years, the hotel achieved an 80% occupancy rate, increased its ADR by 50%, and received consistently positive guest reviews. The property's value doubled, and the investor was able to refinance at favorable terms, resulting in a substantial return on investment.

Key Takeaways:

- Acquiring distressed properties in desirable locations provides a solid foundation for a successful turnaround.

- Strategic renovations, rebranding, and marketing efforts are essential for transforming a distressed hotel into a profitable asset.

- Hiring experienced management and improving operational efficiency are critical factors in achieving a successful turnaround.

Investing in distressed hotels offers significant opportunities for high returns, value creation, and market growth. By understanding why investors seek out distressed properties, how to identify turnaround opportunities, assess profitability, and evaluate risks and rewards, investors can make informed decisions that lead to successful acquisitions and revitalizations. The case study demonstrates that with strategic planning, effective management, and a commitment to quality, distressed hotels can be transformed into thriving, profitable assets, providing substantial rewards for investors and stakeholders alike.

Challenges of Managing a Distressed Hotel

Managing a distressed hotel is a complex undertaking that involves navigating a variety of obstacles, from operational inefficiencies to financial constraints. Understanding these challenges and developing strategies to address them is essential for hotel owners, investors, and managers looking to restore profitability and stability. This section provides an in-depth analysis of the common obstacles faced by distressed hotels, the complexities of managing such properties, legal and regulatory challenges, handling negative guest perceptions, practical tips for overcoming these difficulties, and a real-life example of how a hotel manager successfully tackled operational challenges.

Common Obstacles Faced by Distressed Hotels

Distressed hotels often face a multitude of challenges that hinder their ability to operate efficiently and profitably. These challenges can include:

- Financial Constraints: Distressed hotels frequently struggle with cash flow issues, which limit their ability to invest in necessary improvements, pay staff, or cover operating expenses. This financial strain often leads to deferred maintenance, reduced service quality, and ultimately, lower guest satisfaction.

- Operational Inefficiencies: Inefficient processes, inadequate staffing levels, and outdated technology can exacerbate a hotel's distress. These inefficiencies lead to longer wait times, reduced service quality, and higher operating costs, making it difficult to compete with more efficient competitors.

- High Staff Turnover: Financial difficulties often result in low employee morale, reduced training opportunities, and a lack of job security, contributing to high staff turnover. This turnover disrupts operations, affects service quality, and further impacts the hotel's reputation.

- Declining Guest Satisfaction: Distressed hotels often receive negative reviews due to outdated amenities, poor service, or cleanliness issues. These negative perceptions can deter potential guests, reducing occupancy rates and revenue.

Actionable Step: Conduct an operational audit to identify areas of inefficiency and implement targeted strategies to address staffing, technology, and service quality. Improving these areas can help reduce costs and enhance guest satisfaction.

The Complexities of Distressed Property Management

Managing a distressed hotel is significantly more complex than managing a stable or profitable property. Some of the unique complexities include:

- Balancing Immediate Needs with Long-Term Goals: Distressed hotels require immediate interventions to address critical issues such as cash flow shortages, guest complaints, or safety concerns. However, managers must also develop long-term strategies to restore the hotel's profitability and reputation, which requires careful planning and resource allocation.

- Dealing with Multiple Stakeholders: Distressed hotels often have multiple stakeholders with varying interests, including investors, lenders, employees, suppliers, and guests. Balancing these interests while making necessary changes can be challenging, as each group may have different priorities and expectations.

- Implementing Cost-Saving Measures: Cutting costs is essential for distressed hotels, but doing so without compromising service quality can be difficult. Managers must identify areas where expenses can be reduced, such as renegotiating supplier contracts, implementing energy-saving practices, or optimizing staffing levels, while ensuring that guest experiences remain positive.

Practical Example: A distressed hotel managed to cut operating expenses by 15% by implementing energy-efficient lighting, automating check-in processes, and cross-training staff to handle multiple roles. These changes improved efficiency without negatively impacting guest satisfaction.

Actionable Step: Prioritize cost-saving measures that do not compromise guest experience, such as investing in energy-efficient technology, renegotiating vendor contracts, and implementing technology-driven solutions to streamline operations.

Legal and Regulatory Challenges

Distressed hotels often face legal and regulatory challenges that complicate management efforts. These challenges can include:

- Compliance Issues: Distressed hotels may struggle to maintain compliance with health, safety, labor, and environmental regulations due to financial constraints. Non-compliance can result in fines, legal actions, or even temporary closure, further exacerbating financial distress.

- Contractual Obligations: Existing contracts with suppliers, lenders, employees, or franchisors may impose financial burdens or operational restrictions on distressed hotels. Renegotiating these contracts or meeting contractual obligations can be challenging, especially if the hotel is already struggling financially.

- Lender Involvement: Lenders may impose additional requirements or restrictions on distressed hotels to protect their investments. This can include demands for increased reporting, operational changes, or oversight, making it more difficult for hotel managers to implement turnaround strategies.

Practical Example: A distressed hotel facing regulatory fines for outdated fire safety systems was able to negotiate a payment plan with the local authorities and secure a short-term loan to finance the necessary upgrades. By addressing this compliance issue, the hotel avoided further penalties and improved guest safety.

Actionable Step: Conduct a comprehensive legal and regulatory review to identify potential compliance issues, contractual obligations, and lender requirements. Engage legal or financial advisors to negotiate favorable terms and ensure compliance with all regulations.

Dealing with Negative Guest Perceptions and Reviews

Negative guest perceptions and reviews can significantly impact a distressed hotel's ability to attract new guests and generate revenue. Addressing these perceptions is critical to improving occupancy rates and restoring the hotel's reputation.

- Identifying Common Guest Complaints: Analyze guest feedback, online reviews, and social media comments to identify recurring complaints. Common issues may include outdated amenities, cleanliness problems, unresponsive staff, or poor service quality.

- Developing a Guest Experience Improvement Plan: Create a plan to address the issues identified, focusing on areas that have the greatest impact on guest satisfaction. For example, if guests frequently complain about cleanliness, prioritize improvements in housekeeping standards and training.

- Responding to Negative Reviews: Respond promptly and professionally to negative reviews, demonstrating that the hotel is committed to addressing concerns and improving guest experiences. Offering a solution or compensation can help rebuild trust and encourage guests to give the hotel another chance.

Case Study Example: A distressed hotel received numerous negative reviews about slow check-in processes and unclean rooms. The management team implemented a new, user-friendly check-in system and retrained housekeeping staff, resulting in a significant improvement in guest satisfaction scores within three months.

Actionable Step: Monitor online reviews regularly and develop a proactive plan to address guest complaints. Consider implementing guest satisfaction surveys to gather direct feedback and identify areas for improvement.

Practical Tips for Overcoming These Challenges

Overcoming the challenges of managing a distressed hotel requires a strategic approach and a commitment to continuous improvement. Here are some practical tips:

- Focus on Quick Wins: Identify areas where small changes can lead to immediate improvements, such as upgrading bedding, enhancing staff training, or improving cleanliness. These quick wins can help boost guest satisfaction and generate positive reviews, which are crucial for attracting more bookings.

- Leverage Technology: Invest in technology solutions that improve operational efficiency, such as property management systems (PMS), revenue management software, or guest communication platforms. These tools can help streamline processes, reduce costs, and enhance the guest experience.

- Engage with Staff: Employees are an essential asset in the turnaround process. Engage with staff by providing training, incentives, and opportunities for growth. A motivated and well-trained team is more likely to deliver exceptional service and contribute to the hotel's recovery.

- Develop a Clear Turnaround Plan: Create a comprehensive turnaround plan that outlines specific goals, timelines, and strategies for addressing operational, financial, and guest experience challenges. Regularly review and adjust the plan as needed to ensure progress is being made.

Actionable Step: Implement a monthly performance review process to monitor progress toward turnaround goals, identify areas for improvement, and celebrate successes with staff to maintain motivation and momentum.

Real-Life Example: How a Hotel Manager Tackled Operational Challenges

Background: A distressed hotel in a busy urban location was experiencing low occupancy rates, negative guest reviews, and high staff turnover. The hotel's reputation had suffered due to poor service, outdated amenities, and a lack of cleanliness.

Challenges Faced:

- Guest complaints about unresponsive staff and unclean rooms

- High employee turnover leading to inconsistent service quality

- Limited budget for renovations and marketing

Actions Taken:

- Staff Training and Engagement: The hotel manager invested in comprehensive staff training programs, focusing on customer service, housekeeping standards, and problem-solving skills. Incentives were introduced to reward employees who received positive guest feedback.

- Improved Cleaning Protocols: The manager implemented new cleaning protocols and checklists to ensure rooms were cleaned to a high standard. Housekeeping supervisors conducted regular inspections, and feedback was shared with the team to maintain quality.

- Technology Upgrades: A cloud-based property management system was introduced to streamline check-in/check-out processes, allowing staff to focus more on guest interaction and service delivery.

- Addressing Guest Feedback: The manager personally responded to all guest reviews, both positive and negative, demonstrating a commitment to addressing concerns and improving the guest experience.

Outcome: Within six months, the hotel's guest satisfaction scores improved by 40%, staff turnover decreased by 25%, and occupancy rates increased by 30%. The property's improved reputation attracted more bookings, helping to stabilize the hotel's financial performance.

Managing a distressed hotel presents numerous challenges, from financial constraints and operational inefficiencies to legal hurdles and negative guest perceptions. However, with a strategic approach, effective management practices, and a commitment to continuous improvement, these challenges can be overcome. By addressing common obstacles, engaging with stakeholders, leveraging technology, and implementing targeted strategies, hotel managers can transform distressed properties into profitable and successful assets. The real-life examples and actionable steps provided in this section serve as a guide for navigating the complexities of managing a distressed hotel and achieving a successful turnaround.

Chapter 2: Analyzing Distressed Hotels

Analyzing a distressed hotel is a crucial step in understanding the factors that have led to its decline and in formulating a strategy for its recovery. This chapter provides an in-depth examination of how to conduct a comprehensive analysis of distressed hotel properties, enabling owners, operators, and investors to identify the root causes of distress and determine the best course of action for revitalization. The process begins with conducting a comprehensive operational audit, where the efficiency of core departments such as the front desk, housekeeping, food and beverage (F&B), and maintenance is evaluated. By assessing these operations, managers can identify inefficiencies and develop actionable steps to improve operational efficiency. A focus on key performance indicators (KPIs) and the use of technology can streamline the audit process, making it easier to pinpoint areas in need of improvement.

Next, a thorough financial analysis is essential for gaining a clear picture of a hotel's financial health. This includes examining income statements, balance sheets, and cash flow to understand debt structures and financial obligations. Real-life examples highlight how hidden losses can be uncovered through financial analysis, and strategies for improving financial performance are presented. In addition to internal assessments, it's critical to conduct a market and competitive analysis to understand the local hotel market, demand drivers, and competitor positioning.

This allows distressed hotels to identify target markets and guest segments, develop strategies for differentiation, and leverage market trends to gain a competitive edge.

Identifying the root causes of distress is another vital component, as operational inefficiencies, financial mismanagement, inadequate marketing, and poor guest experiences often contribute to a hotel's challenges. By examining case studies, readers will gain insight into how addressing these root causes can lead to successful turnarounds. Understanding stakeholder interests is equally important, as distressed hotels must balance the concerns of investors, lenders, employees, guests, and the local community. Tips for effective communication and strategies for managing competing interests are discussed in detail.

Finally, the chapter addresses the importance of risk assessment and mitigation strategies in revitalizing a distressed hotel. By identifying potential risks—whether operational, financial, legal, or market-related—and developing a comprehensive risk management plan, hotel operators can build resilience and prevent future challenges. Real-life examples and practical tools are provided to guide hoteliers in navigating these complex issues. This chapter offers a holistic approach to analyzing distressed hotels, equipping readers with the knowledge and tools needed to identify challenges, opportunities, and actionable steps for transforming struggling properties into successful ventures.

Conducting a Comprehensive Operational Audit

A comprehensive operational audit is a crucial step in assessing a distressed hotel's performance and identifying areas that require improvement. This process provides insight into the operational inefficiencies that may be contributing to the hotel's distress, enabling hotel owners and managers to implement targeted strategies to enhance productivity, reduce costs, and improve the guest experience. This section offers a step-by-step guide to conducting an operational audit, evaluating key hotel departments, providing practical examples, identifying key performance indicators (KPIs), using technology to streamline the audit, and actionable steps for improving operational efficiency.

Step-by-Step Guide to Operational Audits

Conducting an operational audit involves a systematic evaluation of all aspects of the hotel's operations. The following steps provide a structured approach to carrying out a thorough audit:

- Preparation and Planning: Define the scope of the audit by identifying the departments, processes, and specific areas that need evaluation. Set clear objectives for the audit, such as identifying inefficiencies, assessing staff performance, or evaluating guest service quality. Collect relevant data, including operational reports, financial statements, guest feedback, and employee performance records, to understand the hotel's current situation.

- Data Collection: Gather information through various methods, such as direct observation, staff interviews, guest surveys, and reviewing operational reports. This step helps you identify discrepancies between expected and actual performance, as well as uncover hidden issues affecting productivity.

- Analysis of Findings: Analyze the collected data to identify patterns, bottlenecks, and areas of inefficiency. Evaluate each department's processes, workflows, and performance metrics to understand how they contribute to the overall operations.

- Identification of Issues: Identify key areas that require improvement. This could include staffing shortages, outdated technology, poor maintenance practices, or suboptimal guest service. Prioritize these issues based on their impact on the hotel's performance and guest experience.

- Developing Recommendations: Based on the audit findings, create a list of actionable recommendations for each department. These recommendations should address the identified inefficiencies, streamline processes, and improve overall operational efficiency.

- Implementation and Monitoring: Work with department heads and staff to implement the recommended changes. Monitor the progress over time and adjust the strategies as needed to ensure sustained improvements.

Actionable Tip: Regularly schedule operational audits (e.g., quarterly or biannually) to maintain high standards and quickly address emerging issues. Evaluating Front Desk, Housekeeping, F&B, and Maintenance

A comprehensive operational audit should focus on evaluating the key departments of the hotel, as they play a significant role in guest satisfaction and overall performance:

- Front Desk: The front desk is the first point of contact for guests and sets the tone for their stay. Evaluate staff communication skills, check-in/check-out processes, guest handling, and the efficiency of reservation systems. Assess the wait times, handling of guest inquiries, and accuracy of billing to identify areas for improvement.

- Housekeeping: Cleanliness and room maintenance are vital to guest satisfaction. Review housekeeping schedules, staff productivity, and quality control measures. Ensure that cleaning procedures are efficient, and rooms are prepared promptly and thoroughly for guest arrivals. Look for signs of wear and tear, and identify opportunities to streamline housekeeping operations.

- Food & Beverage (F&B): Evaluate the F&B department's menu variety, quality of service, kitchen efficiency, inventory management, and waste control. Examine guest feedback on food quality, service speed, and overall dining experience to identify gaps and areas for enhancement.

- Maintenance: Regular maintenance is essential to ensure that the property remains in good condition. Assess the hotel's preventive maintenance schedules, response times to maintenance requests, equipment efficiency, and the effectiveness of maintenance staff. Identify recurring issues and ensure that they are addressed promptly to avoid disruptions to guest services.

Actionable Tip: Establish clear standards and expectations for each department, and communicate these expectations to the staff to ensure consistency and quality in service delivery.
Practical Example: How an Operational Audit Revealed Inefficiencies

An independent 150-room hotel located near a popular tourist destination experienced declining guest satisfaction scores, mainly due to delayed check-ins, inconsistent room cleanliness, and slow restaurant service. A comprehensive operational audit revealed several inefficiencies:

- The front desk staff lacked training in using the property management system (PMS), leading to frequent errors during the check-in/check-out process.

- Housekeeping staff were understaffed, resulting in delayed room preparation and inconsistent cleaning quality.

- The F&B department had an overcomplicated menu that increased kitchen preparation time and resulted in higher food wastage.

By identifying these inefficiencies, the hotel implemented targeted improvements, such as training front desk staff on the PMS, hiring additional housekeeping staff, and simplifying the F&B menu. These changes led to a 30% reduction in guest check-in times, a 25% increase in room cleanliness scores, and a 15% decrease in food wastage within six months.

Actionable Tip: Use guest feedback and reviews to identify operational issues that may be affecting the guest experience, and prioritize these issues during the audit process.

Identifying Key Performance Indicators (KPIs)

KPIs are essential metrics that help measure the performance of different hotel departments. Identifying and tracking KPIs allows hotel managers to monitor operational efficiency, identify areas for improvement, and evaluate the impact of implemented changes. Key KPIs for each department include:

- Front Desk: Average check-in/check-out time, guest satisfaction scores, reservation accuracy, and occupancy rate.

- Housekeeping: Room turnaround time, cleaning quality scores, productivity per housekeeper (rooms cleaned per shift), and guest complaints related to cleanliness.

- F&B: Average time to serve guests, food waste percentage, revenue per available seat hour (RevPASH), and guest satisfaction scores for dining experiences.

- Maintenance: Average response time to maintenance requests, equipment downtime, completion rate of preventive maintenance tasks, and guest complaints related to maintenance issues.

Actionable Tip: Regularly review KPIs for each department and set performance targets to motivate staff and drive continuous improvement.
Using Technology to Streamline the Audit Process

Technology plays a vital role in streamlining the operational audit process and enhancing efficiency. Several technology solutions can be utilized during the audit, such as:

- Property Management Systems (PMS): Use PMS data to analyze guest check-in/check-out times, reservation accuracy, and occupancy rates. This data helps identify front desk inefficiencies and areas for improvement.

- Housekeeping Management Software: Track room turnaround times, cleaning schedules, and staff productivity using housekeeping management software. This software allows managers to monitor housekeeping performance in real time and identify bottlenecks.

- F&B Inventory Management Systems: F&B management systems help track inventory levels, monitor food waste, and analyze menu performance. These insights help optimize inventory management and reduce waste.

- Maintenance Management Software: Use maintenance software to track work orders, preventive maintenance tasks, and response times. This technology ensures that maintenance issues are addressed promptly, reducing equipment downtime and guest complaints.

Actionable Tip: Invest in technology solutions that integrate with existing hotel systems to provide real-time insights into operational performance and streamline the audit process.
Actionable Steps for Improving Operational Efficiency

Based on the findings of the operational audit, hotel managers can implement the following actionable steps to improve efficiency across key departments:

- Front Desk: Streamline check-in/check-out processes by training staff on the use of PMS, implementing mobile check-in options, and reducing paperwork. Create a standardized script for guest interactions to ensure consistent communication and service delivery.

- Housekeeping: Optimize housekeeping

schedules by aligning them with guest check-in/check-out times. Provide additional training to staff on efficient cleaning techniques and establish quality control measures to maintain cleanliness standards. Consider using housekeeping management software to assign tasks and monitor performance.

- F&B: Simplify the menu to reduce preparation time and minimize food waste. Train kitchen staff on efficient cooking techniques and introduce cross-training for waitstaff to handle peak times effectively. Implement inventory management systems to monitor stock levels and reduce waste.

- Maintenance: Establish a preventive maintenance schedule to address potential issues before they become critical problems. Train maintenance staff to prioritize urgent tasks and monitor the completion rate of maintenance requests using maintenance management software.

Practical Example: After implementing these actionable steps, a 200-room hotel improved its operational efficiency by reducing average check-in times by 40%, increasing room cleanliness scores by 25%, and reducing food waste by 20% within six months. This led to a significant increase in guest satisfaction and a 15% rise in overall revenue.

Actionable Tip: Regularly monitor the impact of these improvements using KPIs and make adjustments as needed to ensure sustained operational efficiency.

Conducting a comprehensive operational audit is a critical step in revitalizing a distressed hotel and improving its performance. By following a structured audit process, evaluating key departments, identifying KPIs, utilizing technology, and implementing actionable steps, hotel managers can address operational inefficiencies, enhance guest satisfaction, and ultimately restore profitability. This process not only identifies areas of weakness but also creates a clear roadmap for driving continuous improvement and achieving long-term success.

Financial Analysis of Distressed Hotels

Conducting a thorough financial analysis is crucial when assessing a distressed hotel, as it provides valuable insights into the hotel's financial health, identifies the root causes of distress, and helps develop strategies for a successful turnaround. This section explores how to assess financial health, understand debt structures and obligations, analyze key financial metrics, identify turnaround opportunities, and implement strategies to improve financial performance. A case study will illustrate how a financial analysis revealed hidden losses in a distressed hotel, offering actionable steps for hotel owners and managers.

Assessing Financial Health (Income Statements, Balance Sheets, Cash Flow)

The first step in conducting a financial analysis is to evaluate the hotel's core financial statements: the income statement, balance sheet, and cash flow statement.

- Income Statement: The income statement shows the hotel's revenue, expenses, and profitability over a specific period. Analyzing this statement allows you to identify trends in revenue, costs, and profit margins. Key areas to review include:

- Revenue streams: Identify the primary sources of revenue (e.g., room sales, F&B, ancillary services) and examine how they have changed over time.

- Cost of goods sold (COGS): Evaluate the costs associated with providing services, such as room cleaning, F&B supplies, and utilities.

- Operating expenses: Analyze expenses like payroll, marketing, maintenance, and administration to identify areas where costs have risen disproportionately.

- Balance Sheet: The balance sheet provides a snapshot of the hotel's assets, liabilities, and equity at a specific point in time. Key elements to review include:

- Current assets and liabilities: Assess cash reserves, accounts receivable, and short-term debts to evaluate liquidity and the ability to cover immediate expenses.

- Long-term assets and liabilities: Examine the value of property, equipment, and long-term debt obligations to understand the hotel's financial stability.

- Equity: Analyze the equity position to determine the hotel's overall net worth and the level of investment by owners or shareholders.

- Cash Flow Statement: The cash flow statement tracks the inflow and outflow of cash within the hotel, providing insight into its ability to generate cash from operations, investments, and financing activities. Key areas to review include:

- Operating activities: Assess whether the hotel's core operations generate sufficient cash flow to cover expenses.

- Investing activities: Analyze capital expenditures and investments in property or equipment.

- Financing activities: Examine cash flow related to debt repayment, loans, or equity injections.

Actionable Tip: Regularly monitor these financial statements to identify trends, anomalies, and areas where cost reductions or revenue enhancements are possible.

Understanding Debt Structures and Obligations

Distressed hotels often face significant debt obligations that contribute to financial strain. Understanding the hotel's debt structure is essential for developing strategies to manage and renegotiate debt. Key aspects to consider include:

- Types of Debt: Identify the different types of debt, such as mortgages, equipment loans, lines of credit, and unsecured loans. Each type of debt may have different interest rates, repayment terms, and covenants.

- Debt Maturity: Assess the maturity dates of existing loans to determine when payments are due. Short-term debt with upcoming maturity dates may require immediate attention, while long-term debt allows more time for restructuring.

- Interest Rates: Review the interest rates on outstanding loans to understand the cost of borrowing. High-interest rates can significantly impact cash flow, making it challenging to meet financial obligations.

- Loan Covenants: Examine any loan covenants or conditions imposed by lenders, such as maintaining specific financial ratios or restrictions on additional borrowing. Violating these covenants can lead to penalties or loan default.

Practical Example: A distressed hotel facing high monthly debt payments successfully negotiated with its lender to extend the loan term and reduce interest rates. This adjustment eased cash flow pressures and allowed the hotel to allocate resources toward operational improvements.

Actionable Tip: Engage with financial advisors or debt restructuring experts to explore options for renegotiating loan terms, consolidating debt, or seeking alternative financing solutions.

Case Study: A Hotel's Financial Analysis That Revealed Hidden Losses

A 250-room luxury hotel located in a competitive urban market experienced declining profits and struggled to meet its debt obligations. The hotel's management conducted a comprehensive financial analysis, which revealed several hidden losses:

- Underperforming F&B Department: The hotel's F&B department was losing money due to high food waste, inefficient staffing, and a lack of cost controls. The income statement showed that the F&B department's costs exceeded revenue by 20%.

- High Labor Costs: The hotel had excessive staffing levels, resulting in high payroll expenses that reduced profitability. Labor costs accounted for 45% of total operating expenses, well above the industry average.

- Inadequate Pricing Strategies: The hotel's room rates were inconsistent with market trends, leading to missed revenue opportunities. Despite high occupancy rates, the hotel's average daily rate (ADR) was significantly lower than that of its competitors.

By identifying these issues, the hotel developed targeted strategies to reduce food waste, optimize staffing levels, and adjust room pricing. As a result, the hotel improved its gross operating profit (GOP) by 15% within six months, leading to improved financial stability.

Actionable Tip: Conduct a detailed financial analysis to uncover hidden losses and develop targeted strategies for addressing inefficiencies.

Calculating Key Metrics (e.g., ADR, RevPAR, GOP)

Key financial metrics provide valuable insights into a hotel's performance and profitability. Understanding and tracking these metrics is essential for identifying opportunities for improvement:

- Average Daily Rate (ADR): Measures the average revenue earned per occupied room. Calculate ADR using the formula:

    - ADR=Total Room RevenueNumber of Rooms Sold

    - ADR=Number of Rooms SoldTotal Room Revenue

- Monitoring ADR helps assess pricing strategies and the hotel's ability to attract high-paying guests.

- Revenue per Available Room (RevPAR): Measures the hotel's revenue-generating ability across all available rooms. Calculate RevPAR using the formula:

- RevPAR=Total Room RevenueTotal Available Rooms

- RevPAR=Total Available RoomsTotal Room Revenue

- Alternatively, RevPAR can be calculated by multiplying ADR by the occupancy rate. It provides a comprehensive view of the hotel's revenue performance.

- Gross Operating Profit (GOP): Represents the hotel's profit after deducting all operating expenses. Calculate GOP using the formula:

- GOP=Total Revenue−Total Operating Expenses

- Monitoring GOP helps evaluate overall profitability and operational efficiency.

Actionable Tip: Regularly review these metrics to identify trends, benchmark performance against industry standards, and develop strategies to improve financial outcomes.

Using Financial Data to Identify Turnaround Opportunities

Analyzing financial data can reveal opportunities for turning around a distressed hotel. Some areas to explore include:

- Revenue Enhancement: Identify opportunities to increase revenue by adjusting room rates, targeting higher-paying guests, or introducing value-added services. For example, offering bundled packages, such as spa treatments or dining experiences, can increase overall guest spending.

- Cost Control: Analyze expense categories to identify areas where cost reductions are possible, such as renegotiating vendor contracts, reducing food waste, or optimizing energy consumption.

- Debt Restructuring: Use financial data to negotiate with lenders, demonstrating the hotel's potential for improved profitability if debt payments are reduced or extended.

Practical Example: A 100-room hotel facing financial distress increased its RevPAR by 10% by implementing dynamic pricing strategies and targeting corporate travelers. These changes significantly improved the hotel's cash flow and profitability.

Actionable Tip: Use financial analysis to identify quick wins that can generate immediate cash flow improvements, such as optimizing room rates or reducing non-essential expenses.
Strategies for Improving Financial Performance

Based on the financial analysis findings, implement the following strategies to improve the hotel's financial performance:

- Optimize Pricing and Revenue Management: Implement dynamic pricing strategies that adjust room rates based on demand, seasonality, and market trends. Use revenue management software to analyze booking patterns and adjust rates in real time.

- Control Operating Costs: Implement cost-saving measures, such as energy-efficient lighting, waste reduction programs, and optimized staffing levels. Review vendor contracts and negotiate better terms to reduce expenses.

- Increase Ancillary Revenue: Explore opportunities to generate additional revenue through F&B, spa services, event hosting, or retail partnerships. Cross-promote these services to maximize guest spending.

- Renegotiate Debt Obligations: Work with lenders to restructure debt, extend payment terms, or reduce interest rates. Demonstrating a clear turnaround plan can improve the likelihood of successful negotiations.

Case Study: A distressed hotel successfully increased its GOP by 20% within a year by implementing dynamic pricing strategies, reducing labor costs through cross-training, and renegotiating debt terms with its lender.

Actionable Tip: Regularly monitor financial

performance and adjust strategies as needed to ensure sustained improvements in profitability.
Conclusion

Conducting a comprehensive financial analysis is essential for understanding the underlying causes of distress in a hotel and developing strategies for a successful turnaround. By assessing financial health, understanding debt obligations, calculating key metrics, and identifying opportunities for improvement, hotel owners and managers can implement targeted strategies to restore profitability and long-term stability. The actionable steps and case studies provided in this section offer practical guidance for addressing financial challenges and achieving a successful hotel turnaround.

Market and Competitive Analysis

A comprehensive market and competitive analysis is crucial when seeking to turn around a distressed hotel. Understanding the local market, demand drivers, competitors, and target guests allows hoteliers to develop strategies that differentiate their property and position it for success. This section will provide an in-depth analysis of these factors, including real-life examples, practical strategies, and actionable steps.

Understanding the Local Hotel Market and Demand Drivers

The first step in conducting a market analysis is to gain a thorough understanding of the local hotel market and the factors that drive demand. Demand drivers are the elements that influence guests' decisions to stay at a hotel in a specific area, such as:

- Business Travel: If the hotel is located in a business district or near corporate offices, conferences, and trade centers, business travelers may be a significant demand driver.

- Leisure Travel: Attractions like theme parks, historical sites, beaches, or shopping districts attract leisure travelers who seek accommodation close to these points of interest.

- Events and Festivals: Large events, concerts, sports games, or festivals can create temporary spikes in demand for hotel rooms.

- Seasonality: Seasonal factors, such as weather, holidays, and school vacations, impact demand levels at different times of the year.

For example, a hotel located near a convention center might see peak demand during large conferences, while a beachside resort might be busiest during the summer months. Understanding these demand drivers helps hotels adapt their marketing, pricing, and operational strategies to maximize revenue.

Actionable Step: Conduct regular market research to identify demand drivers in your local area. This can be done through online searches, interviews with local tourism boards, and analyzing historical occupancy data.

Analyzing Competitors and Market Positioning

Competitor analysis involves identifying other hotels in your area and evaluating their strengths, weaknesses, pricing strategies, amenities, and target markets. The goal is to understand how these competitors are positioned in the market and how your hotel compares.

- Identify Competitors: Create a list of direct and indirect competitors in the local area. Direct competitors are hotels that offer similar services, amenities, and price points, while indirect competitors may be alternatives such as short-term rentals or budget accommodations.

- Evaluate Competitors' Offerings: Analyze competitors' room types, amenities, pricing, promotions, guest reviews, and online presence. Identify what they do well and where they fall short.

- Assess Competitors' Market Positioning: Understand how competitors position themselves in terms of luxury, budget, boutique, family-friendly, or business-oriented accommodations. This will help you identify your hotel's unique selling proposition (USP) and areas where you can differentiate.

Practical Example: A mid-range hotel discovered that its primary competitors offered complimentary breakfast and Wi-Fi, while it charged extra for these services. By providing these amenities as part of the room rate, the hotel was able to improve its value proposition and increase bookings.

Actionable Step: Use SWOT (Strengths, Weaknesses, Opportunities, Threats) analysis to evaluate your hotel in comparison to competitors and identify ways to gain a competitive advantage.

Real-Life Example: How a Market Analysis Influenced a Hotel's Turnaround Plan

A 120-room hotel located in a downtown area faced low occupancy rates and declining revenue. The hotel conducted a comprehensive market analysis, which revealed that:

- Business travelers were the primary demand driver in the area, but the hotel lacked amenities such as a business center, meeting rooms, and high-speed internet.

- The hotel's pricing was inconsistent, leading to confusion among potential guests.

- Competitors in the area offered complimentary breakfast, a feature that was highly valued by business travelers.

- Using this information, the hotel implemented the following changes:

- Converted an underutilized space into a small business center and meeting rooms.

- Introduced a consistent pricing structure with corporate discounts and bundled packages.

- Offered a complimentary breakfast for business guests.

As a result, the hotel saw a 20% increase in occupancy and a 15% increase in revenue over six months. The market analysis allowed the hotel to better align its offerings with demand drivers, differentiate itself from competitors, and attract more business travelers.

Actionable Step: Regularly conduct market analyses to identify shifts in demand drivers and adapt your offerings accordingly.

Identifying Target Markets and Guest Segments

Identifying target markets and guest segments is essential for tailoring your marketing, sales, and service strategies. Common guest segments include:

- Business Travelers: Typically look for amenities like free Wi-Fi, meeting rooms, early check-in/late check-out options, and convenient locations near business districts.

- Leisure Travelers: Often prioritize amenities such as pools, spas, restaurants, and proximity to tourist attractions.

- Families: Seek family-friendly amenities like larger rooms, cribs, and kid-friendly menus.

- Solo Travelers/Backpackers: Value affordability, safety, and access to essential amenities.

Understanding the needs and preferences of each segment allows hotels to develop targeted marketing campaigns, personalized services, and tailored packages. For example, a hotel located near a theme park may offer family packages with discounted tickets, while a city-center hotel might offer corporate packages for business travelers.

Actionable Step: Analyze booking data, guest feedback, and demographic information to identify your hotel's target markets and create tailored marketing strategies to attract these segments.

Strategies for Differentiating from Competitors

Differentiation is essential for standing out in a crowded market. Successful differentiation involves highlighting your hotel's unique selling propositions (USPs) and creating a brand identity that resonates with your target audience. Strategies for differentiation include:

- Offering Unique Amenities: Introduce amenities that competitors don't offer, such as a rooftop bar, wellness spa, or eco-friendly initiatives (e.g., a zero-waste program). Highlight these features in marketing campaigns.

- Providing Exceptional Service: Invest in staff

training to deliver outstanding guest experiences. Personal touches, such as welcome gifts, handwritten notes, or complimentary upgrades, can create memorable stays and generate positive reviews.

- Emphasizing Local Experiences: Position your hotel as an authentic local experience by partnering with nearby attractions, restaurants, and tour operators. Offer curated experiences that showcase the destination's culture, cuisine, and activities.

Case Study Example: A boutique hotel in a major city differentiated itself by offering themed rooms inspired by local artists, along with guided city tours and personalized itineraries. This approach attracted guests looking for a unique and immersive experience, leading to increased bookings and positive reviews.

Actionable Step: Conduct guest surveys to understand what makes your hotel stand out and incorporate these insights into your branding and marketing strategies.

Leveraging Market Trends for a Competitive Edge

Keeping up with market trends allows hotels to stay relevant and capitalize on emerging opportunities. Current trends impacting the hotel industry include:

- Sustainability: Guests increasingly prioritize eco-friendly accommodations. Hotels can leverage this trend by implementing green initiatives, such as energy-efficient lighting, recycling programs, and locally sourced F&B options.

- Technology Integration: Contactless check-ins, mobile key access, and virtual concierge services have become more popular, especially post-pandemic. Investing in technology can enhance the guest experience and streamline operations.

- Health and Wellness: Hotels offering wellness amenities, such as fitness centers, yoga classes, healthy dining options, and in-room exercise equipment, can attract health-conscious travelers.

- Remote Work and "Workcations": The rise of remote work has led to the concept of "workcations," where guests combine work and leisure travel. Hotels that provide work-friendly amenities, such as high-speed internet, co-working spaces, and extended stay packages, can tap into this trend.

Practical Example: A hotel noticed the trend of workcations and introduced a "Remote Work Package" that included high-speed Wi-Fi, a quiet workspace, daily breakfast, and discounted rates for extended stays. This package attracted digital nomads and remote workers, resulting in a 25% increase in bookings during off-peak seasons.

Actionable Step: Stay informed about industry trends by subscribing to hospitality publications, attending conferences, and participating in industry forums. Adapt your offerings to align with these trends to stay ahead of competitors.

Conducting a thorough market and competitive analysis is essential for understanding demand drivers, analyzing competitors, and identifying opportunities for differentiation in the hotel industry. By leveraging insights gained from this analysis, hoteliers can make informed decisions that align their offerings with market trends, target the right guest segments, and position their property for success. Real-life examples, case studies, and actionable steps provided in this section demonstrate how market and competitive analysis can play a pivotal role in turning around a distressed hotel and achieving long-term profitability.

Identifying the Root Causes of Distress

Understanding the root causes of distress is essential for turning around a struggling hotel. By identifying the underlying issues—whether they are operational inefficiencies, financial mismanagement, inadequate marketing strategies, or poor guest experiences—hotel owners and managers can develop targeted solutions that address these challenges. This section provides an in-depth analysis of these common root causes, offers practical examples and a case study of a hotel turnaround based on root cause analysis, and concludes with actionable steps for addressing the identified problems.

Operational Inefficiencies

Operational inefficiencies are one of the most common causes of distress in hotels. These inefficiencies can stem from outdated processes, poor staff management, or inadequate use of technology. Symptoms of operational inefficiencies may include slow check-in/check-out processes, inconsistent housekeeping, wasteful food and beverage (F&B) operations, and underutilized amenities.

For example, a hotel with an inefficient housekeeping schedule may face delays in room turnover, resulting in guests waiting longer for room availability. Additionally, an F&B department that over-orders supplies or fails to monitor inventory can lead to waste and increased costs.

Practical Example: A 150-room hotel experienced operational inefficiencies in its housekeeping department, leading to delays in preparing rooms for incoming guests. The hotel conducted an audit that revealed miscommunication between the front desk and housekeeping staff, resulting in cleaning delays and guest dissatisfaction. By implementing a property management system (PMS) that streamlined communication between departments, the hotel improved room turnover times and increased guest satisfaction.

Actionable Step: Conduct a comprehensive operational audit to identify inefficiencies in each department. Implement technology solutions like PMS or point-of-sale (POS) systems to streamline processes and enhance communication.

Financial Mismanagement

Financial mismanagement can lead to distress, even if a hotel appears to be performing well on the surface. This issue often arises from poor budgeting, excessive debt, or a failure to monitor expenses and revenue streams effectively. Common signs of financial mismanagement include cash flow problems, mounting debt, unpaid bills, and poor profitability.

For instance, a hotel may suffer financial distress if it takes on excessive debt for renovations without adequately projecting future revenue streams. This debt burden can overwhelm the hotel's finances, especially during low-occupancy periods.

Practical Example: A mid-sized hotel in a suburban area borrowed heavily to finance an ambitious renovation project. However, the hotel's management failed to conduct a thorough financial analysis to ensure that projected revenue would cover the increased debt obligations. As a result, the hotel struggled to make loan payments and experienced cash flow issues.

Actionable Step: Regularly monitor key financial statements, such as the income statement, balance sheet, and cash flow statement, to ensure a clear understanding of the hotel's financial health. Implement budgeting practices that account for seasonal fluctuations, and avoid taking on debt without a comprehensive financial analysis.

Inadequate Marketing Strategies

Inadequate marketing strategies can prevent a hotel from reaching its target audience, resulting in low occupancy rates and reduced revenue. Common marketing challenges include ineffective online presence, failure to differentiate from competitors, lack of targeted advertising, and underutilization of digital marketing channels.

For example, a hotel that does not actively engage with potential guests on social media or fails to optimize its website for search engines may miss out on valuable booking opportunities. Similarly, hotels that rely solely on traditional marketing methods may struggle to compete in a digital-first environment.

Practical Example: A boutique hotel located near a popular tourist destination struggled with low occupancy despite its unique offerings. The hotel's management relied solely on print advertisements and word-of-mouth marketing, neglecting online channels. After investing in a digital marketing campaign, which included social media engagement, search engine optimization (SEO), and targeted email campaigns, the hotel's visibility increased, leading to a 30% boost in bookings over six months.

Actionable Step: Develop a comprehensive marketing strategy that includes digital marketing channels, such as social media, SEO, email marketing, and pay-per-click (PPC) advertising. Regularly analyze marketing metrics to evaluate the effectiveness of campaigns and adjust strategies accordingly.

Poor Guest Experiences

Guest experiences play a crucial role in a hotel's success, as they directly impact reviews, repeat business, and referrals. Poor guest experiences—such as unclean rooms, unresponsive staff, slow service, or outdated amenities—can lead to negative reviews, damaging the hotel's reputation and driving potential guests away.

Hotels that fail to prioritize guest experience often see a decline in bookings and revenue, as dissatisfied guests share their experiences online. These reviews can quickly become a red flag for potential guests researching accommodations.

Practical Example: A 200-room hotel received numerous complaints about its outdated rooms, slow Wi-Fi, and unresponsive staff. Guest satisfaction scores dropped, and negative online reviews began to affect the hotel's reputation. In response, the hotel invested in room upgrades, provided staff training, and improved its Wi-Fi infrastructure. Over time, guest satisfaction improved, and positive reviews began to replace the negative ones, leading to increased bookings.

Actionable Step: Regularly monitor guest feedback through online reviews, surveys, and direct interactions. Use this feedback to identify areas for improvement and prioritize initiatives that enhance guest experiences, such as staff training, room upgrades, or technology improvements.

Case Study: A Hotel Turnaround Based on Root Cause Analysis

A 250-room hotel located in a tourist area faced declining occupancy rates, mounting debt, and a deteriorating reputation. The management conducted a root cause analysis to identify the key issues contributing to the hotel's distress:

- Operational Inefficiencies: Housekeeping staff frequently missed their cleaning targets, leading to delays in room availability.

- Financial Mismanagement: The hotel had taken on a high-interest loan for renovations without accurately projecting the impact on cash flow, resulting in an inability to meet monthly payments.

- Inadequate Marketing Strategies: The hotel's marketing efforts were limited to local print advertisements, and it lacked an online presence, making it difficult to reach out-of-town tourists.

- Poor Guest Experiences: Negative reviews indicated that guests were unhappy with the hotel's outdated amenities, unresponsive staff, and inconsistent service quality.

By addressing each of these root causes, the hotel developed a comprehensive turnaround plan:

- Operational Improvements: The hotel introduced a new PMS to improve communication between departments, resulting in faster room turnovers and increased efficiency.

- Financial Restructuring: The management renegotiated the terms of the high-interest loan, reducing monthly payments and easing cash flow pressures.

- Marketing Strategy: The hotel launched a digital marketing campaign, optimized its website, and engaged with potential guests on social media, which increased online visibility and bookings.

- Guest Experience Enhancements: The hotel invested in staff training and upgraded outdated amenities, leading to improved guest satisfaction and positive reviews.

Within a year, the hotel's occupancy rates increased by 25%, and profitability improved significantly, demonstrating the effectiveness of addressing root causes.

Actionable Steps for Addressing the Root Causes

To successfully address the root causes of distress, hotel owners and managers should implement the following actionable steps:

- Conduct Regular Audits: Perform comprehensive operational and financial audits to identify inefficiencies, financial mismanagement, and areas for improvement.

- Develop a Clear Marketing Strategy: Invest in digital marketing, optimize your website, and leverage social media to reach target audiences effectively. Tailor your messaging to highlight the hotel's unique selling propositions (USPs).

- Engage with Guests: Actively seek guest feedback through surveys, online reviews, and direct interactions. Use this feedback to address issues and improve guest experiences.

- Monitor Financial Health: Regularly review financial statements and key metrics, such as ADR, RevPAR, and cash flow, to detect signs of financial distress early. Implement budgeting practices and avoid taking on excessive debt without proper analysis.

- Invest in Staff Training: Ensure that staff members are well-trained, responsive, and capable of delivering exceptional guest experiences. Empower employees to resolve guest issues promptly.

Identifying and addressing the root causes of distress is the foundation of a successful hotel turnaround strategy. By recognizing and tackling operational inefficiencies, financial mismanagement, inadequate marketing strategies, and poor guest experiences, hotel owners and managers can develop targeted solutions that drive recovery and long-term profitability. The real-life case study and actionable steps provided in this section offer practical guidance for transforming a distressed hotel into a thriving and competitive business.

Understanding Stakeholder Interests

Successfully turning around a distressed hotel requires a comprehensive understanding of the interests and concerns of all stakeholders involved. These stakeholders include investors, lenders, creditors, hotel employees and management, the hotel brand or franchise, guests, and the local community. Each group has its own priorities, and addressing their needs is crucial for implementing an effective turnaround strategy. This section provides an in-depth analysis of each stakeholder group, real-world examples, and actionable steps for balancing competing interests and maintaining effective communication.

Investors, Lenders, and Creditors

Investors, lenders, and creditors are often the most financially invested stakeholders in a distressed hotel. Their primary concern is the return on their investment or loan, as well as the hotel's ability to repay debts. In distressed situations, they are particularly focused on preserving their capital, minimizing losses, and finding ways to restore profitability.

Key Considerations:

- Investors want to see a clear turnaround strategy that demonstrates potential profitability and growth. They may be open to additional funding if they believe the plan is viable.

- Lenders are concerned with the hotel's ability to meet loan obligations. They may consider restructuring loans, extending repayment terms, or negotiating interest rates if they believe the turnaround is achievable.

- Creditors, such as suppliers and vendors, want assurance that outstanding payments will be made and future transactions will be honored.

Practical Example: A distressed hotel had a significant loan from a financial institution, but the loan terms became unmanageable due to declining revenue. The hotel's management team proactively engaged with the lender and presented a detailed turnaround plan that included cost-saving measures, revenue growth strategies, and a timeline for repayment. Impressed by the plan, the lender agreed to restructure the loan by reducing the interest rate and extending the repayment period, providing the hotel with the necessary financial breathing room to implement its turnaround strategy.

Actionable Step: Engage investors, lenders, and creditors early in the turnaround process. Clearly communicate your strategy, provide transparent financial data, and be prepared to negotiate loan terms or payment schedules to maintain their support.

Hotel Employees and Management

Employees and management play a pivotal role in a hotel's success, but during periods of distress, they often face uncertainty, low morale, and job insecurity.

Ensuring that employees remain motivated and committed is essential for a successful turnaround.

Key Considerations:

- Employees want job security, fair wages, and a positive work environment.

- Management is focused on operational efficiency, guest satisfaction, and profitability but may struggle to maintain employee morale during challenging times.

Practical Example: A distressed hotel experienced high staff turnover due to uncertainty about its future. The management team addressed this issue by implementing transparent communication, providing regular updates on the turnaround progress, and offering incentives, such as performance-based bonuses. By involving employees in the decision-making process and recognizing their contributions, the hotel improved morale, reduced turnover, and saw improvements in service quality.

Actionable Step: Foster open communication with employees and management, and involve them in the turnaround process. Provide training and development opportunities, offer incentives for high performance, and create a positive work culture that encourages teamwork and collaboration.
Brand Reputation and Franchise Obligations

For hotels that are part of a larger brand or franchise, maintaining brand reputation and meeting franchise obligations is crucial. The brand represents a promise of quality and consistency to guests, and any deviation from these standards can have a negative impact on both the individual hotel and the larger brand.

Key Considerations:

- Franchise agreements may include requirements for marketing, operational standards, renovations, and royalty payments. Failing to meet these obligations can lead to penalties or even termination of the franchise agreement.

- A distressed hotel may have difficulty maintaining brand standards, leading to a decline in guest satisfaction and a tarnished reputation.

Practical Example: A distressed hotel part of a national brand was struggling to meet the franchise's quality standards due to budget constraints. To address this, the hotel's management reached out to the franchisor and negotiated a temporary reduction in royalty fees, allowing the hotel to allocate funds toward necessary renovations and service improvements. This cooperation helped the hotel maintain brand standards while working toward financial recovery.

Actionable Step: Communicate regularly with the brand or franchisor and be transparent about the hotel's challenges. Seek support in terms of marketing, training, or financial relief to help maintain brand standards during the turnaround process.

Guests and the Local Community

Guests are the lifeblood of any hotel, and their experiences determine the hotel's reputation, occupancy rates, and revenue. Additionally, the local community often plays a significant role in a hotel's success, especially if it relies on local businesses, events, and attractions.

Key Considerations:

- Guests expect a high level of service, cleanliness, and comfort. Negative experiences can lead to poor reviews, which can further damage a distressed hotel's reputation.

- The local community benefits from the hotel's operations through employment opportunities, business partnerships, and tourism. A distressed hotel can have a ripple effect on the local economy.

Practical Example: A distressed hotel facing declining guest satisfaction scores due to outdated amenities took steps to improve the guest experience by investing in essential renovations, training staff to be more responsive to guest needs, and launching a "Stay Local" campaign that partnered with nearby restaurants and attractions. This initiative not only improved guest satisfaction but also strengthened ties with the local community, leading to increased bookings and a more positive reputation.

Actionable Step: Prioritize guest experience by

addressing service quality, cleanliness, and amenities. Engage with the local community through partnerships, sponsorships, and events to build goodwill and attract local business.

Balancing Competing Stakeholder Interests

Balancing the competing interests of stakeholders is one of the most challenging aspects of managing a distressed hotel. Each stakeholder group has unique priorities, and addressing one group's needs may conflict with the interests of another. For example, investors may push for aggressive cost-cutting measures, while employees may resist changes that impact their wages or job security.

Actionable Strategies:

- Prioritize Communication: Maintain open lines of communication with all stakeholders. Be transparent about the hotel's challenges, the steps being taken to address them, and the progress made.

- Seek Collaborative Solutions: Involve stakeholders in decision-making processes, especially when implementing changes that affect them directly. For instance, engage employees in identifying cost-saving opportunities, or involve investors in discussions about potential revenue-generating strategies.

- Align Interests: Find common ground among stakeholders to align their interests. For example, if improving guest satisfaction is a shared goal, demonstrate how operational changes can benefit both guests and employees, ultimately leading to increased revenue and profitability.

Case Study Example: A distressed resort hotel faced pressure from investors to cut costs, but employees feared job losses. The hotel's management held meetings with both groups to find solutions that balanced cost savings with job retention. By implementing flexible work schedules, cross-training staff, and offering voluntary unpaid leave, the hotel was able to reduce expenses without resorting to layoffs, ultimately satisfying both investors and employees.

Tips for Effective Stakeholder Communication

Effective communication is the foundation for building trust, managing expectations, and maintaining stakeholder support during a turnaround. Here are some tips for communicating effectively with stakeholders:

- Be Transparent and Honest: Share both positive and negative updates with stakeholders. Transparency builds trust and demonstrates your commitment to addressing challenges.

- Provide Regular Updates: Keep stakeholders informed of progress, setbacks, and changes in strategy through regular reports, meetings, or newsletters.

- Tailor Communication: Customize your communication style and messaging based on the stakeholder group. For example, investors may require detailed financial data, while employees may appreciate information about how changes will impact their roles.

- Listen to Feedback: Encourage stakeholders to share their concerns, suggestions, and insights. Listening to feedback fosters collaboration and helps identify potential solutions.

Actionable Step: Establish a communication plan that outlines how and when you will engage with each stakeholder group. Ensure that communication is consistent, timely, and tailored to meet their needs.
Conclusion

Understanding and addressing the interests of all stakeholders—investors, lenders, creditors, employees, management, the brand or franchise, guests, and the local community—is crucial for a successful hotel turnaround. By balancing competing interests, maintaining transparent communication, and involving stakeholders in the decision-making process, hotel owners and managers can build the trust, support, and collaboration needed to navigate the complexities of a distressed hotel and achieve long-term success. The case studies, practical examples, and actionable steps provided in this section offer valuable insights into effectively managing stakeholder relationships during a hotel turnaround.

Risk Assessment and Mitigation Strategies

Risk management is a crucial component of turning around a distressed hotel, as it helps identify, assess, and address potential threats that can hinder recovery. This section delves into identifying potential risks, strategies for mitigating them, a case study of how effective risk management saved a distressed hotel, and practical steps for developing a comprehensive risk management plan. Additionally, we explore tools for risk assessment and ways to build resilience in hotel operations.

Identifying Potential Risks

Understanding the risks that can impact a distressed hotel is the first step toward developing an effective risk management strategy. These risks can be categorized into four primary areas:

- Operational Risks: These risks stem from internal inefficiencies or disruptions in hotel operations, such as staffing shortages, equipment breakdowns, poor service quality, and supply chain issues. For example, understaffing during peak seasons can lead to delayed room turnovers and reduced guest satisfaction.

- Financial Risks: Financial risks include challenges like insufficient cash flow, rising operational costs, high debt levels, or fluctuations in revenue due to seasonality. A distressed hotel with a significant loan burden may face the risk of defaulting on payments, resulting in foreclosure or bankruptcy.

- Legal Risks: These involve compliance with local regulations, health and safety standards, labor laws, and contractual obligations. Legal risks can arise from negligence in maintaining safety standards, leading to potential lawsuits, fines, or loss of licenses.

- Market Risks: Market risks are external factors such as changes in guest preferences, increased competition, economic downturns, or shifts in tourism trends. For example, a downturn in tourism due to a natural disaster, pandemic, or geopolitical event can drastically impact a hotel's revenue.

Actionable Step: Conduct a comprehensive risk assessment to identify all potential risks specific to your hotel. Engage with different departments and stakeholders to gain insights into the various threats that could affect operations, finances, legal compliance, or market performance.

Strategies for Mitigating Risks

Once risks are identified, implementing mitigation strategies can help minimize their impact. Here are some effective strategies for each type of risk:

- Operational Risks Mitigation:

  - Cross-Training Staff: Train employees to handle multiple roles, ensuring that operations can continue smoothly even during staffing shortages.

- o Regular Maintenance: Conduct preventive maintenance on equipment and facilities to avoid unexpected breakdowns and disruptions.

- o Streamline Operations: Implement technology solutions, such as property management systems (PMS) and point-of-sale (POS) systems, to improve efficiency and reduce human error.

- Financial Risks Mitigation:

  - o Cash Flow Management: Develop a detailed cash flow forecast and monitor expenses closely to avoid financial shortfalls.

  - o Diversify Revenue Streams: Explore additional revenue opportunities, such as offering event spaces, spa services, or F&B promotions, to reduce dependence on room bookings alone.

  - o Renegotiate Loan Terms: Work with lenders to restructure debt, reduce interest rates, or extend repayment terms, providing more financial flexibility.

- Legal Risks Mitigation:

  - o Compliance Audits: Conduct regular

> audits to ensure adherence to local regulations, safety standards, and contractual obligations.

  - o Legal Counsel: Engage with legal experts to review contracts, leases, and agreements to avoid potential legal pitfalls.

  - o Staff Training: Train employees on compliance issues, such as safety protocols, health regulations, and anti-discrimination laws.

- Market Risks Mitigation:

  - o Monitor Market Trends: Stay informed about market conditions, competitor activities, and guest preferences to adjust strategies accordingly.

  - o Flexible Pricing: Implement dynamic pricing strategies to adjust room rates based on demand fluctuations, local events, or seasonal trends.

  - o Adapt Marketing Strategies: Regularly update marketing campaigns and offerings to target new guest segments and address changing preferences.

Actionable Step: Create a risk mitigation plan that includes specific strategies for each identified risk, assign responsibilities to team members, and set timelines for implementation.

Case Study: How Risk Management Saved a Distressed Hotel

A 200-room hotel located in a popular tourist destination faced severe financial distress due to an unexpected drop in occupancy rates, rising operational costs, and poor guest reviews. The hotel's management team conducted a comprehensive risk assessment and discovered several critical issues:

- Operational Risks: Staff shortages during peak seasons led to delays in room turnovers and negative guest experiences.

- Financial Risks: The hotel was struggling to meet its loan obligations due to decreased revenue and high-interest payments.

- Market Risks: Increased competition from nearby hotels offering lower rates and better amenities further impacted occupancy levels.

In response, the hotel developed a risk management plan that included cross-training staff, renegotiating loan terms with the lender, and implementing a dynamic pricing strategy to compete with neighboring hotels. Additionally, the hotel invested in improving its marketing campaigns, targeting new guest segments, and offering unique amenities to differentiate itself from competitors.

Within 18 months, the hotel's occupancy rates increased by 30%, and its financial position stabilized, demonstrating how proactive risk management can

save a distressed hotel from failure.
Developing a Risk Management Plan

A risk management plan is a strategic document outlining how a hotel will identify, assess, and address potential risks. Here's a step-by-step guide to developing an effective plan:

- Identify Risks: Conduct a comprehensive risk assessment to identify potential threats across operational, financial, legal, and market areas.

- Assess Risks: Evaluate the likelihood and impact of each risk on hotel operations. Prioritize risks based on their potential severity and urgency.

- Develop Mitigation Strategies: Create specific strategies to address each risk, including preventive measures, contingency plans, and response actions.
- Assign Responsibilities: Assign team members to manage and monitor different aspects of the risk management plan.

- Monitor and Review: Regularly review and update the risk management plan to reflect changes in the hotel's operations, market conditions, or regulatory environment.

Actionable Step: Implement the risk management plan as a living document that evolves with the hotel's circumstances. Schedule regular risk assessments and adjust the plan accordingly.

Practical Tools for Risk Assessment

Several tools can help hotels conduct effective risk assessments and implement mitigation strategies:

- SWOT Analysis: Use a SWOT (Strengths, Weaknesses, Opportunities, Threats) analysis to identify internal and external factors that may impact the hotel.

- Risk Matrix: Create a risk matrix to evaluate risks based on their likelihood and potential impact, helping prioritize risk management efforts.

- Scenario Planning: Develop different scenarios (e.g., economic downturn, staffing shortages, natural disasters) and create contingency plans for each situation.

- Financial Analysis Software: Utilize financial analysis tools to monitor cash flow, profitability, and debt obligations, helping identify financial risks early on.

- Guest Feedback Platforms: Leverage online review platforms, guest surveys, and feedback tools to monitor guest experiences and address operational issues before they escalate.

Actionable Step: Incorporate these tools into regular risk assessments and decision-making processes, ensuring a proactive approach to identifying and addressing risks.

Building Resilience in Hotel Operations

Building resilience means preparing the hotel to adapt to and recover from potential risks and challenges. This requires a culture of continuous improvement, flexibility, and responsiveness:

- Invest in Staff Training: Equip employees with the skills and knowledge needed to handle unexpected situations, such as guest complaints, emergencies, or operational disruptions.

- Embrace Technology: Implement technology solutions like property management systems, revenue management software, and digital marketing platforms to streamline operations, improve decision-making, and respond quickly to market changes.

- Develop Strong Partnerships: Build relationships with suppliers, vendors, and industry contacts who can provide support or resources during challenging times.

- Diversify Revenue Streams: Explore opportunities to diversify revenue, such as offering event spaces, F&B services, or wellness amenities, to reduce reliance on a single source of income.

Actionable Step: Encourage a culture of resilience by empowering staff, investing in technology, and continuously seeking opportunities for growth and improvement.

Effective risk assessment and mitigation strategies are essential for the successful turnaround of a distressed hotel. By identifying potential risks, implementing mitigation strategies, developing a comprehensive risk management plan, and utilizing practical tools, hotel owners and managers can proactively address threats and build resilience in their operations. The case study demonstrates the power of proactive risk management in saving a distressed hotel, providing valuable insights for those facing similar challenges. Embracing a culture of resilience, continuous improvement, and adaptability can help ensure that the hotel is prepared to navigate future uncertainties and achieve long-term success.

Chapter 3: Creating a Turnaround Plan for Distressed Hotels

In any effort to bring a distressed hotel back to profitability, developing a well-structured turnaround plan is essential. This chapter focuses on the critical steps needed to create and implement a comprehensive plan that addresses the unique challenges faced by struggling hotel properties. It emphasizes the importance of setting clear, realistic goals and objectives that are tailored to the hotel's market opportunities. By defining measurable goals, hotel owners and managers can create a roadmap that guides every aspect of the turnaround process. The chapter will also explore how aligning these goals with both short-term and long-term strategies ensures that progress is sustainable and on track, as illustrated by a case study of a hotel that achieved a successful turnaround through well-defined objectives.

Financial restructuring plays a significant role in stabilizing a distressed hotel. This chapter provides insights into creating a financial plan that reduces expenses, improves cash flow, and renegotiates terms with lenders and creditors. It offers practical tips for managing debt obligations and introduces revenue-enhancing strategies that can bolster the hotel's financial health. A real-life case study is presented to showcase how effective financial restructuring saved a hotel from the brink of bankruptcy, underscoring the importance of prudent financial management and forecasting for long-term sustainability.

Operational improvements are another critical component of a successful turnaround plan. This chapter delves into strategies for streamlining hotel operations to enhance efficiency and improve guest experiences. Real-life examples illustrate how operational changes can transform a struggling hotel by implementing cost-saving measures and utilizing technology to boost operational performance. The chapter provides actionable steps that can be applied to optimize various aspects of hotel operations, from housekeeping to front desk management.

Marketing and rebranding are equally vital for breathing new life into a distressed hotel. This section covers the development of a compelling brand identity and effective digital marketing strategies that help reposition the hotel in the market. By engaging with guests through social media, creating attractive packages, and building relationships with travel agencies and distribution channels, hotels can significantly increase bookings and revenue. A case study of a successful rebranding effort demonstrates how a revitalized image can lead to a hotel's resurgence.

Employee engagement and training are often overlooked but are crucial in executing a turnaround plan. This chapter highlights the importance of investing in staff training programs to improve service quality and empower employees to take ownership of the turnaround process. Real-life examples show how staff engagement can lead to increased guest satisfaction, while tips for maintaining morale during challenging times offer guidance on keeping employees motivated. Recognizing and rewarding employee contributions can help build a culture of commitment and excellence that is essential for a successful turnaround.

Finally, the chapter emphasizes the importance of monitoring and adjusting the turnaround plan regularly. By tracking progress through key performance indicators (KPIs) and conducting regular performance reviews, hotel managers can stay on course and adapt to changing market conditions. Learning from setbacks and celebrating successes are crucial elements that help maintain momentum and keep the turnaround process moving forward. This chapter will provide actionable steps and practical insights to ensure that the turnaround plan is not only effective but also flexible enough to respond to any challenges that may arise.

Establishing Goals and Objectives

Establishing clear, realistic, and measurable goals is the foundation of any successful hotel turnaround strategy. These goals serve as the guiding principles that direct the actions and decisions of all stakeholders involved in revitalizing a distressed property. This section will explore how to define realistic and measurable goals, align objectives with market opportunities, and set both short-term and long-term goals. We'll delve into a case study of a hotel that successfully turned around by establishing clear goals, outline strategies for engaging stakeholders in the goal-setting process, and discuss methods for tracking progress.

Defining Realistic and Measurable Goals

The first step in establishing goals and objectives for a distressed hotel is to define what success looks like in clear, quantifiable terms. Goals should be Specific, Measurable, Achievable, Relevant, and Time-bound (SMART). This approach ensures that goals are realistic and attainable, allowing the team to track progress and adjust strategies as needed.

For example, rather than setting a vague goal like "increase revenue," a SMART goal would be: "Increase the hotel's monthly revenue by 20% within the next six months by targeting new corporate clients and implementing a dynamic pricing strategy." This goal is specific (targeting new corporate clients and using dynamic pricing), measurable (20% increase), achievable (based on market research), relevant (to the hotel's financial turnaround), and time-bound (six months).

Actionable Step: Conduct a SWOT (Strengths, Weaknesses, Opportunities, Threats) analysis to gain a comprehensive understanding of the hotel's current situation. Use this analysis to identify realistic and measurable goals that address weaknesses, leverage strengths, and capitalize on market opportunities. Aligning Objectives with Market Opportunities

For a hotel turnaround to be successful, goals and objectives must align with existing and emerging market opportunities. This involves understanding the hotel's competitive landscape, guest preferences, and local demand drivers. By tailoring objectives to these opportunities, a distressed hotel can position itself to attract the right target audience and achieve sustainable growth.

For instance, if the local market shows a growing demand for eco-friendly accommodations, the hotel might set a goal to "achieve Green Key certification within the next 12 months by implementing sustainable practices in energy consumption, waste management, and water conservation." This goal not only aligns with market opportunities but also differentiates the hotel from competitors.

Practical Example: A hotel located near a convention center identified an opportunity to attract business travelers and conference attendees. The management team set a goal to increase corporate bookings by 30% over the next year by creating tailored business packages, enhancing meeting facilities, and partnering with local event organizers. This targeted approach allowed the hotel to tap into a lucrative market segment and drive consistent revenue.

Actionable Step: Conduct thorough market research to identify trends, preferences, and demand drivers within your hotel's target audience. Use this data to set objectives that align with these opportunities, ensuring that your turnaround plan is market-responsive.

Case Study: How Clear Goals Led to a Hotel's Successful Turnaround

A luxury beachfront hotel in distress faced declining occupancy rates, negative guest reviews, and financial losses. The management team decided to implement a turnaround strategy, starting with setting clear, measurable goals. Their goals included:

- Increase average occupancy rates from 55% to 75% within 12 months by improving guest experience, offering seasonal promotions, and targeting local travelers.

- Achieve a guest satisfaction score of 85% within six months by enhancing staff training, upgrading amenities, and responding promptly to guest feedback.

- Reduce operational costs by 15% within nine months through energy-saving initiatives, renegotiating vendor contracts, and streamlining housekeeping processes.

The team developed specific action plans to achieve each goal. They introduced a loyalty program for repeat guests, partnered with travel agencies to promote weekend packages, and invested in staff training to improve service quality. By continuously monitoring progress and making data-driven adjustments, the hotel not only met its goals but exceeded them. Occupancy rates reached 80%, guest satisfaction scores improved to 90%, and operational costs were reduced by 18%. This turnaround transformed the hotel's financial performance and reputation, demonstrating the power of setting clear, measurable goals.

Actionable Step: Use SMART goals as the foundation of your turnaround strategy. Break down each goal into actionable steps and assign responsibilities to

team members. Regularly review progress and make adjustments based on performance metrics.
Setting Short-Term and Long-Term Goals

Effective turnaround strategies involve setting both short-term and long-term goals. Short-term goals are designed to generate quick wins and build momentum, while long-term goals focus on sustained growth and profitability.

Short-Term Goals: These typically span 3 to 6 months and address immediate challenges or opportunities. Examples include:

- Increasing occupancy rates by 15% within the next three months by offering discounts and promotions.

- Improving guest satisfaction scores by 10% in the next quarter through enhanced staff training and service delivery.

- Reducing food and beverage costs by 8% within six months by renegotiating supplier contracts.

Long-Term Goals: These extend beyond six months and focus on building a solid foundation for the hotel's future. Examples include:

- Achieving an annual revenue growth rate of 25% over the next two years by expanding corporate bookings and diversifying revenue streams.

- Attaining a four-star rating on major travel

websites within 12 months by enhancing amenities, services, and guest experiences.

- Reducing energy consumption by 20% over the next year through sustainable practices and energy-efficient technologies.

Actionable Step: Develop a timeline for both short-term and long-term goals, with specific milestones and deadlines. This timeline should serve as a roadmap for the turnaround process, ensuring that each objective is met systematically.

Strategies for Engaging Stakeholders in Goal-Setting

Engaging stakeholders in the goal-setting process is crucial for gaining buy-in, fostering accountability, and ensuring a shared vision. This involves collaborating with employees, management, investors, lenders, and even guests to create goals that reflect their perspectives and expectations.

Practical Example: A hotel facing financial difficulties involved its employees in the goal-setting process by conducting brainstorming sessions. Employees were encouraged to suggest ways to improve operational efficiency and reduce costs. One of the ideas—replacing single-use toiletries with refillable dispensers—helped the hotel save $10,000 annually and aligned with the hotel's sustainability goals.

Engaging investors and lenders is also vital, as their support may be needed for funding or restructuring debt. Presenting clear, measurable goals and a well-defined turnaround strategy can build confidence among these stakeholders, increasing the likelihood of financial assistance.

Actionable Step: Organize goal-setting workshops or meetings with key stakeholders. Encourage open dialogue, listen to feedback, and incorporate their suggestions into the final objectives. This collaborative approach fosters a sense of ownership and commitment to achieving the turnaround plan.

Tracking Progress Toward Goals

Tracking progress is essential to ensure that the turnaround plan stays on course and goals are met. Regular monitoring allows hotel management to identify areas of success, address challenges, and make data-driven adjustments.

Key Performance Indicators (KPIs): Use KPIs to track progress toward goals. For example:

- Occupancy Rate for measuring room sales performance.

- Revenue per Available Room (RevPAR) for assessing revenue efficiency.

- Guest Satisfaction Scores from surveys and online reviews to monitor service quality.

- Operating Expenses as a Percentage of Revenue to evaluate cost efficiency.

Regular Performance Reviews: Schedule monthly or

quarterly performance reviews to assess progress, identify barriers, and adjust strategies as needed. Involving stakeholders in these reviews can provide valuable insights and ensure continued alignment with the turnaround plan.

Case Study Example: A hotel struggling with declining guest satisfaction scores implemented a bi-weekly review process to monitor progress toward its goal of achieving an 85% satisfaction rate. By analyzing guest feedback and identifying service gaps, the hotel made targeted improvements, such as enhancing staff training and upgrading in-room amenities. This proactive approach allowed the hotel to reach its satisfaction goal within four months.

Actionable Step: Create a tracking system that includes KPIs, timelines, and responsible parties. Regularly update the tracking system to reflect progress and share updates with stakeholders to maintain momentum and accountability.

Establishing clear, realistic, and measurable goals is the foundation of any hotel turnaround strategy. By aligning objectives with market opportunities, engaging stakeholders, and tracking progress, distressed hotels can create a roadmap to recovery and long-term success. The case study and practical examples provided demonstrate the transformative power of goal-setting in achieving a successful turnaround. With a well-defined plan, consistent monitoring, and the commitment of all stakeholders, distressed hotels can navigate the challenges they face and emerge stronger and more profitable.

Developing a Financial Restructuring Plan

Developing a financial restructuring plan is a crucial step in turning around a distressed hotel, as it directly addresses the financial challenges that threaten the property's viability. A well-crafted financial restructuring plan focuses on reducing expenses, improving cash flow, negotiating with lenders and creditors, identifying revenue-enhancing strategies, managing debt obligations, and creating a sustainable financial forecast. This section provides in-depth analysis, practical examples, a real-life case study, and actionable steps to guide you through the process of developing an effective financial restructuring plan.

Reducing Expenses and Improving Cash Flow

The first step in financial restructuring is to conduct a thorough review of all expenses to identify opportunities for cost savings. A detailed examination of operational, administrative, and maintenance costs can uncover inefficiencies and areas where expenses can be reduced without compromising service quality.

Practical Example: A hotel struggling with high utility bills conducted an energy audit and discovered that outdated lighting and HVAC systems were consuming excessive amounts of electricity. By switching to LED lighting and installing programmable thermostats, the hotel reduced its monthly energy costs by 20%, resulting in annual savings of $50,000. Similarly, implementing a linen reuse program reduced laundry expenses by 15%.

Actionable Steps:

- Conduct a comprehensive review of all expense categories, including utilities, staffing, food and beverage, maintenance, and administrative costs.

- Identify high-cost areas and implement cost-saving measures such as energy-efficient upgrades, renegotiating vendor contracts, or reducing waste.

- Monitor expenses regularly to ensure that cost-saving measures are effective and sustainable.

In addition to reducing expenses, improving cash flow is essential for maintaining day-to-day operations. This can be achieved by accelerating receivables, delaying payables, and managing inventory levels efficiently.

Example: A hotel introduced early payment incentives for guests who booked directly through the hotel's website. This initiative improved cash flow by reducing the average collection period from 30 days to 15 days, providing the hotel with the funds needed to cover immediate expenses.

Actionable Steps:

- Offer discounts or incentives for early payments to improve cash flow.

- Negotiate extended payment terms with suppliers to delay cash outflows.

- Monitor cash flow projections weekly to identify potential shortfalls and take corrective action.

Negotiating with Lenders and Creditors

Negotiating with lenders and creditors is a critical component of a financial restructuring plan, especially for distressed hotels with significant debt obligations. Lenders may be willing to offer more favorable terms if they believe the hotel has a viable turnaround plan and is committed to improving its financial position.

Practical Example: A distressed hotel with an outstanding loan balance of $2 million was facing the threat of foreclosure. The hotel's management team approached the lender with a detailed financial restructuring plan that included cost-saving measures, revenue-enhancing strategies, and a commitment to making regular payments. As a result, the lender agreed to restructure the loan by reducing the interest rate and extending the repayment period by five years, which eased the hotel's financial burden and provided time to implement the turnaround plan.

Actionable Steps:

- Prepare a comprehensive financial restructuring plan that demonstrates how the hotel will improve its financial position.

- Communicate openly and honestly with lenders and creditors about the challenges faced by the hotel and your proposed solutions.

- Explore options such as interest rate reductions, loan extensions, payment deferrals, or debt-for-equity swaps.

Case Study: A Financial Restructuring That Saved a Hotel from Bankruptcy

A mid-sized hotel in a popular tourist destination faced financial distress due to a combination of declining occupancy rates, high debt levels, and operational inefficiencies. The hotel's management recognized the need for a financial restructuring plan to avoid bankruptcy and regain profitability.

Step 1: Reducing Expenses – The management team conducted a comprehensive review of all expenses and identified several cost-saving opportunities. They implemented an energy-saving program that reduced utility costs by 25%, renegotiated contracts with suppliers, and introduced more efficient inventory management practices.

Step 2: Improving Cash Flow – The hotel launched a marketing campaign to attract more direct bookings, which improved cash flow by reducing commission fees paid to third-party booking platforms. Additionally, the hotel offered discounts for early payments, which helped accelerate receivables.

Step 3: Negotiating with Lenders – The hotel's management approached its primary lender with a detailed turnaround plan that demonstrated how cost reductions and revenue enhancements would improve profitability. The lender agreed to restructure the loan, reducing monthly payments and providing the hotel with a six-month grace period to stabilize its finances.

Outcome: Within 18 months, the hotel had achieved a 30% increase in occupancy rates, reduced operating expenses by 20%, and returned to profitability. The successful financial restructuring plan saved the hotel from bankruptcy and restored its financial health.

Key Takeaway: A well-executed financial restructuring plan, combined with open communication with lenders and a commitment to cost-saving measures, can enable a distressed hotel to overcome financial challenges and achieve long-term stability.
Identifying Revenue-Enhancing Strategies

While reducing expenses is crucial, identifying opportunities to increase revenue is equally important in a financial restructuring plan. Revenue-enhancing strategies can help generate additional cash flow, allowing the hotel to cover its financial obligations and reinvest in improvements.

Practical Example: A hotel struggling with low occupancy rates identified an opportunity to attract local residents by offering "staycation" packages. By promoting weekend getaways and family-friendly activities, the hotel increased weekend occupancy from 40% to 70% within three months, generating an additional $60,000 in revenue.

Actionable Steps:

- Analyze guest demographics and preferences to

identify potential revenue opportunities (e.g., themed packages, corporate events, seasonal promotions).

- Implement dynamic pricing strategies to adjust room rates based on demand, maximizing revenue during peak periods.

- Partner with local businesses, tour operators, or travel agencies to offer bundled packages and experiences.

Practical Tips for Managing Debt Obligations

Effective debt management is a key aspect of financial restructuring. Hotels with high levels of debt must prioritize managing their obligations to avoid default and maintain positive relationships with creditors.

Practical Example: A hotel with multiple loans consolidated its debt by obtaining a single, low-interest loan to pay off existing debts. This move reduced monthly payments by 30%, allowing the hotel to allocate more funds toward operational improvements and marketing efforts.

Actionable Steps:

- Create a detailed debt repayment schedule that outlines payment due dates, amounts, and interest rates.

- Prioritize paying off high-interest debt first to reduce overall interest expenses.

- Explore options for refinancing or consolidating debt to lower monthly payments.

Financial Forecasting for Long-Term Sustainability

Financial forecasting is essential for ensuring the long-term sustainability of a distressed hotel. By developing accurate financial projections, hotel owners and managers can identify potential challenges, plan for future investments, and make informed decisions.

Practical Example: A hotel undergoing financial restructuring created a three-year financial forecast that included projected revenue, expenses, and cash flow. By regularly comparing actual performance against the forecast, the hotel management team was able to identify deviations early, make necessary adjustments, and stay on track toward financial stability.

Actionable Steps:

- Develop financial projections for at least three years, including revenue, expenses, cash flow, and profitability.

- Regularly review and update the forecast based on actual performance and market conditions.

- Use the forecast to guide decision-making, identify potential financial risks, and plan for future investments.

Developing a financial restructuring plan is a critical step in turning around a distressed hotel. By focusing on reducing expenses, improving cash flow, negotiating with lenders, identifying revenue-enhancing strategies, managing debt obligations, and creating a financial forecast, hotels can regain financial stability and position themselves for long-term success. The case study and practical examples provided in this section demonstrate the effectiveness of a well-executed financial restructuring plan, offering actionable steps that can be applied to any distressed hotel facing financial challenges. Through careful planning, open communication with creditors, and a commitment to improving financial performance, a distressed hotel can successfully navigate financial challenges and achieve profitability.

Operational Improvements

Operational improvements are often the cornerstone of a successful hotel turnaround strategy, as they directly impact a hotel's ability to deliver exceptional service, reduce costs, and ultimately improve profitability. By streamlining operations, enhancing guest experiences, implementing cost-saving measures, and leveraging technology, a distressed hotel can significantly boost its performance and regain competitiveness in the market. This section will delve into practical examples, a real-life case study, and actionable steps for implementing operational improvements to transform a struggling hotel.

Streamlining Operations for Efficiency

Streamlining operations involves identifying

inefficiencies in daily processes and implementing changes to optimize workflows, reduce costs, and improve productivity. Every department, from front desk operations to housekeeping and food and beverage services, plays a critical role in achieving overall efficiency.

Practical Example: A hotel struggling with long check-in and check-out times found that the manual data entry process was causing delays and frustrating guests. By implementing an automated check-in system with self-service kiosks, the hotel reduced check-in times by 50%, improved staff productivity, and enhanced the guest experience. This change also allowed front desk staff to focus on personalized guest interactions, improving overall service quality.

Actionable Steps:

- Conduct a thorough operational audit to identify bottlenecks, redundancies, and inefficiencies in each department.

- Implement standardized processes and procedures to ensure consistency across all operations.

- Provide cross-training opportunities for staff to enhance flexibility and responsiveness during peak periods.

Key Takeaway: Streamlining operations not only reduces costs but also enables staff to deliver a more consistent and efficient level of service, which can have a direct impact on guest satisfaction and retention.

Enhancing Guest Experience and Service Quality

Guest experience is a critical factor in a hotel's success, and distressed hotels often face challenges with maintaining high service quality. Enhancing the guest experience can lead to positive reviews, repeat business, and increased revenue.

Practical Example: A hotel experiencing declining guest satisfaction scores identified that a lack of personalized service was contributing to negative reviews. In response, the hotel introduced a guest preferences program, where staff members collected and recorded information about guest preferences (e.g., room temperature, pillow type, dietary restrictions). This data was used to personalize each guest's stay, resulting in a 20% increase in guest satisfaction scores within six months.

Actionable Steps:

- Train staff on the importance of delivering exceptional service and how to anticipate guest needs.

- Implement a guest feedback system to capture insights and identify areas for improvement.

- Introduce personalized touches, such as welcome notes, room upgrades for loyal guests, or complimentary amenities, to create a memorable experience.

Key Takeaway: Enhancing the guest experience requires a commitment to delivering personalized service, attention to detail, and a genuine desire to exceed guest expectations. When guests feel valued and cared for, they are more likely to return and recommend the hotel to others.

Real-Life Example: How Operational Changes Transformed a Struggling Hotel

A mid-range hotel in a popular tourist destination was facing operational inefficiencies, declining guest satisfaction, and mounting financial losses. The hotel's management recognized the need for a turnaround and implemented several operational changes to improve performance.

Step 1: Streamlining Housekeeping Operations – The hotel conducted a time-and-motion study to analyze housekeeping tasks and identified that staff members were spending excessive time traveling between floors to collect supplies. To address this issue, the hotel introduced supply carts on each floor, which reduced travel time and increased productivity. As a result, the average room cleaning time decreased by 30%, allowing the hotel to accommodate early check-ins more efficiently.

Step 2: Implementing a Revenue Management Strategy – The hotel introduced dynamic pricing based on demand patterns and local events. This change led to an increase in occupancy rates during off-peak periods and maximized revenue during high-demand seasons.

Step 3: Enhancing the Guest Experience – The hotel launched a "Service Excellence" training program for staff, focusing on proactive communication, problem-solving, and personalized interactions. This training improved guest satisfaction scores by 25% within three months.

Outcome: Within 12 months, the hotel achieved a 40% increase in revenue, improved guest satisfaction scores, and reduced operational costs by 15%. These operational changes transformed the hotel's financial performance and reputation, allowing it to regain a competitive edge in the market.

Implementing Cost-Saving Measures

Reducing operational costs is essential for improving profitability, especially for distressed hotels. Cost-saving measures can be implemented across various departments without compromising the quality of service.

Practical Example: A hotel facing high food and beverage costs implemented portion control measures and conducted regular inventory checks to reduce waste. By standardizing portion sizes and using inventory management software, the hotel reduced food waste by 20% and saved $25,000 annually.

Actionable Steps:

- Conduct regular audits of inventory, energy usage, and labor expenses to identify cost-saving opportunities.

- Negotiate contracts with suppliers to secure better rates or bulk discounts.

- Implement sustainable practices, such as energy-efficient lighting, water-saving devices, and waste reduction programs, to reduce utility costs.

Key Takeaway: Implementing cost-saving measures requires a proactive approach to monitoring expenses, negotiating with suppliers, and finding innovative ways to reduce waste. These measures contribute to improved profitability and financial stability.

Utilizing Technology for Operational Efficiency

Technology plays a crucial role in improving operational efficiency, streamlining processes, and enhancing the guest experience. By adopting modern technology solutions, hotels can automate repetitive tasks, reduce manual errors, and free up staff time to focus on guest service.

Practical Example: A hotel implemented a property management system (PMS) that integrated with its reservation, housekeeping, and accounting systems. This technology allowed for real-time updates on room availability, automated billing, and efficient communication between departments. As a result, the hotel reduced administrative workload, improved accuracy, and enhanced the overall guest experience.

Actionable Steps:

- Invest in a PMS that offers integrated functionality for reservations, housekeeping, billing, and reporting.

- Implement a customer relationship management (CRM) system to track guest preferences, interactions, and feedback.

- Use data analytics to monitor performance metrics, identify trends, and make data-driven decisions.

Key Takeaway: Leveraging technology not only streamlines operations but also provides valuable insights into guest behavior, preferences, and operational performance. This data can be used to make informed decisions that improve efficiency and enhance the guest experience.

Actionable Steps for Boosting Operational Performance

To successfully implement operational improvements, hotel management must adopt a structured approach that involves evaluating existing processes, identifying areas for improvement, and making data-driven changes. Here are some actionable steps for boosting operational performance:

- Conduct an Operational Audit: Regularly review all operational processes to identify inefficiencies, bottlenecks, and opportunities for improvement. This audit should cover all departments, including front desk, housekeeping, food and beverage, and maintenance.

- Set Clear Operational Goals: Establish specific, measurable, achievable, relevant, and time-bound (SMART) goals for each department. For example, set a target to reduce average room cleaning time by 15% within three months or improve guest satisfaction scores by 10% over the next quarter.

- Train and Empower Staff: Invest in ongoing training programs to equip staff with the skills needed to deliver exceptional service and adapt to changing operational requirements. Empower employees to make decisions and take ownership of their roles, fostering a culture of accountability and continuous improvement.

- Monitor and Measure Performance: Use key performance indicators (KPIs) to track operational efficiency, such as average check-in times, housekeeping turnaround, food and beverage costs, and guest satisfaction scores. Regularly review these metrics and adjust strategies as needed.

- Implement Technology Solutions: Adopt technology solutions that streamline operations, enhance communication, and improve guest experiences. Monitor the effectiveness of these solutions and make adjustments to ensure they align with the hotel's goals.

- Solicit Guest Feedback: Encourage guests to provide feedback through surveys, online reviews, and in-person interactions. Use this feedback to identify areas for improvement and implement changes that address guest concerns.

Operational improvements are a critical component of any hotel turnaround strategy, as they directly impact efficiency, guest experience, and profitability. By streamlining operations, enhancing service quality, implementing cost-saving measures, and leveraging technology, distressed hotels can transform their performance and regain a competitive edge. The practical examples, real-life case study, and actionable steps provided in this section offer a comprehensive roadmap for implementing operational improvements that drive positive results. Through continuous monitoring, staff engagement, and a commitment to excellence, distressed hotels can achieve sustainable growth and long-term success.

Marketing and Rebranding Strategies

Effectively marketing and rebranding a distressed hotel is crucial to transforming its image and attracting guests. This section delves into strategies that can breathe new life into a hotel, focusing on brand identity, digital marketing, social media engagement, crafting compelling offers, and building partnerships with travel agencies and distribution channels.

Developing a Compelling Brand Identity

The foundation of any successful rebranding strategy lies in establishing a compelling brand identity. For a distressed hotel, this process begins with evaluating the current brand's strengths, weaknesses, and the unique value proposition that can set it apart from competitors. It's essential to answer the following questions:

- What unique experiences or amenities can the hotel offer?

- Who is the target audience, and what are their preferences?

- How can the hotel's story and history be woven into a brand narrative?

A strong brand identity extends beyond just a logo or tagline; it encapsulates the hotel's values, guest experience, and personality. For instance, if a hotel is located near a beautiful beachfront, the brand identity might emphasize a relaxed, coastal lifestyle, catering to travelers looking for a tranquil escape. This approach influences everything from the visual aesthetics (color schemes, website design, marketing materials) to the tone of voice used in communications.

Actionable Steps:

- Conduct a brand audit to understand current perceptions.

- Develop a brand persona that aligns with target demographics.

- Redesign visual elements like logos, signage, and marketing materials to reflect the new brand identity.

- Train staff to embody the brand's values in every guest interaction.

Digital Marketing Strategies for Distressed Hotels

In today's digital age, leveraging online platforms is vital for reaching potential guests. A strong digital marketing strategy can turn around the fortunes of a distressed hotel by creating awareness, driving bookings, and building brand loyalty.

1. Search Engine Optimization (SEO): Ensuring the hotel's website ranks high on search engines is crucial. Keywords related to location, amenities, and unique offerings should be strategically embedded in the website content. For example, if the hotel offers pet-friendly accommodation, optimizing for phrases like "pet-friendly hotels near [city]" can attract guests searching for this specific feature.

2. Pay-Per-Click (PPC) Advertising: PPC campaigns on Google and social media platforms can be highly effective, particularly when targeting potential guests in specific geographical areas. The budget should be adjusted based on peak booking seasons and major events in the area.

3. Content Marketing: Publishing high-quality content such as blogs, videos, and virtual tours can engage potential guests and improve SEO rankings. For example, creating blog posts about "Top Attractions Near [Hotel Name]" or "How to Have a Perfect Weekend Stay at [Hotel Name]" can showcase the hotel's proximity to points of interest and amenities.

4. Email Marketing: Building an email list of past and potential guests allows for targeted marketing. Sending personalized offers, such as discounts for returning guests or exclusive promotions, can drive repeat business.

Actionable Steps:

- Audit the hotel's website for SEO improvements.
- Create a content calendar with topics that resonate with target guests.

- Invest in PPC campaigns during high-traffic seasons.

- Build and segment an email marketing list for tailored promotions.

Case Study: A Successful Rebranding That Revitalized a Hotel's Image

One notable example of successful hotel rebranding is the transformation of the Marriott Renaissance Pittsburgh Hotel. Initially seen as an outdated property, it struggled to attract guests in a competitive market. The hotel's management invested in a complete rebranding effort that focused on its rich history and prime riverfront location.

Key Strategies:

- The hotel adopted a modern yet classic brand identity, reflecting the blend of historic architecture and contemporary amenities.

- It leveraged digital marketing, using professional photography and videos to highlight the property's unique features, such as panoramic river views and luxury suites.

- The team created a series of social media campaigns that shared stories of the hotel's past, intertwining them with modern amenities, thus appealing to both business travelers and leisure guests.

As a result, the hotel experienced a 35% increase in bookings within the first year of rebranding and significantly improved its online reputation.

Key Takeaway: Effective rebranding isn't just about changing the logo or updating the website. It involves telling a story that resonates with the target audience, supported by consistent and strategic digital marketing efforts.

Engaging with Guests Through Social Media

Social media is a powerful tool for engaging with guests and building a community around the hotel brand. It allows distressed hotels to showcase improvements, share guest experiences, and provide real-time updates.

1. Consistent Posting: Hotels should maintain an active presence on platforms like Instagram, Facebook, and Twitter. Posting daily updates, behind-the-scenes looks at renovations, or sharing guest testimonials can keep followers engaged.

2. User-Generated Content: Encouraging guests to share their experiences through photos and reviews, and reposting this content on the hotel's social media channels, creates a sense of authenticity. For instance, incentivizing guests to share their stay experiences with a branded hashtag can generate organic exposure.

3. Engaging Stories and Reels: Utilizing Instagram Stories and Reels to showcase amenities, room tours, or dining experiences can make potential guests feel more connected to the brand.

Actionable Steps:

- Develop a social media calendar with regular posts.
- Create a unique hashtag for guests to use during their stay.

- Respond promptly to guest comments and inquiries on social media to build relationships.

Creating Packages and Promotions to Drive Bookings

Special packages and promotions can be an effective way to attract guests, especially during off-peak periods or when a hotel is recovering from financial distress. The key is to craft offers that provide value and align with guests' interests.

Examples of Packages:

- Staycation Deals: Target locals with discounted rates for extended stays, breakfast-included packages, or spa treatments.

- Themed Packages: Create packages around holidays, local events, or unique experiences, such as "Romantic Getaway," "Family Adventure," or "Golf and Relaxation."

- Loyalty Programs: Offering a loyalty program that provides discounts, free nights, or room upgrades for returning guests can foster repeat business.

Actionable Steps:

- Analyze booking trends to identify peak and off-peak periods.

- Collaborate with local businesses to create joint packages (e.g., a partnership with a local restaurant or attraction).

- Promote these packages through the hotel's

website, email marketing, and social media.

Building Relationships with Travel Agencies and Distribution Channels

Partnering with travel agencies and leveraging online travel agencies (OTAs) can significantly expand a hotel's reach, especially when targeting international travelers.

1. Establish Relationships with Local Travel Agencies: Offering travel agencies a competitive commission or exclusive deals can encourage them to recommend the hotel to their clients.

2. Leverage OTAs: Listing the hotel on platforms like Booking.com, Expedia, and Agoda ensures visibility among a broader audience. Ensure the hotel's profile is complete, with high-quality images, detailed descriptions, and up-to-date pricing.

3. Dynamic Pricing Strategies: Using dynamic pricing tools that adjust rates based on demand, local events, or market trends can maximize revenue and occupancy.

Actionable Steps:

- Reach out to local travel agencies with partnership proposals.

- Regularly update listings on OTAs with fresh images and content.

- Invest in revenue management software to

optimize pricing strategies.

Marketing and rebranding distressed hotels require a multi-faceted approach, combining compelling brand identity development, digital marketing, social media engagement, attractive packages, and strategic partnerships. By implementing these strategies, distressed hotels can re-establish their market presence, attract new guests, and ultimately achieve a successful turnaround.

Engaging and Training Staff

One of the most critical components of a successful turnaround for a distressed hotel is the engagement and training of staff. Employees are the face of the hotel, and their attitudes, skills, and commitment can make or break the guest experience. This section explores the importance of employee engagement, effective training programs, empowerment, recognition, and strategies for maintaining high morale during challenging times.

The Importance of Employee Engagement in Turnarounds

Employee engagement is often the difference between a hotel that merely survives and one that thrives. Engaged employees are more likely to deliver exceptional service, exhibit a positive attitude, and go the extra mile to ensure guest satisfaction. In a turnaround situation, where the stakes are high, fostering engagement is even more crucial. Engaged staff can act as brand ambassadors, helping to rebuild the hotel's reputation and create a welcoming environment for guests.

A disengaged workforce, on the other hand, can lead to poor guest experiences, low productivity, and higher turnover rates—all of which can further exacerbate a hotel's challenges. To foster engagement, management must involve employees in the turnaround process, communicate openly about the hotel's goals, and provide them with a sense of purpose.

Actionable Steps:

- Conduct regular staff meetings to update employees on the hotel's progress and goals.

- Encourage feedback from employees, demonstrating that their opinions are valued.

- Share success stories and celebrate small wins to keep morale high.

Training Programs for Improving Service Quality

Training is essential to ensure that staff have the skills and knowledge necessary to provide excellent service, which is often the deciding factor in whether a guest chooses to return. Comprehensive training programs should cover areas such as customer service, communication skills, problem-solving, and understanding the brand's values.

1. Customer Service Training: Focus on teaching staff how to anticipate guest needs, handle complaints, and

create memorable experiences. Role-playing exercises can be particularly effective, allowing employees to practice handling various scenarios.

2. Communication Skills: Training staff on how to communicate effectively with guests, colleagues, and management ensures a seamless guest experience. This includes active listening, clear articulation, and maintaining a friendly demeanor, even in challenging situations.

3. Brand Values and Storytelling: Employees should be well-versed in the hotel's brand identity, values, and story. This enables them to communicate these aspects to guests and create a cohesive brand experience.

4. Upselling Techniques: Training staff to identify opportunities to upsell services, such as room upgrades or dining packages, can help increase the hotel's revenue. This not only benefits the hotel but also provides guests with a more personalized experience.

Actionable Steps:

- Develop a comprehensive training manual outlining service standards, brand values, and key skills.

- Implement regular training workshops and refresher courses.

- Utilize e-learning platforms to provide ongoing training that staff can complete at their own pace.

Real-Life Example: How Staff Training Improved Guest Satisfaction

A well-known example of the impact of staff training can be seen in the turnaround of the Ritz-Carlton in New Orleans after Hurricane Katrina. Faced with the challenges of rebuilding in the aftermath of a disaster, the hotel implemented an extensive training program focused on service excellence.

Key Training Strategies:

- The hotel introduced a "Gold Standards" training program, which emphasized personalized service, guest engagement, and problem-solving.

- Employees were empowered to use their discretion to make decisions that would enhance the guest experience, such as providing complimentary services when they identified opportunities to exceed guest expectations.

- Daily team meetings were held to reinforce the brand's core values, share guest feedback, and recognize outstanding performance.

The result was a significant increase in guest satisfaction scores, which led to a rise in repeat bookings and a stronger reputation in the market. This turnaround not only boosted the hotel's financial performance but also solidified its position as a leader in luxury hospitality.

Key Takeaway: Investing in staff training can transform guest experiences, even in the most challenging circumstances, and play a pivotal role in the overall turnaround of a distressed hotel.

Empowering Staff to Take Ownership of the Turnaround Process

Empowerment is about giving employees the authority, resources, and confidence to make decisions that positively impact the guest experience and the hotel's success. When staff feel empowered, they are more likely to take ownership of their roles, contribute ideas, and act in the best interests of the hotel.

1. Decision-Making Authority: Allowing employees to make decisions within their areas of responsibility, such as offering a small discount or complimentary amenity to resolve guest issues, can lead to faster problem resolution and improved guest satisfaction.

2. Encouraging Initiative: Create an environment where staff feel comfortable sharing ideas for improvement. For example, a housekeeper might suggest a more efficient way to prepare rooms, or a front desk agent might identify an opportunity to enhance the check-in experience.

3. Providing the Right Tools: Ensure employees have the resources they need to perform their jobs effectively, whether it's training, technology, or access to information.

Actionable Steps:

- Establish clear guidelines on decision-making authority and encourage staff to take initiative.

- Hold regular brainstorming sessions to gather employee ideas for improving operations.

- Recognize and implement staff suggestions, giving credit to the individuals who proposed them.

Recognizing and Rewarding Employee Contributions

Recognition and rewards play a significant role in maintaining employee motivation and engagement, especially during challenging times. When employees feel appreciated, they are more likely to stay committed to the turnaround process and deliver exceptional service.

1. Public Acknowledgment: Recognize employees' achievements in team meetings, newsletters, or on a recognition board. For example, highlighting a team member who received positive guest feedback can boost morale.

2. Incentive Programs: Offer rewards such as bonuses, gift cards, or additional time off for employees who consistently perform well or contribute to the turnaround effort. This approach incentivizes staff to maintain high standards of service.

3. Employee of the Month: Implementing an

"Employee of the Month" program not only recognizes top performers but also creates healthy competition among staff, encouraging everyone to strive for excellence.

Actionable Steps:

- Create a structured recognition program with clear criteria for rewards.

- Regularly highlight success stories and individual achievements.

- Involve staff in nominating their peers for recognition to foster a sense of community.

Tips for Maintaining High Morale During Challenging Times

Maintaining high morale is essential during a turnaround, as employees are likely to face increased workloads, uncertainty, and stress. High morale leads to better service, reduced turnover, and a more positive work environment, all of which contribute to a successful turnaround.

1. Open Communication: Keeping employees informed about the hotel's progress, challenges, and future plans helps build trust and reduces uncertainty. Regular updates from management demonstrate transparency and a commitment to involving staff in the process.

2. Providing Support: Offer resources to help employees cope with stress, such as access to

counseling services, wellness programs, or flexible scheduling. This support shows that management cares about their well-being.

3. Celebrating Milestones: Celebrate small wins and milestones to maintain momentum. For example, if the hotel reaches a certain occupancy rate or receives positive guest reviews, take the time to acknowledge these achievements with a team celebration.

4. Encouraging Team Bonding: Organize team-building activities that foster camaraderie and strengthen relationships among staff. These activities can be as simple as a team lunch, an after-work social event, or a friendly competition.

Actionable Steps:

- Schedule regular team meetings to communicate progress and celebrate achievements.

- Provide access to wellness resources and encourage staff to take breaks when needed.

- Organize monthly team-building events to foster a sense of unity.

Engaging and training staff is a critical component of any successful hotel turnaround. By prioritizing employee engagement, offering comprehensive training, empowering staff, recognizing contributions, and maintaining high morale, hotels can create a team that is motivated, skilled, and ready to deliver exceptional guest experiences. These strategies not only improve service quality but also build a positive workplace culture that supports long-term success and growth.

Monitoring and Adjusting the Turnaround Plan

A well-executed turnaround plan is crucial for reviving a distressed hotel, but it's the ongoing monitoring and adjustments that ensure the plan remains effective. This section explores how to track progress using key performance indicators (KPIs), conduct regular performance reviews, adapt to changing market conditions, learn from setbacks, and celebrate successes to maintain momentum.

Tracking Progress with Key Performance Indicators (KPIs)

KPIs are essential metrics that provide a quantifiable measure of the hotel's performance. They help management monitor progress, identify areas of improvement, and determine whether the turnaround strategies are working. For a distressed hotel, it's important to focus on KPIs that directly impact profitability, guest experience, and operational efficiency.

1. Occupancy Rate: This metric shows the percentage of available rooms that are occupied over a specific period. An increasing occupancy rate indicates that marketing and sales efforts are attracting guests.

2. Average Daily Rate (ADR): ADR measures the average revenue earned per occupied room. It's

crucial to monitor whether guests are willing to pay more for rooms, which reflects the hotel's perceived value and brand positioning.

3. Revenue Per Available Room (RevPAR): RevPAR combines occupancy rate and ADR, providing a comprehensive view of the hotel's revenue-generating ability. An increasing RevPAR indicates improved performance and is a key measure of a successful turnaround.

4. Guest Satisfaction Score (GSS): Guest feedback is invaluable in tracking service quality. Monitoring online reviews, guest surveys, and ratings on platforms like TripAdvisor, Google, and Booking.com helps gauge whether the hotel's service and amenities meet guest expectations.

5. Employee Turnover Rate: A high turnover rate often signals issues with morale or management. By tracking this KPI, hotels can identify problems and implement strategies to improve employee retention.

Actionable Steps:

- Identify 5-10 critical KPIs that align with the hotel's turnaround objectives.

- Use a dashboard to monitor KPIs in real-time, ensuring all team members have access to the data.

- Establish benchmarks and targets for each KPI to measure progress.

Conducting Regular Performance Reviews

Regular performance reviews are crucial for assessing the effectiveness of the turnaround plan and making necessary adjustments. These reviews should be comprehensive, involving both quantitative and qualitative assessments of progress.

1. Weekly Check-Ins: Conducting weekly meetings with department heads allows for quick identification of issues and immediate action. For instance, if the occupancy rate is lower than expected, marketing strategies can be adjusted promptly.

2. Monthly Performance Reviews: A more detailed review should be conducted monthly to evaluate overall performance against KPIs. This is an opportunity to analyze trends, discuss challenges, and develop strategies to address them.

3. Quarterly Strategy Sessions: Every quarter, conduct a strategic review to evaluate the success of the turnaround plan, identify areas for improvement, and refine goals. These sessions should involve the management team and key stakeholders, ensuring that everyone is aligned with the plan's objectives.

Actionable Steps:

- Schedule regular performance review meetings and ensure all relevant data is available in advance.

- Encourage open discussions during reviews, allowing team members to voice concerns and suggest solutions.

- Document action items and follow up on their implementation in subsequent meetings.

Case Study: How Regular Monitoring Kept a Turnaround on Track

The Hilton Milwaukee City Center is a prime example of how regular monitoring can steer a turnaround plan to success. The hotel, once struggling with declining occupancy rates and guest satisfaction scores, implemented a comprehensive turnaround strategy focused on improving service quality, marketing efforts, and operational efficiency.

Key Monitoring Strategies:

- The hotel established a robust KPI tracking system that provided real-time data on occupancy rates, guest satisfaction, and RevPAR.

- Weekly meetings were held with department heads to review performance metrics, identify areas of concern, and brainstorm solutions.

- Monthly performance reviews highlighted trends, allowing management to adjust marketing campaigns, enhance staff training, and implement cost-saving measures.

By closely monitoring progress, the Hilton Milwaukee City Center managed to increase its occupancy rate by 20% within six months and achieved a significant improvement in guest satisfaction scores. This steady progress helped the hotel regain its position as a preferred accommodation choice in the city.

Key Takeaway: Consistent monitoring and regular performance reviews enable hotels to identify issues early, make timely adjustments, and keep the turnaround plan on track.

Adapting the Plan to Changing Market Conditions

The hospitality industry is dynamic, with market conditions that can change rapidly due to factors like economic fluctuations, seasonality, local events, or even global crises like pandemics. A successful turnaround requires the ability to adapt the plan in response to these changes.

1. Monitoring Market Trends: Stay informed about changes in the market by regularly analyzing competitor performance, local event calendars, economic indicators, and guest booking behaviors. For example, if a nearby hotel launches a new marketing campaign, consider adjusting your pricing strategy or promotions to remain competitive.

2. Flexible Pricing Strategies: Implement a dynamic pricing model that adjusts room rates based on demand, seasonality, and local events. This allows the hotel to maximize revenue during peak periods and attract guests during slower times.

3. Adapting Marketing Strategies: If market trends indicate a shift in traveler preferences, adjust your

marketing strategies accordingly. For instance, during economic downturns, focus on promoting value-for-money packages, while during peak travel seasons, emphasize luxury amenities or unique experiences.

Actionable Steps:

- Conduct regular market analysis to stay informed about changing conditions.

- Maintain flexibility in pricing and marketing strategies to adapt to fluctuations in demand.

- Train staff to handle different types of guests, ensuring service quality remains consistent regardless of market changes.

Learning from Setbacks and Failures

Setbacks are inevitable during a turnaround, but they offer valuable learning opportunities. Instead of viewing failures as roadblocks, use them to refine strategies, improve processes, and strengthen the team's resilience.

1. Conducting Post-Mortem Analyses: After experiencing a setback, conduct a detailed analysis to identify the root causes, what went wrong, and how to prevent similar issues in the future. This might involve reviewing guest complaints, financial reports, or operational inefficiencies.

2. Encouraging a Culture of Learning: Foster a culture that views mistakes as opportunities for growth. Encourage staff to share their experiences and

insights, and involve them in developing solutions.

3. Implementing Changes Based on Learnings: Use the insights gained from setbacks to make informed adjustments to the turnaround plan. For example, if a marketing campaign failed to generate bookings, analyze the messaging, timing, and target audience, and use the findings to improve future campaigns.

Actionable Steps:

- Establish a process for conducting post-mortem analyses after setbacks.

- Involve staff in identifying lessons learned and implementing corrective actions.

- Document lessons learned to build a knowledge base for future reference.

Celebrating Successes and Building Momentum

Celebrating successes, no matter how small, is essential for maintaining morale and building momentum throughout the turnaround process. Recognizing achievements reinforces the team's efforts, boosts motivation, and creates a sense of collective accomplishment.

1. Recognizing Team Achievements: Highlight team achievements during regular meetings, in newsletters, or on notice boards. Recognizing the hard work of employees who contributed to a successful initiative encourages a sense of pride and ownership.

2. Rewarding Milestones: Offer tangible rewards, such as bonuses, gift cards, or extra time off, when the hotel reaches key milestones. This not only motivates staff but also reinforces the idea that their efforts are contributing to the hotel's success.

3. Sharing Success Stories: Share success stories with guests, stakeholders, and the broader community through social media, newsletters, and press releases. This builds positive momentum and enhances the hotel's reputation.

Actionable Steps:

- Create a recognition program that rewards employees for achieving specific goals.

- Celebrate milestones with team events, such as dinners, outings, or awards ceremonies.

- Communicate successes regularly to build a culture of positivity and momentum.

Monitoring and adjusting the turnaround plan is a dynamic, ongoing process that requires vigilance, adaptability, and a commitment to learning. By tracking progress with KPIs, conducting regular reviews, adapting to market conditions, learning from setbacks, and celebrating successes, a distressed hotel can navigate its turnaround journey effectively. These practices not only help maintain momentum but also ensure that the turnaround plan remains relevant and responsive to the ever-changing hospitality landscape.

Chapter 4: Repositioning Distressed Hotels

Repositioning a distressed hotel can be a transformative journey, one that requires a strategic blend of market insight, creativity, and meticulous planning. This chapter delves into the complexities of repositioning, exploring how to turn a struggling property into a profitable, desirable destination that attracts a new target market and establishes a sustainable competitive edge. A distressed hotel often carries the burden of past challenges, whether it's declining guest satisfaction, outdated facilities, or an inability to adapt to evolving market trends. However, with the right approach, these challenges can become opportunities to redefine the hotel's identity and create a fresh, appealing experience that resonates with today's travelers.

The process begins with identifying repositioning opportunities, which entails a deep understanding of market trends, guest preferences, and the competitive landscape. By assessing the hotel's strengths and weaknesses, hoteliers can uncover hidden potential and redefine their target market and guest profile. This crucial first step sets the foundation for a successful repositioning, as it enables hotel owners and managers to recognize gaps in the market that their property can fill. In this section, we'll explore a case study of a boutique hotel that successfully navigated the repositioning process, demonstrating how actionable insights can transform a distressed property into a sought-after destination.

Building on these insights, the next phase involves developing a repositioning strategy that establishes a clear vision and creates a unique value proposition. Repositioning is more than just a facelift; it's about aligning the hotel's operations, design, and guest experience with a new brand identity that speaks to its target market. This section covers how to plan renovations and upgrades, while also sharing a practical example of how a strategic vision led to the successful turnaround of a distressed hotel. Consistency is key in this phase, and we'll provide tips on ensuring that every aspect of the property reflects the new brand.

Renovations and design play a pivotal role in repositioning efforts, as they bring the hotel's vision to life. From budgeting and planning to choosing design elements that reflect the new brand, this section provides insights into how to create a space that appeals to modern travelers. Working with architects, designers, and contractors can be a complex process, especially when trying to minimize disruptions to ongoing operations. Through a real-life case study, we'll illustrate how renovations can breathe new life into a distressed property and pave the way for a successful repositioning, while also exploring sustainable design practices that cater to today's environmentally conscious guests.

Implementing the repositioning plan involves more than physical changes; it requires staff training, marketing efforts, and guest engagement to introduce the repositioned hotel to the market effectively. This section covers practical steps for training staff to embody the new brand experience and launching marketing campaigns that generate excitement and awareness. By engaging with guests and gathering feedback, hotels can refine their approach and ensure the repositioning resonates with the target market. A real-life example of how a marketing campaign boosted a repositioned hotel's visibility will highlight the importance of a well-executed launch.

Repositioning is not without its challenges, and this chapter will address the common obstacles hotels face during the transition. From managing guest expectations to handling negative feedback, it's crucial to maintain momentum and stay committed to the repositioning vision. We'll share a case study of a hotel that successfully overcame these challenges, offering tips and strategies for long-term success.

Finally, we'll examine how to evaluate the success of repositioning efforts by measuring performance against established goals, analyzing guest feedback, and assessing financial metrics. Adjusting strategies for continuous improvement is essential for maintaining the gains achieved through repositioning. Celebrating achievements and preparing for future growth will ensure that the repositioning effort not only revitalizes the hotel but sets the stage for lasting success in a competitive market.

Identifying Repositioning Opportunities

Repositioning a distressed hotel begins with a deep understanding of its current market position, strengths, weaknesses, and the opportunities available to transform it into a more competitive and attractive property. This process involves thorough analysis, strategic thinking, and a willingness to adapt to changing market demands. In this section, we explore how to identify repositioning opportunities by analyzing market trends and guest preferences, assessing the hotel's strengths and weaknesses, understanding the competitive landscape, and defining the target market and guest profile. We will also examine a real-life case study of a successful boutique hotel repositioning and provide actionable steps for implementing these strategies.

Analyzing Market Trends and Guest Preferences

The first step in identifying repositioning opportunities is to gain insight into the broader market trends and evolving guest preferences. The hospitality industry is constantly changing, with shifts driven by factors such as technology, changing demographics, economic conditions, and traveler behaviors. By staying informed about these trends, hoteliers can identify gaps in the market and adapt their offerings to meet emerging demands.

For example, the rise of "bleisure" travel—where guests combine business trips with leisure activities— has led to an increased demand for hotels that offer amenities suited to both work and relaxation. Similarly, the growing preference for eco-friendly accommodations means that travelers are seeking hotels that prioritize sustainability.

To analyze market trends, hoteliers should:

- Monitor industry reports, market research, and

travel publications to identify emerging trends.

- Attend hospitality conferences and webinars to gain insights from industry experts.

- Use tools like Google Trends and social media analytics to understand traveler preferences.

By identifying trends such as wellness tourism, remote work-friendly accommodations, or family-friendly packages, a distressed hotel can reposition itself to cater to a specific niche, creating a unique value proposition that sets it apart from competitors.

Practical Example: Suppose a hotel is located in a city that has recently become a hub for tech startups. By recognizing this trend, the hotel could reposition itself to attract business travelers by offering co-working spaces, high-speed internet, and networking events, transforming from a generic property into a preferred choice for professionals.

Assessing the Property's Strengths and Weaknesses

Once market trends are identified, the next step is to conduct an internal assessment of the hotel's strengths and weaknesses. This honest evaluation helps determine what aspects of the property can be leveraged in a repositioning strategy and what areas need improvement.

Strengths: Consider the unique aspects of the property, such as its location, architecture, history, amenities, or service quality. For instance, a hotel located in a historic building may have architectural charm that can be emphasized in a repositioning strategy to attract guests interested in culture and heritage.

Weaknesses: Identify areas that detract from the guest experience, such as outdated decor, lack of amenities, or inefficient operations. Recognizing these weaknesses allows for targeted improvements that enhance the hotel's appeal.

Actionable Steps:

- Conduct a SWOT analysis (Strengths, Weaknesses, Opportunities, and Threats) with input from various departments.

- Gather feedback from guests through surveys, reviews, and online ratings to identify areas of concern.

- Use guest feedback and operational data to prioritize improvements that align with repositioning goals.

Example: A hotel might discover that its spacious conference facilities are underutilized. This insight could lead to repositioning the property as a premier venue for corporate events, with a focus on upgrading technology and offering tailored business packages. Understanding the Competitive Landscape

Understanding the competitive landscape is crucial to identifying repositioning opportunities. By analyzing competitors, hoteliers can identify what sets their property apart and where there is room to differentiate.

Key Areas to Analyze:

- Competitor Offerings: Study the amenities, services, pricing, and guest experience provided by competitors.

- Market Positioning: Identify which market segments competitors target and how they position themselves in the market.

- Online Reputation: Review competitors' online reviews and ratings to understand their strengths and weaknesses from a guest's perspective.

Conducting a competitive analysis helps hoteliers identify opportunities to fill gaps in the market or offer a superior experience. For example, if competitors focus on budget travelers, there might be an opportunity to reposition the hotel as a mid-range or upscale option catering to a more affluent audience.

Actionable Steps:

- Create a competitive matrix to compare key competitors across various criteria, such as price, amenities, and guest reviews.

- Conduct mystery shopping by visiting competitors to experience their service quality firsthand.

- Monitor competitors' marketing strategies, promotions, and online presence to stay informed about their positioning.

Defining the Target Market and Guest Profile

After analyzing market trends, property strengths and weaknesses, and the competitive landscape, it's time to define the target market and guest profile. This involves identifying the specific group of travelers the hotel aims to attract and understanding their preferences, behaviors, and expectations.

Defining Your Target Market:

- Demographics: Age, gender, income level, and occupation.

- Psychographics: Interests, lifestyle, and travel motivations.

- Travel Purpose: Business, leisure, family, or group travel.

By clearly defining the target market, the hotel can tailor its offerings, marketing strategies, and guest experience to meet their needs. For instance, a hotel targeting young professionals might focus on creating trendy social spaces, while a hotel targeting families would prioritize family-friendly amenities and activities.

Example: If a hotel is located near a university, it could target parents visiting students, offering weekend packages that include discounts on local attractions, complimentary breakfast, and shuttle service to the campus.

Case Study: A Successful Repositioning of a Boutique Hotel

A prime example of successful repositioning is the transformation of The Wythe Hotel in Brooklyn, New York. Originally a factory built in 1901, the building was converted into a hotel but initially struggled to attract guests due to a lack of identity and clear market positioning.

Steps Taken to Reposition:

- Market Analysis: The hotel's management analyzed Brooklyn's evolving market and recognized the growing demand for unique, local experiences among travelers.

- Redefining the Target Market: The Wythe Hotel repositioned itself to attract creative professionals, artists, and travelers looking for an authentic Brooklyn experience.

- Leveraging Strengths: The hotel's industrial architecture and prime location in a trendy neighborhood were emphasized as part of its brand identity.

- Creating a Unique Value Proposition: The hotel introduced features such as locally sourced decor, a rooftop bar with panoramic city views, and partnerships with local artists to showcase their work.

The repositioning was highly successful, turning The Wythe Hotel into one of Brooklyn's most sought-after boutique hotels, with a strong brand identity and loyal guest following.

Key Takeaway: By understanding market trends, leveraging strengths, and defining a clear target market, The Wythe Hotel was able to reposition itself successfully and thrive in a competitive market.

Actionable Steps for Identifying Repositioning Opportunities

- Conduct Market Research: Use industry reports, guest surveys, and social media analytics to identify trends and preferences.

- Perform a SWOT Analysis: Evaluate the hotel's strengths, weaknesses, opportunities, and threats to identify areas for improvement.

- Analyze Competitors: Create a competitive matrix to understand the offerings and positioning of similar hotels in the area.

- Define Your Target Market: Use demographic and psychographic data to create a detailed profile of your ideal guests.

- Engage with Guests: Collect feedback through surveys, focus groups, and online reviews to understand what guests value most.

- Test and Validate: Before fully committing to a

repositioning strategy, test concepts with a small segment of your target market to gather feedback and refine your approach.

Identifying repositioning opportunities is a critical step in transforming a distressed hotel into a thriving, competitive property. By analyzing market trends, assessing strengths and weaknesses, understanding the competitive landscape, and defining a clear target market, hoteliers can uncover opportunities to create a unique and compelling value proposition. As demonstrated by The Wythe Hotel, a successful repositioning strategy not only attracts new guests but also establishes a sustainable competitive advantage in the market.

Developing a Repositioning Strategy

A successful repositioning strategy for a distressed hotel requires more than just cosmetic changes; it demands a clear vision, a strong value proposition, and a comprehensive plan that integrates every aspect of the hotel's operations. By establishing a coherent strategy that resonates with target guests and delivers a distinctive experience, a distressed hotel can transform itself into a thriving property. This section explores how to develop an effective repositioning strategy, including establishing a clear vision, creating a unique value proposition, planning for renovations, aligning operations with the new brand identity, and ensuring consistency throughout the process. Establishing a Clear Vision for the Hotel

The foundation of any repositioning strategy lies in establishing a clear and compelling vision for the hotel. This vision serves as the guiding star for all subsequent decisions and actions, shaping everything from renovations and marketing to guest experience and operational changes. The vision should answer the fundamental question: What do we want this hotel to become?

To craft a vision, consider the following:

- Target Audience: Who is the hotel trying to attract? Is it business travelers, families, couples seeking a romantic getaway, or millennials looking for unique experiences?

- Desired Guest Experience: What kind of experience should guests have? Should the hotel evoke luxury, relaxation, adventure, or a sense of home?

- Market Positioning: How should the hotel be perceived in the marketplace? Is it an upscale boutique, a mid-range family-friendly option, or an affordable yet stylish choice?

A clear vision provides direction and helps differentiate the hotel from competitors. For example, if the vision is to create a luxurious retreat for wellness-focused travelers, every aspect of the hotel—from spa services and healthy dining options to room design and marketing campaigns—should align with this concept.

Actionable Steps:

- Gather input from stakeholders, including

owners, management, staff, and even guests, to create a shared vision.

- Develop a vision statement that articulates the hotel's purpose, target audience, and unique positioning.

- Use the vision statement as a reference point for all decisions throughout the repositioning process.

Creating a Unique Value Proposition

A unique value proposition (UVP) is what sets the hotel apart from competitors and gives guests a compelling reason to choose it over others. The UVP should be a direct reflection of the hotel's vision and encapsulate the essence of the guest experience.

To develop a UVP, focus on aspects that differentiate the hotel, such as:

- Location: Is the hotel situated in a prime location, like a historic district, near major attractions, or on a picturesque beach?

- Amenities: Does the hotel offer exceptional amenities, such as a rooftop pool, a Michelin-starred restaurant, or a state-of-the-art fitness center?

- Personalized Service: Is the hotel known for its personalized service, like dedicated concierge services, unique welcome experiences, or staff trained in multiple languages?

For example, a hotel in a bustling urban area might position itself as a tranquil oasis, offering an exclusive rooftop garden, spa treatments, and soundproofed rooms to provide a serene escape from the city's chaos. This UVP could be the differentiator that attracts guests seeking relaxation in an otherwise hectic environment.

Practical Example: The Smyth Tribeca Hotel in New York City faced challenges as a mid-range property in a competitive market. By repositioning itself with a UVP centered around providing a "home away from home" for creative professionals, it introduced personalized touches like in-room art supplies, curated local guides, and a comfortable, stylish co-working space. This strategy helped the hotel gain traction with its target audience and improved its occupancy rates.

Actionable Steps:

- Identify the hotel's standout features and align them with guest preferences.

- Create a value proposition that emphasizes what makes the hotel unique.

- Incorporate the UVP into all marketing materials, guest communications, and operational processes.

Planning for Renovations and Upgrades

Physical renovations and upgrades play a vital role in repositioning a hotel, as they provide a tangible representation of the new vision and value proposition. However, renovations must be carefully planned to ensure they are both cost-effective and impactful.

1. Identify Priority Areas: Focus on areas that have the most significant impact on guest experience, such as the lobby, guest rooms, and common areas. For example, updating a dated lobby with modern furnishings, lighting, and artwork can create a strong first impression that aligns with the new brand identity.

2. Budgeting and Phasing: Renovations can be expensive, so it's crucial to establish a budget and consider phasing the work over time to minimize disruptions and manage cash flow. For instance, start with high-traffic areas, then move on to guest rooms and other spaces.

3. Working with Designers and Contractors: Collaborate with experienced designers and contractors who understand the vision and can bring it to life. Make sure they have experience in the hospitality industry and can incorporate elements that enhance the guest experience.

Case Study: The Post Oak Hotel at Uptown Houston underwent a multi-million-dollar renovation to reposition itself as a luxury property. By focusing on upscale finishes, state-of-the-art technology, and world-class amenities, the hotel successfully transitioned from an underperforming asset to one of Houston's most prestigious addresses.

Actionable Steps:

- Conduct a property assessment to identify renovation priorities.

- Develop a renovation plan that aligns with the repositioning vision and budget.

- Communicate renovation timelines and updates to guests to manage expectations.

Aligning Operations with the New Brand Identity

For a repositioning strategy to be successful, it's essential that operations are aligned with the new brand identity. This means ensuring that every touchpoint of the guest experience reflects the repositioned hotel's vision and value proposition.

1. Staff Training: Train staff to understand the new brand identity, service standards, and guest expectations. Employees should be able to communicate the hotel's story, values, and offerings to guests confidently.

2. Service Delivery: Align service delivery with the repositioning goals. If the repositioning focuses on luxury, ensure that staff provides personalized, high-touch service at every guest interaction.

3. Operational Processes: Review operational processes to ensure they support the new brand identity. For example, if the repositioning emphasizes sustainability, implement eco-friendly practices, such

as reducing plastic waste, using energy-efficient lighting, and sourcing local, organic ingredients for the restaurant.

Practical Example: The Ace Hotel Group repositioned itself from a traditional budget chain to a trendy, boutique brand by aligning its operations with a "hipster" aesthetic. This included training staff to adopt a laid-back, friendly service style, designing unique interiors that reflect the neighborhood culture, and hosting local art and music events. This comprehensive approach helped the Ace Hotel build a cult following among young, creative travelers.

Actionable Steps:

- Develop training programs that introduce staff to the new brand identity and service standards.

- Implement operational changes that align with the repositioning goals.

- Continuously monitor guest feedback to ensure operations meet expectations.

Practical Example: How a Strategic Vision Transformed a Distressed Hotel

The Fairmont Royal York in Toronto, a historic hotel, faced declining occupancy rates and struggled to compete with newer luxury properties. Recognizing the need for repositioning, the management team established a strategic vision to restore the hotel to its former glory while embracing modern luxury.

Steps Taken:

- The hotel underwent extensive renovations to update guest rooms, common areas, and dining options, blending the building's historic charm with contemporary design.

- It repositioned itself as a luxury destination for business travelers, families, and tourists, emphasizing its unique blend of history and modernity.

- Staff received training to provide high-touch, personalized service, and the hotel invested in marketing campaigns that highlighted its iconic status and new amenities.

The result was a successful transformation that revitalized the hotel's brand, improved occupancy rates, and re-established it as one of Toronto's premier luxury destinations.

Tips for Ensuring Consistency in Repositioning Efforts

- Maintain Brand Guidelines: Develop and distribute brand guidelines to ensure consistency across all touchpoints, from marketing materials to guest interactions.

- Regular Training: Conduct ongoing training sessions to reinforce the brand identity and service standards.

- Monitor Guest Feedback: Regularly collect and

analyze guest feedback to identify areas where the repositioning efforts may be falling short and adjust accordingly.

- Evaluate Progress: Use key performance indicators (KPIs) to measure the success of repositioning efforts and make data-driven adjustments as needed.

Developing a repositioning strategy is a multi-faceted process that requires a clear vision, a unique value proposition, careful planning, and consistent execution. By establishing a vision that guides all aspects of the hotel experience, crafting a compelling value proposition, investing in renovations, and aligning operations with the new brand identity, a distressed hotel can successfully transform into a competitive and desirable property. Through careful planning and unwavering commitment, repositioning can revitalize a hotel, allowing it to attract new guests, generate increased revenue, and achieve long-term success.

Renovations and Design

Renovating a distressed hotel is a pivotal aspect of its repositioning, as it directly impacts the guest experience and reflects the new brand identity. Effective renovations can breathe new life into a property, attract a target market, and create a competitive edge. This section explores the essential steps involved in planning and budgeting for renovations, selecting design elements that align with the new brand, collaborating with architects and contractors, minimizing disruptions to ongoing operations, and implementing sustainable practices. We'll also examine a real-life case study that demonstrates how thoughtful renovations can transform a distressed hotel into a sought-after destination.

Planning and Budgeting for Renovations

The first step in any renovation project is thorough planning and budgeting. A clear, strategic plan ensures that renovations stay on track, meet the hotel's repositioning goals, and deliver a return on investment.

1. Conducting a Property Assessment: Before any renovations begin, conduct a comprehensive assessment of the property to identify areas requiring improvement. This evaluation should consider the hotel's current state, guest feedback, market trends, and the new brand identity. For example, if guests frequently mention outdated bathrooms in reviews, this could be a priority area for renovation.

2. Defining Renovation Objectives: Identify what the renovations aim to achieve. Are you looking to modernize guest rooms, enhance public spaces, improve energy efficiency, or create additional amenities? Clearly defining these objectives will help guide the project and ensure that every dollar spent contributes to the hotel's repositioning goals.

3. Establishing a Budget: Set a realistic budget that aligns with the repositioning strategy. Consider costs for materials, labor, permits, and potential unforeseen expenses. Allocate funds to areas that will have the

greatest impact on guest experience and revenue generation, such as upgrading rooms, renovating the lobby, or enhancing the restaurant.

4. Phasing the Renovations: Renovations can be phased over time to manage costs and minimize disruption. For instance, start with high-traffic areas like the lobby and guest rooms, then move on to less critical spaces.

Practical Example: A distressed hotel may allocate a $1 million renovation budget to focus primarily on guest room upgrades, followed by refurbishing the lobby and restaurant. By prioritizing guest-facing areas, the hotel can create an immediate impact that resonates with guests, improving occupancy rates and revenue.

Actionable Steps:

- Conduct a thorough property assessment to identify renovation needs.

- Develop a detailed renovation plan with clear objectives and a realistic budget.

- Consider phasing renovations to manage costs and minimize disruptions.

Choosing Design Elements That Reflect the New Brand

Design elements play a critical role in communicating the hotel's new brand identity. The chosen style, color scheme, furniture, and decor should reflect the desired guest experience and create a cohesive brand image.

1. Aligning Design with Brand Identity: The design should be an extension of the hotel's vision and target market. For example, a hotel repositioning itself as a chic, upscale property might choose sleek, modern furnishings, elegant lighting, and a neutral color palette with bold accent pieces.

2. Creating a Memorable Guest Experience: Design elements should evoke emotions and create a sense of place. Incorporate unique touches that make the hotel stand out, such as locally inspired artwork, custom furniture, or signature scent diffusers in the lobby.

3. Prioritizing Functionality and Comfort: While aesthetics are important, design elements must also be functional and comfortable for guests. For example, in-room desks with ample charging ports cater to business travelers, while soft lighting and plush bedding enhance relaxation for leisure guests.

Practical Example: The 1 Hotel Brooklyn Bridge successfully repositioned itself as an eco-luxury destination by integrating reclaimed wood, living green walls, and floor-to-ceiling windows offering stunning views of the Brooklyn Bridge. These design elements not only reflected the brand's commitment to sustainability but also created a memorable, luxurious experience that resonated with guests.

Actionable Steps:

- Choose design elements that align with the new

brand identity and target market.

- Incorporate unique touches that create a memorable experience.

- Ensure that design choices balance aesthetics with functionality and comfort.

Working with Architects, Designers, and Contractors

Collaboration with experienced architects, designers, and contractors is crucial to bringing the renovation vision to life. Effective communication and coordination ensure that the project runs smoothly, stays within budget, and meets quality standards.

1. Selecting the Right Partners: Choose architects, designers, and contractors with experience in the hospitality industry, as they understand the unique challenges and requirements of hotel renovations. Check their portfolios, references, and industry reputation before making a decision.

2. Establishing Clear Communication Channels: From the outset, establish clear communication channels and expectations with your team. Regular meetings, progress reports, and site visits help keep everyone aligned and address issues promptly.

3. Involving Stakeholders: Involve key stakeholders, such as hotel management, owners, and brand representatives, in the design and renovation process. Their input ensures that the final product aligns with the hotel's goals and brand identity.

Actionable Steps:

- Choose experienced architects, designers, and contractors with a track record in hospitality projects.

- Establish regular communication and collaboration channels.

- Involve stakeholders in the design and renovation process.

Minimizing Disruption to Ongoing Operations

Renovations can be disruptive to hotel operations, but careful planning and communication can minimize the impact on guests and staff.

1. Phased Renovations: Phasing renovations allows parts of the hotel to remain operational while others are being updated. For example, renovating one floor at a time ensures that guests have access to other areas.

2. Communicating with Guests: Be transparent with guests about renovation activities, and inform them in advance about potential noise or limited access to certain areas. Offer complimentary amenities, discounts, or upgrades to compensate for any inconvenience.

3. Scheduling Work During Off-Peak Hours: Whenever possible, schedule noisy or disruptive work during off-peak hours to minimize disturbance to guests.

Case Study: The Ritz-Carlton Orlando, Grande Lakes underwent a major renovation while maintaining operations. By phasing the work, communicating with guests, and offering alternative amenities, the hotel successfully completed the renovation without significant disruption to its service quality or guest experience.

Actionable Steps:

- Implement phased renovations to keep parts of the hotel operational.

- Communicate renovation plans and timelines with guests.

- Schedule disruptive work during off-peak hours.

Case Study: How Renovations Led to a Hotel's Successful Repositioning

The LINE Hotel in Los Angeles transformed from a dated, struggling property into a trendy, sought-after destination through a well-executed renovation strategy. Originally built in the 1960s, the hotel faced declining occupancy and struggled to compete with newer properties in the area.

Steps Taken:

- The LINE Hotel repositioned itself as a lifestyle brand targeting millennials and young professionals.

- Renovations included modernizing guest rooms, creating an Instagram-worthy lobby, and adding a rooftop pool and bar with panoramic city views.

- Design elements drew inspiration from LA's cultural and artistic scene, featuring eclectic furnishings, local artwork, and a fusion of industrial and contemporary styles.

The result was a dramatic increase in occupancy rates, room rates, and positive guest reviews. By aligning renovations with its repositioning goals, the LINE Hotel became a popular destination for travelers and locals alike.

Sustainable Design Practices for Modern Travelers

Sustainability has become a priority for modern travelers, making it an important consideration in any renovation project. Incorporating sustainable design practices can enhance the hotel's brand image and appeal to environmentally conscious guests.

1. Energy-Efficient Lighting and HVAC Systems: Install LED lighting, smart thermostats, and energy-efficient HVAC systems to reduce energy consumption and lower operating costs.

2. Eco-Friendly Materials: Use sustainable materials, such as reclaimed wood, recycled metal, or low-VOC (volatile organic compound) paint, to minimize the environmental impact.

3. Water Conservation: Incorporate water-saving fixtures, such as low-flow showerheads and faucets, to reduce water usage and costs.

4. Green Spaces: Integrate green spaces, such as rooftop gardens or indoor plants, to improve air quality and create a relaxing environment for guests.

Practical Example: The Hotel Verde in Cape Town, South Africa, is known as "Africa's Greenest Hotel." Its renovations included energy-efficient systems, rainwater harvesting, and sustainable building materials, attracting eco-conscious travelers and earning multiple sustainability awards.

Actionable Steps:

- Incorporate energy-efficient systems, eco-friendly materials, and water-saving fixtures.

- Highlight sustainable practices in marketing materials to attract environmentally conscious guests.

Renovations and design are integral to repositioning a distressed hotel, as they provide a tangible representation of the new brand identity and guest experience. By planning and budgeting carefully, choosing design elements that align with the brand, working closely with architects and contractors, and minimizing disruptions, hotels can transform their properties and attract their target market. Incorporating sustainable practices not only appeals to modern travelers but also contributes to long-term profitability and success. Through thoughtful renovation strategies, a distressed hotel can be revitalized and repositioned as a competitive, desirable destination.

Implementing the Repositioning Plan

After months of planning, designing, and renovating, the success of a hotel repositioning strategy ultimately depends on how effectively it is implemented. Execution is crucial, as it brings the new brand identity to life and communicates the transformation to the market. This section explores the key elements of implementing the repositioning plan, including training staff, launching marketing campaigns, engaging with guests, tracking success, and practical steps for ensuring a seamless transition. A real-life example will demonstrate how an effective marketing campaign can significantly impact the repositioning of a hotel.

Training Staff to Deliver the New Brand Experience

The most beautifully renovated hotel can fall short of success if the staff is not adequately trained to deliver the new brand experience. Employees are the primary touchpoint for guests, and their ability to embody the new brand identity is essential for a successful repositioning.

1. Aligning Staff with the New Brand Identity: It's crucial that staff understand the new brand values, target market, and service standards. Conduct training sessions that explain the vision, mission, and unique value proposition of the repositioned hotel.

This ensures that every team member—from the front desk to housekeeping—is aligned with the hotel's goals and can communicate them effectively to guests.

2. Emphasizing Customer Service Excellence: Exceptional service is often the differentiator between a successful hotel and a struggling one. Provide staff with training on how to anticipate guest needs, handle complaints, and create personalized experiences. For example, if the hotel is repositioning itself as a luxury destination, staff should be trained in delivering high-touch service, such as addressing guests by name, offering personalized recommendations, and promptly responding to special requests.

3. Role-Playing and Real-Life Scenarios: Role-playing exercises are an effective way to prepare staff for various guest interactions. Create scenarios that reflect typical guest experiences at the repositioned hotel, allowing staff to practice delivering the new brand experience in a controlled environment.

Practical Example: A luxury hotel in New York repositioned itself as a high-end wellness retreat. To support this shift, staff received training on mindfulness, relaxation techniques, and how to create a tranquil environment. As a result, they were better equipped to engage with guests who were looking for a rejuvenating experience, enhancing the overall brand consistency.

Actionable Steps:

- Conduct comprehensive training sessions to introduce staff to the new brand identity and

service standards.
- Use role-playing exercises to practice delivering the brand experience.

- Regularly evaluate and reinforce training through follow-up sessions and guest feedback.

Launching Marketing Campaigns to Introduce the Repositioned Hotel

A successful repositioning requires a strategic marketing campaign to communicate the hotel's transformation and attract the target audience. The campaign should highlight the hotel's new identity, features, and value proposition, ensuring that the market is aware of the changes.

1. Developing a Multi-Channel Marketing Strategy: Utilize a mix of marketing channels—social media, email marketing, search engine optimization (SEO), pay-per-click advertising, influencer partnerships, and public relations—to reach a broad audience. Tailor the messaging for each platform to ensure consistency while adapting to the nuances of each channel.

2. Creating Compelling Visual Content: Invest in professional photography and videography to showcase the renovated spaces, upgraded amenities, and overall guest experience. Visual content is crucial for capturing the attention of potential guests and conveying the new brand identity.

3. Engaging with Influencers and Media: Collaborate with travel influencers, bloggers, and journalists to

generate buzz around the repositioned hotel. Invite them to experience the hotel and share their experiences with their followers, amplifying your reach.

Practical Example: The Hoxton Hotel chain repositioned itself as a trendy, community-focused brand. The marketing campaign featured vibrant images of their redesigned lobbies, guest rooms, and local artwork. They hosted launch parties, collaborated with travel influencers, and shared guest testimonials, which generated substantial social media engagement and increased bookings.

Actionable Steps:

- Develop a multi-channel marketing plan to introduce the repositioned hotel.

- Invest in high-quality visuals that reflect the new brand identity.

- Engage with influencers, media, and bloggers to expand your reach.

Engaging with Guests and Gathering Feedback

Guest feedback is invaluable during the implementation of a repositioning plan, as it provides insights into how well the changes are resonating with the target market. Engaging with guests and actively seeking their opinions helps refine the guest experience and ensures the repositioning efforts are meeting expectations.

1. Encouraging Guest Feedback: Encourage guests to share their feedback through surveys, online reviews, social media, and in-person interactions. Consider offering incentives, such as discounts on future stays, to encourage participation.

2. Monitoring Online Reviews and Social Media: Track guest reviews on platforms like TripAdvisor, Google, and Booking.com, as well as comments on social media channels. Respond promptly to both positive and negative feedback, demonstrating that the hotel values guest opinions and is committed to continuous improvement.

3. Adapting Based on Feedback: Use guest feedback to make necessary adjustments to the repositioning strategy. For example, if guests mention that they love the new room designs but find the check-in process slow, implement measures to streamline the check-in experience.

Practical Example: A boutique hotel in Miami that repositioned itself as an art-inspired destination received guest feedback that the art installations were captivating, but guests desired more interaction with local artists. The hotel responded by organizing weekly art workshops and meet-and-greet events with artists, which enhanced the guest experience and reinforced the brand identity.

Actionable Steps:

- Implement feedback channels such as surveys, social media, and review sites.

- Regularly monitor guest feedback and respond promptly.

- Use feedback to make continuous improvements to the guest experience.

Tracking the Success of Repositioning Efforts

Measuring the success of a repositioning plan is crucial to ensure that the strategy is delivering the desired results. Tracking key performance indicators (KPIs) helps gauge progress and identify areas that need adjustment.

1. Occupancy Rate and Average Daily Rate (ADR): Monitor changes in occupancy rates and ADR to determine if the repositioning has attracted more guests and justified higher pricing. An increase in these metrics suggests that the hotel is successfully attracting its target market.

2. Revenue Per Available Room (RevPAR): RevPAR provides a comprehensive view of how well the hotel is performing in terms of both occupancy and pricing. A rising RevPAR is a positive indicator that the repositioning is driving revenue growth.

3. Guest Satisfaction Scores: Track guest satisfaction scores through surveys, online reviews, and feedback to measure how well the repositioning efforts have enhanced the guest experience.

4. Brand Awareness and Online Engagement: Monitor metrics such as website traffic, social media engagement, and media coverage to evaluate the

effectiveness of marketing campaigns in raising awareness about the repositioned hotel.

Actionable Steps:

- Identify and track key KPIs to measure the success of the repositioning.

- Use data analytics tools to monitor progress and identify trends.

- Adjust strategies based on KPI performance to ensure continuous improvement.

Real-Life Example: How a Marketing Campaign Boosted a Repositioned Hotel

The Palace Hotel in San Francisco serves as an excellent example of how an effective marketing campaign can boost a repositioned hotel. After extensive renovations to restore its historic grandeur while incorporating modern luxury elements, the hotel launched a comprehensive marketing campaign to reintroduce itself to the market.

Key Strategies:

- A series of high-quality videos and images showcased the renovated spaces, including the opulent Garden Court, luxurious suites, and the revitalized lobby.

- The hotel partnered with travel influencers and bloggers who shared their experiences on social media, generating buzz and excitement.

- A grand reopening event was held, inviting media, travel agents, and industry influencers, resulting in widespread media coverage.

The campaign led to a significant increase in occupancy rates, with the hotel becoming a top choice for both leisure and business travelers seeking a blend of historic charm and modern luxury.
Practical Steps for Ensuring a Seamless Repositioning

- Consistent Communication: Keep staff, guests, stakeholders, and partners informed about the repositioning process. Consistent communication helps build excitement and ensures everyone is aligned with the hotel's new direction.

- Monitor and Adapt: Regularly monitor progress and be prepared to adapt the strategy based on feedback and performance metrics.

- Celebrate Milestones: Celebrate key milestones during the repositioning process to maintain momentum and motivate staff.

- Maintain Quality: Ensure that every aspect of the guest experience—service, amenities, and facilities—reflects the new brand identity and meets the highest quality standards.

Actionable Steps:

- Communicate consistently with all stakeholders.

- Monitor progress, adapt strategies, and celebrate successes.

- Ensure quality and brand consistency in every aspect of the hotel experience.

Implementing the repositioning plan is a multifaceted process that requires careful execution, from training staff and launching marketing campaigns to engaging with guests and tracking progress. By focusing on these key areas and using real-life examples as a guide, distressed hotels can successfully transform their brand and attract a new audience. With the right strategies and a commitment to delivering an exceptional guest experience, the repositioned hotel can thrive in a competitive market and achieve long-term success.

Overcoming Challenges in Repositioning

Repositioning a distressed hotel can be a transformative process, but it's rarely a smooth journey. The path is often fraught with challenges that can hinder progress and threaten the success of the repositioning efforts. Overcoming these obstacles requires strategic planning, adaptability, and a proactive approach to managing guest expectations, handling negative feedback, addressing operational challenges, and maintaining momentum. In this section, we'll explore how to navigate these hurdles with practical examples, case studies, and actionable steps to ensure a successful repositioning and long-term success.

Managing Guest Expectations During the Transition

During the repositioning process, guests may experience disruptions, such as renovations, changes in services, or inconsistencies in the brand experience. Managing guest expectations is crucial to maintaining satisfaction and preventing negative perceptions of the hotel during this period.

1. Clear Communication: Transparent communication is essential when managing guest expectations. Inform guests about ongoing changes, renovations, or service modifications through multiple channels, such as emails, website updates, signage, and in-person interactions. For instance, if the lobby is undergoing renovations, inform guests at check-in and provide an alternative route or space for relaxation.

2. Offering Compensation or Incentives: Guests who experience disruptions should feel valued and appreciated. Offering compensations like room upgrades, discounted rates, complimentary amenities, or free dining experiences can help mitigate any inconvenience caused by the repositioning process.

3. Training Staff to Handle Guest Concerns: Equip staff with the skills to handle guest concerns empathetically and professionally. Staff should be well-informed about the repositioning process and capable of addressing questions, offering solutions, and reassuring guests.

Practical Example: When a luxury hotel in Miami underwent major renovations, management proactively informed guests about the changes in advance, offered complimentary breakfast vouchers, and provided access to nearby partner facilities. This transparent approach resulted in positive feedback from guests who appreciated the honesty and gestures of goodwill.

Actionable Steps:

- Communicate all changes and disruptions through multiple channels.

- Offer compensation or incentives to guests affected by the repositioning process.

- Train staff to address guest concerns with empathy and professionalism.

Handling Negative Reviews and Feedback

Negative reviews and feedback are inevitable during the repositioning process, as guests may be affected by ongoing changes or inconsistencies. However, how a hotel responds to this feedback can significantly impact its reputation and repositioning success.

1. Responding Promptly and Professionally: Respond to negative reviews and feedback promptly, showing genuine concern and a willingness to address the issues raised. A personalized response demonstrates that the hotel values guest opinions and is committed to improving the guest experience.

2. Learning from Feedback: Negative feedback provides valuable insights into areas that need

improvement. Use this feedback to identify trends, make adjustments to operations, and enhance the repositioning process. For example, if guests consistently complain about noise from renovations, consider adjusting work hours or providing noise-canceling amenities.

3. Highlighting Positive Changes: Leverage online platforms to showcase positive changes resulting from the repositioning efforts. Share before-and-after photos, guest testimonials, or stories about the hotel's transformation to shift the narrative from negative to positive.

Practical Example: A boutique hotel in Los Angeles received negative feedback about inconsistent service quality during its repositioning. The management team took immediate action by implementing additional staff training, which led to improved service. They responded to negative reviews by highlighting these changes and inviting guests to experience the enhanced service, which eventually improved their online reputation.

Actionable Steps:

- Respond to negative reviews promptly and professionally.

- Use feedback to identify and address problem areas.

- Highlight positive changes to shift the narrative and improve perceptions.

Addressing Operational Challenges

Repositioning often brings operational challenges, such as coordinating renovations, managing costs, and maintaining service quality. Addressing these challenges requires strategic planning and adaptability to ensure smooth operations during the transition.

1. Coordinating Renovations and Daily Operations: Renovations can disrupt daily operations, affecting guest experiences and staff productivity. To minimize disruptions, schedule renovations during off-peak hours, and prioritize high-traffic areas first. Phasing renovations ensures that only a portion of the property is under construction at any given time, allowing other areas to remain fully operational.

2. Managing Costs and Budgets: Repositioning projects can strain financial resources, especially if unexpected costs arise. Establish a contingency budget to handle unforeseen expenses and monitor spending closely to prevent cost overruns. Regularly review the budget and make adjustments as needed to stay on track.

3. Maintaining Service Quality: Service quality should not be compromised during the repositioning process. Train staff to adapt to changing circumstances, and encourage them to remain attentive and responsive to guest needs. Implementing temporary solutions, such as portable check-in stations or pop-up dining areas, can help maintain service standards.

Case Study: The Ritz-Carlton, Grand Cayman faced

significant operational challenges during a multi-million-dollar renovation. By scheduling renovations during low-occupancy periods, maintaining open communication with guests, and offering alternative dining options, the hotel was able to complete the project without compromising service quality or guest satisfaction.

Actionable Steps:

- Coordinate renovations to minimize disruption to daily operations.

- Monitor budgets closely and establish a contingency fund.

- Train staff to maintain service quality during the transition.

Case Study: How a Hotel Overcame Obstacles During Repositioning

The Ace Hotel New Orleans offers a compelling example of overcoming obstacles during repositioning. Originally, the property was a neglected warehouse struggling to find its place in a competitive market. Management decided to reposition the hotel as a trendy, boutique destination that catered to young, creative professionals.

Challenges Encountered:

- Extensive renovations were required to transform the outdated space into a modern, stylish hotel.

- Negative perceptions of the neighborhood posed a challenge in attracting the target market.

- Staff initially struggled to adapt to the hotel's unique brand identity and service expectations.

Solutions Implemented:

- The hotel partnered with local artists, musicians, and designers to create a space that reflected New Orleans' vibrant culture, which helped shift perceptions and attract the target market.

- Management invested in extensive staff training to ensure employees understood and embodied the new brand experience.

- A robust marketing campaign highlighted the hotel's transformation, incorporating storytelling that emphasized the connection to local culture.

The repositioning was a success, with the Ace Hotel New Orleans gaining popularity among travelers seeking an authentic, culturally immersive experience.

Key Takeaway: Overcoming obstacles requires a combination of creativity, adaptability, and a commitment to delivering a unique brand experience that resonates with guests.

Tips for Maintaining Momentum

Maintaining momentum during the repositioning process is crucial for sustaining progress and keeping the team motivated. Repositioning can be a long and complex journey, but with the right strategies, you can maintain enthusiasm and drive results.

1. Celebrate Milestones: Recognize and celebrate key achievements, such as completing renovations, reaching occupancy targets, or receiving positive feedback. Celebrating successes boosts morale and encourages staff to remain committed to the repositioning goals.

2. Regularly Review Progress: Conduct regular progress reviews to assess the effectiveness of repositioning efforts and identify areas for improvement. Adjust strategies as needed to address challenges and capitalize on opportunities.

3. Engage with the Community: Engaging with the local community can help build momentum and generate interest in the repositioned hotel. Host events, collaborate with local businesses, and participate in community initiatives to raise awareness and foster connections.

Actionable Steps:

- Celebrate milestones to maintain team motivation.

- Conduct regular progress reviews and adjust strategies as needed.

- Engage with the local community to build momentum and awareness.

Strategies for Long-Term Success

Achieving long-term success in repositioning requires a commitment to continuous improvement and adapting to changing market conditions.

1. Continuously Monitor Performance: Regularly monitor key performance indicators (KPIs) such as occupancy rates, RevPAR, guest satisfaction scores, and online reviews. Use this data to make informed decisions and adjust strategies to ensure sustained success.

2. Invest in Ongoing Staff Training: Staff training should not end once the repositioning process is complete. Provide ongoing training to ensure employees continue to deliver the brand experience and adapt to evolving guest expectations.

3. Stay Ahead of Market Trends: The hospitality industry is dynamic, and staying ahead of trends is essential for long-term success. Monitor industry developments, guest preferences, and emerging technologies to remain competitive and relevant.

Practical Example: The Savoy Hotel in London has maintained its status as a luxury destination by continuously adapting to changing trends, investing in staff training, and enhancing its services. This proactive approach has enabled the Savoy to remain a leader in the luxury hotel market for over a century.

Actionable Steps:

- Monitor KPIs and adjust strategies for continuous improvement.

- Invest in ongoing staff training to maintain service quality.

- Stay informed about industry trends and adapt to changing market conditions.

Overcoming challenges in repositioning is an ongoing process that requires resilience, adaptability, and strategic planning. By managing guest expectations, handling feedback, addressing operational issues, and maintaining momentum, hotels can navigate the repositioning journey successfully. Adopting strategies for long-term success ensures that the repositioned hotel remains competitive, profitable, and capable of meeting the evolving needs of guests in an ever-changing market.

Evaluating the Success of the Repositioning Efforts

Evaluating the success of a hotel's repositioning efforts is a crucial step that determines whether the transformation has achieved its objectives. This evaluation not only helps in assessing the impact of the changes but also provides insights for future growth and continuous improvement. In this section, we'll explore how to measure performance against repositioning goals, analyze guest feedback, assess financial metrics, adjust strategies, celebrate achievements, and prepare for future expansion.

Measuring Performance Against Repositioning Goals

The first step in evaluating repositioning success is to measure performance against the goals established at the outset of the repositioning process. These goals typically include improved occupancy rates, enhanced guest satisfaction, increased average daily rate (ADR), and a stronger brand presence in the market.

1. Establishing Key Performance Indicators (KPIs): KPIs should be aligned with the hotel's repositioning objectives. Common KPIs include:

- Occupancy Rate: Has there been an increase in room occupancy since the repositioning?

- Average Daily Rate (ADR): Has the hotel been able to command higher room rates?

- Revenue Per Available Room (RevPAR): This metric combines occupancy and ADR to measure overall revenue performance.

- Guest Satisfaction Scores: Have guest reviews and ratings improved, reflecting a positive perception of the repositioning?

2. Monitoring Brand Awareness and Market Positioning: Track metrics such as website traffic, social media engagement, and media mentions to gauge how well the repositioned hotel is resonating with the target audience.

Practical Example: A boutique hotel in Chicago repositioned itself as a luxury art-themed destination, targeting affluent travelers. After repositioning, they monitored KPIs like ADR and occupancy rate, which increased by 15% and 20%, respectively, indicating that the hotel had successfully attracted a more upscale clientele.

Actionable Steps:

- Identify and track KPIs that align with repositioning goals.

- Regularly review performance data to assess progress.

- Compare pre- and post-repositioning metrics to measure success.

Analyzing Guest Feedback and Satisfaction

Guest feedback is one of the most valuable indicators of repositioning success, as it provides insights into how well the new brand experience meets guest expectations.

1. Monitoring Online Reviews and Ratings: Track guest reviews on platforms such as TripAdvisor, Booking.com, and Google. Look for recurring themes and sentiments in feedback to understand what guests appreciate about the repositioned hotel and where there might be room for improvement.

2. Conducting Guest Satisfaction Surveys: Implement surveys that capture guests' perceptions of the hotel's new brand identity, amenities, and services. Surveys can be conducted during the stay, at check-out, or via

email post-stay. Ask specific questions about aspects of the repositioning, such as the updated design, service quality, and overall experience.

3. Engaging Directly with Guests: Encourage guests to share their experiences with staff during their stay. Frontline staff can gather valuable feedback, which can then be analyzed to identify trends and areas for enhancement.

Practical Example: A hotel that repositioned itself as a wellness retreat introduced a guest survey asking for feedback on its new spa facilities, healthy dining options, and wellness activities. The survey results revealed high satisfaction with the spa but highlighted a demand for more vegetarian and vegan dining choices, prompting the hotel to expand its menu.

Actionable Steps:

- Regularly monitor online reviews and guest satisfaction scores.

- Conduct targeted surveys to gather feedback on the repositioning experience.

- Analyze feedback trends to identify strengths and areas for improvement.

Financial Metrics for Evaluating Repositioning Success

Financial metrics are a crucial component of evaluating repositioning success, as they provide a clear picture of the hotel's profitability and return on investment (ROI).

1. Revenue Growth: Measure total revenue growth, including room revenue, food and beverage sales, and other ancillary services. An increase in revenue indicates that the repositioning is driving more business to the hotel.

2. Profit Margins: Analyze profit margins to determine if the repositioning has improved the hotel's profitability. Higher margins suggest that the hotel is successfully attracting higher-paying guests or operating more efficiently.

3. ROI on Renovations and Marketing: Calculate the ROI of the renovation and marketing investments made during repositioning. This metric helps determine whether the capital spent on upgrades, design, and marketing campaigns has translated into increased revenue and profitability.

Practical Example: A mid-range hotel that repositioned itself as a business-friendly property invested $500,000 in renovations and marketing. Within a year, the hotel experienced a $700,000 increase in revenue, resulting in a 40% ROI, indicating that the repositioning strategy was financially successful.

Actionable Steps:

- Track revenue, profit margins, and ROI on repositioning investments.

- Compare financial performance before and

after repositioning to assess the impact.

- Adjust strategies based on financial outcomes to maximize profitability.

Adjusting Strategies for Continuous Improvement

Repositioning is not a one-time event but an ongoing process that requires continuous monitoring and adjustments. Evaluating success provides insights into what works and what doesn't, allowing the hotel to refine its strategy.

1. Analyzing Data and Trends: Regularly review KPIs, guest feedback, and financial metrics to identify trends and areas for improvement. For instance, if guest satisfaction scores are consistently low for a specific service, address the issue promptly.

2. Adapting to Market Changes: Stay informed about market trends, competitor activities, and changing guest preferences. Adapt the repositioning strategy to stay relevant and meet evolving demands.

3. Implementing Incremental Changes: Make small, incremental changes based on feedback and performance data. For example, if guests express interest in more local experiences, consider partnering with nearby attractions or restaurants.

Practical Example: A hotel repositioned as a family-friendly resort initially focused on offering kid-centric activities but noticed an increasing demand for family bonding experiences. In response, the hotel introduced family-oriented cooking classes and craft workshops, which boosted guest satisfaction and increased bookings.

Actionable Steps:

- Regularly analyze performance data and guest feedback.

- Stay informed about market trends and adjust strategies accordingly.

- Implement incremental changes to enhance the guest experience.

Celebrating Achievements and Sharing Success Stories

Recognizing and celebrating achievements is essential for maintaining momentum and motivating staff. Sharing success stories also helps build the hotel's reputation and reinforces the brand identity.

1. Recognizing Staff Contributions: Celebrate staff contributions to the repositioning process by acknowledging their efforts in team meetings, newsletters, or through incentive programs. This boosts morale and encourages continued dedication to the brand's success.

2. Sharing Success Stories with Guests: Share success stories, testimonials, and milestones with guests through newsletters, social media, and website updates. Highlighting achievements, such as awards won, improved guest ratings, or increased occupancy

rates, builds credibility and reinforces the repositioned brand.

3. Engaging with Media and Influencers: Leverage media coverage and influencer partnerships to share the repositioning success story. This increases brand visibility and attracts potential guests who are interested in experiencing the transformation.

Practical Example: After successfully repositioning as a luxury wellness resort, a hotel celebrated by hosting a grand reopening event, inviting media, influencers, and loyal guests. The event generated positive press coverage, social media buzz, and a surge in bookings.

Actionable Steps:

- Recognize and reward staff contributions to the repositioning effort.

- Share success stories with guests and the broader community.

- Engage with media and influencers to increase brand visibility.

Preparing for Future Growth and Expansion

Evaluating repositioning success also involves planning for future growth and expansion. A successful repositioning lays the foundation for continued development, allowing the hotel to build on its achievements.

1. Expanding the Brand Offering: Consider expanding

the hotel's offerings to attract a broader market segment. For example, introduce new amenities, services, or packages that align with the repositioned brand identity.

2. Exploring New Revenue Streams: Identify opportunities to generate additional revenue streams, such as hosting events, offering corporate retreats, or partnering with local businesses for experiential packages.

3. Scaling the Repositioning Strategy: If the repositioning strategy has proven successful, consider scaling it to other properties within the portfolio or franchising the concept to expand the brand's reach.

Practical Example: After repositioning itself as a destination for culinary tourism, a hotel in Napa Valley expanded its offerings by introducing cooking classes, wine tasting events, and partnerships with local vineyards. These additional experiences attracted more guests and increased revenue, positioning the hotel for long-term success.

Actionable Steps:

- Expand the hotel's offerings to attract new market segments.

- Explore additional revenue streams that align with the brand.
- Consider scaling the repositioning strategy to other properties or markets.

Evaluating the success of a hotel's repositioning

efforts is an ongoing process that requires a comprehensive analysis of KPIs, guest feedback, financial performance, and market trends. By measuring success against repositioning goals, adjusting strategies for continuous improvement, celebrating achievements, and preparing for future growth, hotels can ensure that their repositioning efforts lead to sustained success and profitability. This evaluation not only validates the repositioning strategy but also sets the stage for continued growth and expansion in a competitive hospitality market.

Chapter 5: Bank Workouts for Distressed Hotels

Navigating financial distress in the hotel industry requires a strategic and collaborative approach, particularly when dealing with lenders. This chapter delves into the complexities of bank workouts for distressed hotels, offering a comprehensive guide on how to work with lenders to resolve financial challenges and steer the property toward recovery. Bank workouts represent a critical lifeline for distressed hotel owners, providing a pathway to restructure debt, negotiate more favorable terms, and avoid foreclosure.

The chapter begins by explaining what a bank workout entails and why it's a viable solution for distressed hotels. We'll explore the lender's perspective on distressed assets, shedding light on the various types of bank workouts, such as forbearance agreements and loan modifications. Understanding these options is essential for hotel owners seeking to determine their eligibility for a workout and preparing themselves for the process ahead. Real-world examples will illustrate how a successful bank workout can restore financial stability, along with actionable steps for preparing and initiating discussions with lenders.

Next, we delve into the process of initiating a workout, emphasizing the importance of building rapport with lenders and preparing comprehensive financial documentation. We'll identify common challenges that arise during this stage and how to present a compelling case for restructuring. Through a detailed case study, you'll learn how a distressed hotel successfully negotiated a workout, overcoming obstacles and managing lender relationships effectively.

Negotiating with lenders requires a thorough understanding of their priorities and concerns. In this section, we'll outline strategies for effective negotiation, addressing potential objections, and finalizing terms that are mutually beneficial. A practical example will highlight a successful negotiation that saved a hotel from financial ruin, demonstrating how to approach discussions with confidence and clarity. Actionable steps will be provided to help you improve negotiation outcomes and achieve favorable results.

Once the workout plan is in place, implementing it effectively is crucial for the long-term success of the hotel. We'll cover how to monitor compliance with workout terms, manage cash flow, and report progress to lenders. Adjusting strategies as needed is part of maintaining financial health, and a case study will illustrate how a well-executed workout plan can turn around a distressed hotel, offering tips for ensuring successful implementation.

While bank workouts are a common solution, they aren't the only option available to distressed hotel owners. We'll explore alternatives such as refinancing, asset sales, and bankruptcy, examining the pros and cons of each. By comparing these options, you'll gain insights into when it might be appropriate to pursue an alternative route. A practical example will show how a hotel avoided foreclosure through refinancing, providing valuable lessons on weighing different paths to recovery.

The chapter concludes with an exploration of lessons learned from bank workouts, including common pitfalls and how to build resilience against future financial challenges. Through a case study of a hotel that emerged stronger after a workout, we'll highlight the importance of developing a proactive financial management strategy and learning from past experiences. By the end of this chapter, you'll be equipped with the knowledge and tools needed to navigate the complexities of bank workouts and steer your distressed hotel toward a more secure financial future.

Understanding Bank Workouts

When a hotel faces financial distress and is unable to meet its debt obligations, a bank workout can be a lifeline, allowing the property to avoid foreclosure while regaining financial stability. Understanding the nuances of bank workouts is essential for hotel owners who wish to navigate financial challenges effectively and maintain their assets. This section delves into what a bank workout entails, the lender's perspective on distressed assets, the different types of workouts available, and how to assess eligibility. We'll also explore a practical example of a successful bank workout and provide actionable steps to prepare for the process.

What Is a Bank Workout?
A bank workout is a negotiated agreement between a borrower (the hotel owner) and a lender to modify the terms of a loan when the borrower is facing financial difficulties. The objective is to create a mutually beneficial arrangement that allows the borrower to avoid foreclosure and continue operating the business while providing the lender with a structured plan to recover the outstanding debt.

Bank workouts are not a one-size-fits-all solution. They require careful negotiation, thorough preparation, and a clear understanding of both the borrower's financial situation and the lender's expectations. Successful workouts often involve adjusting loan terms, repayment schedules, interest rates, or other conditions to provide temporary relief while the hotel regains profitability.

Key Benefits of a Bank Workout:

- Avoiding foreclosure and bankruptcy, which can be costly and damaging to the hotel's reputation.

- Providing breathing room to stabilize cash flow and improve financial performance.

- Preserving the relationship between the hotel owner and the lender, which can be crucial for long-term financing needs.

The Lender's Perspective on Distressed Hotel Assets

Understanding the lender's perspective is a critical component of a successful bank workout. Lenders are in the business of lending money, not managing or owning hotels. When a hotel defaults on its loan, the lender faces the risk of financial loss, which is why they may be willing to negotiate a workout rather than pursuing foreclosure.

Key Considerations for Lenders:

Recovery of the Outstanding Debt: Lenders are primarily concerned with recovering as much of the outstanding loan as possible. They will evaluate whether a workout provides a better chance of recovery than foreclosure.

- Hotel's Potential for Recovery: Lenders will assess the hotel's potential for returning to profitability. They will consider factors such as location, market conditions, management capabilities, and any planned improvements.

- Collateral Value: The value of the hotel as collateral is a significant factor. If the property's value has declined, lenders may be more inclined to negotiate a workout to avoid the costs and delays associated with foreclosure and selling the asset.

- Minimizing Risk: Lenders seek to minimize risk by ensuring that any workout agreement includes safeguards, such as regular reporting, financial monitoring, and conditions that protect their interests.

By demonstrating a clear plan for financial recovery and a commitment to meeting new terms, hotel owners can build credibility and increase the likelihood of securing a favorable workout agreement.

Types of Bank Workouts

There are several types of bank workouts, each designed to address different aspects of financial distress. Understanding these options allows hotel owners to negotiate the most appropriate solution for their situation.

1. Forbearance Agreements: In a forbearance agreement, the lender agrees to temporarily suspend or reduce loan payments, giving the borrower time to address financial challenges. For example, a lender might agree to suspend principal payments for six months, allowing the hotel to stabilize its cash flow.

2. Loan Modification: Loan modification involves permanently changing one or more terms of the loan, such as extending the repayment period, reducing the interest rate, or adjusting the payment schedule. This option provides long-term relief and makes loan payments more manageable for the borrower.

3. Interest-Only Payments: In this arrangement, the borrower makes interest-only payments for a specified period, reducing the monthly payment amount. This option can help improve cash flow during a temporary downturn in business.

4. Debt Restructuring: Debt restructuring involves reorganizing the hotel's debt obligations, which may include consolidating multiple loans, renegotiating terms, or exchanging debt for equity. This option is more complex but can significantly reduce the hotel's financial burden.

5. Deed in Lieu of Foreclosure: As a last resort, a hotel owner may voluntarily transfer ownership of the property to the lender to satisfy the debt. While this option avoids the legal process of foreclosure, it results in the loss of the hotel.

Practical Example: A hotel owner in Orlando facing financial distress due to a decline in tourism successfully negotiated a loan modification. The lender agreed to extend the loan term by five years and reduce the interest rate, which lowered the monthly payments and allowed the hotel to improve cash flow. Over time, the hotel stabilized its operations, increased occupancy rates, and returned to profitability.

Assessing Eligibility for a Workout

Not all distressed hotels qualify for a bank workout. Lenders assess eligibility based on several factors, and it's essential for hotel owners to evaluate their situation before approaching the lender.

1. Financial Viability: The hotel must demonstrate its potential for financial recovery. Lenders will scrutinize financial statements, cash flow projections, and market conditions to assess whether the hotel can meet revised loan terms.

2. Asset Value: The property's current value relative to the outstanding debt plays a crucial role in determining eligibility. If the hotel's value is significantly lower than the loan balance, the lender may be less willing to negotiate.

3. Management Capability: The lender must have confidence in the hotel management's ability to implement a successful turnaround plan. Demonstrating experience, expertise, and a track record of effective management can improve eligibility.

4. Willingness to Collaborate: A borrower who is proactive, transparent, and willing to work with the lender is more likely to be considered for a workout. Open communication and a genuine commitment to resolving financial challenges build trust with the lender.

Actionable Steps:

- Prepare detailed financial statements and cash flow projections to demonstrate the hotel's potential for recovery.

- Conduct a property valuation to understand how the hotel's value compares to the outstanding debt.
- Develop a turnaround plan that outlines strategies for improving profitability, managing expenses, and increasing revenue.

- Approach the lender proactively and express a

willingness to collaborate on finding a solution.

Practical Example: A Successful Bank Workout for a Hotel

The Seaside Inn, a mid-range hotel located in a coastal town, faced financial distress due to declining occupancy rates during the off-season. The hotel's management approached the lender with a comprehensive turnaround plan that included cost-cutting measures, targeted marketing campaigns, and partnerships with local businesses to drive bookings.

The lender agreed to a forbearance agreement, suspending principal payments for six months and reducing the interest rate temporarily. During this period, the Seaside Inn executed its turnaround plan, improved occupancy rates, and increased revenue. By the end of the forbearance period, the hotel was in a much stronger financial position and resumed regular loan payments, ultimately avoiding foreclosure.

Key Takeaway: A proactive approach, combined with a well-prepared turnaround plan, can lead to a successful workout that benefits both the hotel owner and the lender.

Actionable Steps for Preparing for a Bank Workout

- Assess Financial Health: Conduct a thorough analysis of the hotel's financial situation, including cash flow, expenses, debt obligations, and profitability.

- Develop a Turnaround Plan: Create a detailed plan that outlines strategies for improving financial performance, reducing costs, and increasing revenue.

- Prepare Financial Documentation: Compile accurate financial statements, tax returns, cash flow projections, and property valuations to present to the lender.

- Engage with the Lender: Approach the lender proactively, demonstrating a willingness to collaborate and negotiate a workout.

- Build Credibility: Be transparent, communicate regularly, and provide updates on the hotel's progress throughout the workout process.

Understanding bank workouts is essential for distressed hotel owners seeking to regain financial stability and avoid foreclosure. By recognizing the lender's perspective, exploring different types of workouts, assessing eligibility, and taking a proactive approach, hotel owners can negotiate effective solutions that provide much-needed relief. With the right strategies, preparation, and collaboration, a bank workout can be a turning point that helps a distressed hotel recover and thrive.

Initiating the Workout Process

Initiating the bank workout process can be a daunting task for distressed hotel owners, but it's a crucial step in regaining financial stability and avoiding foreclosure. Engaging with lenders requires a strategic approach, thorough preparation, and effective communication to build trust and confidence. This section delves into the essential elements of starting the workout process, from engaging with lenders and preparing financial documentation to presenting a compelling case for restructuring. We'll also examine common challenges, offer practical tips for managing lender relationships, and highlight a case study that demonstrates how a hotel successfully negotiated a workout.

Engaging with Lenders and Building Rapport

The foundation of a successful bank workout lies in establishing a strong, collaborative relationship with the lender. Engaging with lenders early and building rapport can significantly increase the chances of reaching a favorable workout agreement. Remember, lenders want to recover their funds, and demonstrating a genuine willingness to cooperate can help build trust.

1. Approach the Lender Proactively: Don't wait until the situation becomes dire before reaching out to the lender. Engaging with them at the first sign of financial distress shows responsibility and transparency, which can foster a more positive and cooperative relationship.

2. Be Transparent and Honest: Share the hotel's current financial situation, challenges, and reasons for distress openly. Lenders appreciate honesty and are more likely to work with owners who provide a clear picture of their circumstances.

3. Communicate Regularly: Consistent communication is key to maintaining rapport. Keep the lender informed about your efforts to improve the hotel's financial health, including any steps you've taken to cut costs, increase revenue, or address operational inefficiencies.

Practical Example: A hotel owner in Denver noticed occupancy rates declining due to increased competition. Instead of waiting until debt obligations became unmanageable, they proactively reached out to their lender, explained the situation, and expressed a willingness to collaborate on a workout plan. This proactive approach made the lender more receptive to restructuring the loan terms, resulting in a successful outcome.

Actionable Steps:

- Reach out to your lender at the first sign of financial distress.

- Be transparent about your financial challenges and the reasons behind them.

- Maintain regular communication and provide updates on your efforts to improve the hotel's performance.

Preparing Financial Documentation and Projections

Lenders will scrutinize your financial position before agreeing to any workout, making it essential to present comprehensive and accurate financial documentation. Being well-prepared with detailed financial statements and projections demonstrates professionalism and increases the lender's confidence in your ability to manage the hotel's finances.

1. Compile Accurate Financial Statements: Prepare income statements, balance sheets, cash flow statements, and tax returns for at least the past three years. These documents provide the lender with a clear picture of your financial history and current status.

2. Create Cash Flow Projections: Develop cash flow projections for the next 12 to 24 months, showing how you plan to generate sufficient revenue to meet your financial obligations under the proposed workout plan. Include various scenarios (best case, worst case, and most likely) to demonstrate that you've considered potential risks.

3. Prepare a Detailed Business Plan: Include a comprehensive business plan that outlines your strategy for improving the hotel's financial performance. This plan should cover revenue growth strategies, cost-cutting measures, marketing initiatives, and any planned renovations or upgrades.

Practical Example: A hotel in Las Vegas facing financial distress due to declining tourism prepared detailed financial statements and a business plan that outlined a strategy to attract local guests through targeted marketing and special packages. By presenting this data to the lender, the hotel owner demonstrated a clear path to recovery, which helped secure a favorable workout agreement.

Actionable Steps:

- Gather and organize all relevant financial statements and tax returns.

- Develop detailed cash flow projections for the next 12 to 24 months.

- Create a business plan that outlines your strategy for financial recovery and growth.

Identifying Common Challenges in Bank Workouts

The workout process is rarely straightforward, and hotel owners often face several challenges that can hinder negotiations. Identifying these challenges in advance allows you to prepare and address them effectively.

1. Lender Reluctance: Lenders may be hesitant to negotiate, especially if they believe foreclosure offers a better chance of recovering their funds. To overcome this, demonstrate that a workout is a more viable option by presenting a compelling case for the hotel's potential recovery.

2. Inadequate Financial Documentation: Insufficient or inaccurate financial documentation can undermine your credibility and delay the workout process. Ensure all financial records are accurate, up-to-date, and well-organized before engaging with the lender.

3. Unrealistic Projections or Expectations: Overly optimistic cash flow projections or unrealistic

expectations about the workout terms can erode trust with the lender. Be realistic about what you can achieve and present achievable goals backed by data.

4. Market Uncertainty: External factors, such as economic downturns, changing travel patterns, or regional crises, can impact the workout process. Acknowledge these challenges in your negotiations and outline how you plan to mitigate their effects.

Actionable Steps:

- Prepare thoroughly to address potential lender concerns.

- Ensure financial documentation is accurate and comprehensive.

- Be realistic in your projections and expectations.

Presenting a Compelling Case for Restructuring

To secure a favorable workout agreement, you must present a compelling case that demonstrates the hotel's potential for financial recovery and profitability. Lenders need to be convinced that the proposed restructuring plan is in their best interest.

1. Highlight the Hotel's Strengths: Emphasize aspects of the hotel that make it a valuable asset, such as its prime location, unique amenities, or potential to attract a specific target market. Show how these strengths can be leveraged to improve financial

performance.

2. Address Operational Improvements: Demonstrate how you plan to address operational inefficiencies, reduce costs, and increase revenue. For example, you might outline plans to streamline staffing, implement energy-saving measures, or launch targeted marketing campaigns.

3. Provide a Clear Repayment Plan: Present a clear and realistic repayment plan that outlines how you will meet the revised loan terms. Include detailed timelines, payment amounts, and contingencies for potential setbacks.

Practical Example: A beachfront resort in Florida, struggling due to seasonal fluctuations, presented a compelling case by highlighting its unique location, outlining plans to introduce off-season events, and showcasing partnerships with local businesses to drive year-round traffic. This approach convinced the lender that the resort had the potential to recover, resulting in a successful workout agreement.

Actionable Steps:

- Emphasize the hotel's strengths and potential for recovery.

- Present a realistic and achievable repayment plan.

- Address operational improvements and cost-saving measures.

Case Study: How a Hotel Negotiated a Successful Workout

The Willow Creek Inn, a 200-room hotel in a suburban area, experienced financial distress due to a combination of market saturation and a decrease in corporate travel. Recognizing the challenges ahead, the hotel's management team proactively engaged with their lender, providing transparent financial records and a comprehensive turnaround plan.

Steps Taken:

- The management team initiated open communication with the lender, acknowledging the hotel's financial difficulties and expressing their commitment to finding a solution.

- They presented detailed financial documentation and cash flow projections that demonstrated a realistic path to profitability.

- The turnaround plan included strategies such as targeting weekend leisure travelers, offering staycation packages, and forming partnerships with local businesses to host events at the hotel.

The lender agreed to a forbearance agreement, reducing the monthly payments for 12 months while the hotel executed its turnaround plan. The hotel's management team successfully increased occupancy rates, enhanced revenue streams, and met the adjusted payment terms, ultimately restoring financial stability.

Key Takeaway: By being proactive, transparent, and presenting a well-prepared plan, Willow Creek Inn secured a workout agreement that allowed it to overcome financial challenges.

Tips for Managing Lender Relationships

- Maintain Open Communication: Keep the lender informed about your progress, challenges, and any adjustments made to the workout plan. Regular updates help build trust and demonstrate your commitment to the agreement.

- Be Transparent and Honest: If you encounter setbacks, inform the lender promptly and outline the steps you're taking to address them. Lenders are more willing to work with borrowers who are honest about their challenges.

- Show Progress: Demonstrate that you're actively implementing your turnaround plan by sharing positive developments, such as improved occupancy rates, cost savings, or increased revenue.

Actionable Steps:

- Schedule regular meetings or updates with your lender.

- Be transparent about challenges and how you

plan to address them.
- Share progress reports to demonstrate your commitment to the workout plan.

Initiating the workout process requires a proactive approach, thorough preparation, and the ability to build rapport with lenders. By engaging early, presenting comprehensive financial documentation, addressing common challenges, and presenting a compelling case for restructuring, hotel owners can increase their chances of negotiating a successful workout agreement. Through effective communication, transparency, and a commitment to the workout plan, distressed hotels can navigate financial challenges and regain stability.

Negotiating with Lenders

Successfully negotiating with lenders is a critical step in securing a bank workout that enables a distressed hotel to regain financial stability. This process requires a deep understanding of lender priorities, a well-thought-out negotiation strategy, and the ability to address potential objections effectively. In this section, we will explore the nuances of negotiating with lenders, providing practical examples, actionable steps, and a case study that demonstrates how a hotel successfully negotiated a workout that saved the property.

Understanding Lender Priorities and Concerns

Before entering into negotiations, it's crucial to understand what drives the lender's decision-making process. Lenders are primarily concerned with minimizing risk and maximizing their chances of recovering the loan amount. Recognizing these priorities allows you to frame your negotiation strategy in a way that aligns with the lender's interests.

1. Loan Repayment: Lenders want assurance that they will eventually recover the funds they lent, along with any accrued interest. They are more likely to agree to a workout if they believe it increases the likelihood of repayment over time, compared to the uncertainty and costs associated with foreclosure.

2. Collateral Value: The hotel serves as collateral for the loan, so lenders will be concerned about the current market value of the property. If the value has declined significantly, they may be more hesitant to negotiate favorable terms. Demonstrating the potential to enhance the property's value through repositioning or operational improvements can help ease these concerns.

3. Risk Mitigation: Lenders are risk-averse and want to minimize the chance of further financial losses. They will carefully assess your management capability, the hotel's future revenue potential, and your ability to execute a turnaround plan. Presenting a credible plan that addresses risks and outlines clear steps for recovery can make lenders more receptive to negotiations.

4. Legal and Regulatory Compliance: Lenders are bound by regulatory requirements and internal policies that may limit their flexibility in negotiations.

Understanding these constraints helps set realistic expectations about what they can and cannot agree to.

Practical Example: A hotel owner seeking to negotiate a workout understood that the lender's top concern was the hotel's declining cash flow. The owner presented a detailed plan to boost revenue by targeting new market segments, cutting operational costs, and implementing strategic marketing campaigns. This approach directly addressed the lender's priority of loan repayment, making them more willing to negotiate favorable terms.

Actionable Steps:

- Research the lender's priorities and concerns before entering negotiations.

- Demonstrate how your proposal addresses the lender's need for loan repayment and risk mitigation.

- Be prepared to discuss how your plan will enhance the property's value over time.

Developing a Negotiation Strategy

A well-prepared negotiation strategy is essential for achieving a successful workout agreement. This strategy should outline your objectives, the terms you're willing to accept, and potential areas for compromise.

1. Define Your Goals and Objectives: Clarify what you want to achieve from the workout, such as reduced

interest rates, extended loan terms, or temporary payment forbearance. Having clear objectives allows you to focus your negotiations and avoid unnecessary concessions.

2. Identify Areas for Flexibility: Determine which aspects of the workout are negotiable and where you can be flexible. For example, you might be open to making interest-only payments for a period or agreeing to a slightly higher interest rate in exchange for an extended loan term.

3. Develop a Data-Driven Approach: Support your negotiation strategy with data, including financial statements, cash flow projections, market analysis, and a detailed turnaround plan. Presenting factual evidence strengthens your credibility and demonstrates your commitment to recovery.

4. Prepare for Counteroffers: Anticipate the lender's counteroffers and be ready to adjust your approach accordingly. Consider potential objections or concerns they might raise and develop responses that address these issues.

Practical Example: A hotel owner negotiating with a lender aimed to secure a 12-month forbearance agreement. The owner supported this request with financial projections showing how the hotel could stabilize cash flow and meet loan obligations within the proposed timeframe. By having a clear goal and presenting data, the owner successfully negotiated favorable terms.

Actionable Steps:

- Define your primary goals and objectives for the workout.

- Identify areas where you can be flexible and prepare for potential counteroffers.

- Use data to support your negotiation strategy and build credibility.

Addressing Potential Objections

Lenders may raise objections during negotiations, questioning the feasibility of your turnaround plan or expressing concerns about the hotel's financial outlook. Addressing these objections promptly and effectively is crucial to maintaining momentum in the negotiation process.

1. Lack of Confidence in Management: Lenders may doubt your ability to execute the turnaround plan, especially if the hotel has experienced prolonged financial distress. Address this by highlighting your experience, expertise, and any operational improvements already implemented.

2. Uncertain Market Conditions: Lenders may be concerned about broader market trends, such as economic downturns or changes in travel patterns. Provide data that shows how your strategy accounts for these trends and how you plan to adapt.

3. Inadequate Cash Flow Projections: If the lender questions your cash flow projections, provide detailed

explanations of your assumptions, revenue-generating strategies, and cost-cutting measures. Offer alternative scenarios to demonstrate that you've considered various possibilities.

Practical Example: During a negotiation, a lender expressed concerns about a hotel's ability to recover in a post-pandemic environment. The hotel owner addressed this by presenting a marketing plan targeting local travelers, corporate events, and staycation packages, showcasing a clear path to revenue growth despite market uncertainty.

Actionable Steps:

- Anticipate potential objections and prepare responses that address them.

- Use data and real-world examples to validate your assumptions and projections.

- Be transparent about challenges and demonstrate how you plan to overcome them.

Finalizing Workout Terms and Agreements

Once both parties have agreed on the workout terms, it's essential to finalize the agreement with clear and comprehensive documentation. This step ensures that all aspects of the negotiation are legally binding and that there is mutual understanding of the terms.

1. Review the Agreement Thoroughly: Carefully review the workout agreement, paying close attention to details such as interest rates, payment schedules, and

any conditions or covenants. Ensure that all terms are accurately reflected and aligned with what was negotiated.

2. Seek Legal Advice: Engage a legal advisor with experience in workout agreements to review the document. Their expertise can help identify potential issues, ensure compliance, and protect your interests.

3. Establish a Monitoring and Reporting Framework: The lender will likely require regular updates on your progress. Establish a clear framework for monitoring compliance with the workout terms and reporting financial performance to maintain transparency.

Practical Example: A hotel owner successfully negotiated a loan modification that reduced the interest rate and extended the repayment period. Before finalizing the agreement, the owner's legal advisor identified a clause that could have led to penalties if the hotel missed even one payment. The owner negotiated a more lenient clause, which allowed for a brief grace period in case of unforeseen delays.

Actionable Steps:

- Review the workout agreement carefully and ensure all negotiated terms are accurately reflected.

- Consult with a legal advisor to protect your interests.

- Establish a reporting framework to monitor

compliance with the workout terms.

Practical Example: A Successful Negotiation That Saved a Hotel

The Seabreeze Resort, a 150-room beachfront property, was struggling with declining occupancy rates and mounting debt. Faced with the threat of foreclosure, the hotel owner engaged in negotiations with the lender to explore workout options.

The owner presented a detailed turnaround plan that included marketing campaigns targeting staycation travelers, partnerships with local businesses, and plans to introduce new revenue-generating amenities like a rooftop bar and wellness spa. By demonstrating the hotel's potential to recover, addressing the lender's concerns, and proposing realistic repayment terms, the owner successfully negotiated a loan modification that reduced the monthly payments and extended the loan term by five years.

Over the next 18 months, the Seabreeze Resort improved its occupancy rates, increased revenue, and stabilized its cash flow, ultimately meeting the revised loan obligations and avoiding foreclosure.

Key Takeaway: A combination of thorough preparation, effective communication, and a credible turnaround plan can lead to successful negotiations that save a distressed hotel.

Actionable Steps for Improving Negotiation Outcomes

- Understand the lender's priorities and tailor your proposal accordingly.
- Prepare a data-driven negotiation strategy supported by financial statements, projections, and a turnaround plan.

- Anticipate objections and develop responses that address lender concerns.

- Engage a legal advisor to review the agreement and protect your interests.

- Maintain open communication and transparency throughout the negotiation process.

Negotiating with lenders is a critical step in securing a workout agreement that allows a distressed hotel to regain financial stability. By understanding lender priorities, developing a data-driven negotiation strategy, addressing objections, and finalizing the terms effectively, hotel owners can significantly improve their chances of achieving a favorable outcome. With careful preparation and a proactive approach, it is possible to negotiate terms that benefit both the lender and the hotel, ultimately paving the way for a successful financial turnaround.

Implementing the Workout Plan

Once a workout plan has been successfully negotiated with the lender, the real challenge begins:

implementing the plan effectively to ensure the hotel's financial recovery. This phase requires careful monitoring, disciplined cash flow management, regular communication with the lender, and the flexibility to adjust strategies as necessary. This section provides an in-depth guide on how to implement a workout plan, with practical examples, a case study, and actionable steps to ensure successful execution.

Monitoring Compliance with Workout Terms

The first step in implementing the workout plan is to monitor compliance with the agreed-upon terms. Failure to adhere to the workout agreement can lead to severe consequences, including the lender taking legal action or reverting to foreclosure proceedings.

1. Establish a Compliance Tracking System: Create a system that tracks all workout terms and conditions, including repayment schedules, financial reporting requirements, and any performance targets specified in the agreement. This could be a simple spreadsheet or a more sophisticated software solution, depending on the complexity of the workout.

2. Assign Responsibilities: Designate team members responsible for monitoring compliance, such as the hotel's financial manager or accountant. Their role is to ensure that all payments are made on time and that all obligations are met according to the workout terms.

3. Regularly Review Compliance: Hold regular meetings to review the hotel's compliance with the

workout agreement. Identify any areas where the hotel is falling short and take immediate corrective action to prevent further issues.

Practical Example: A hotel in Miami entered into a workout agreement with reduced monthly payments for 12 months, contingent on maintaining a minimum occupancy rate of 70%. The hotel's financial team developed a dashboard to monitor occupancy rates in real-time, allowing management to take quick action, such as launching marketing campaigns during slow periods to meet the required targets.

Actionable Steps:

- Create a system for tracking compliance with workout terms.

- Assign a team member responsible for monitoring compliance.

- Conduct regular meetings to review compliance and address issues.

Managing Cash Flow and Expenses

Effective cash flow management is essential for implementing a successful workout plan. Since financial distress often stems from cash flow issues, ensuring that the hotel operates within its means is critical.

1. Prioritize Expenses: Identify and prioritize essential expenses, such as payroll, utilities, and loan payments, ensuring that these obligations are met

first. Non-essential expenses, such as discretionary marketing spend or minor renovations, should be deferred until the hotel's financial situation improves.

2. Implement Cost-Cutting Measures: Review all operating expenses to identify areas where costs can be reduced without compromising guest experience. This may include renegotiating contracts with suppliers, reducing energy consumption, or streamlining staffing levels during low-occupancy periods.

3. Monitor Cash Flow Closely: Maintain a detailed cash flow forecast that projects income and expenses for the next 12 months. Update this forecast regularly to identify potential shortfalls and take proactive measures to address them.

Practical Example: A resort facing financial distress during the off-season reduced its operating costs by renegotiating vendor contracts, implementing energy-saving initiatives, and adjusting staffing schedules based on occupancy rates. These measures helped the resort maintain positive cash flow during the slower months.

Actionable Steps:

- Prioritize essential expenses and defer non-essential spending.

- Implement cost-cutting measures without compromising guest experience.

- Maintain and regularly update a cash flow

forecast.

Reporting Progress to Lenders

Regular communication with the lender is essential for maintaining a positive relationship and demonstrating your commitment to the workout plan. Providing transparent and accurate reports helps build trust and keeps the lender informed about the hotel's progress.

1. Provide Regular Financial Reports: Submit monthly or quarterly financial reports that include income statements, balance sheets, cash flow statements, and key performance indicators (KPIs). These reports should clearly show how the hotel is progressing toward the goals outlined in the workout agreement.

2. Highlight Achievements and Challenges: Share any successes, such as increased occupancy rates or cost savings, to demonstrate progress. At the same time, be transparent about any challenges or setbacks, explaining how you plan to address them. This approach shows the lender that you are proactive and dedicated to overcoming obstacles.

3. Schedule Regular Meetings: Arrange regular check-ins with the lender to discuss the hotel's progress, answer questions, and address any concerns. These meetings provide an opportunity to strengthen the relationship and ensure that the lender remains confident in your ability to meet the workout terms.

Practical Example: A hotel owner implemented a weekly reporting system to track the hotel's financial performance, which was shared with the lender at monthly meetings. By consistently demonstrating progress and addressing any concerns, the owner built a strong relationship with the lender, which proved beneficial when requesting an extension on the workout agreement.

Actionable Steps:

- Submit regular financial reports to the lender.

- Highlight both achievements and challenges in your reports.

- Schedule regular meetings to maintain open communication with the lender.

Adjusting Strategies as Needed

Implementing a workout plan requires flexibility, as unexpected challenges or changes in market conditions may necessitate adjustments to the original strategy. Being willing to adapt and respond proactively to these changes is key to ensuring the success of the workout plan.

1. Monitor Market Conditions: Stay informed about changes in the market that could impact the hotel's performance, such as shifts in travel patterns, economic trends, or competitive activity. Adjust your strategies to respond to these changes and maintain momentum.

2. Review and Adjust Operational Strategies: Regularly assess the effectiveness of your operational

strategies, such as marketing campaigns, pricing structures, or service offerings. If a particular strategy is not yielding the expected results, be prepared to adjust or replace it with a more effective approach.

3. Communicate Changes to the Lender: If adjustments to the workout plan are necessary, communicate these changes to the lender promptly. Provide a rationale for the adjustments and explain how they will contribute to the hotel's long-term financial stability.

Practical Example: A hotel that relied heavily on business travelers experienced a drop in occupancy due to changes in travel patterns. In response, the hotel adjusted its strategy by targeting the leisure market with special weekend packages and staycation promotions, which helped fill rooms and maintain cash flow.

Actionable Steps:

- Monitor market conditions and adjust strategies accordingly.

- Regularly review operational strategies and make necessary adjustments.

- Communicate any changes to the workout plan with the lender.

Case Study: How a Workout Plan Turned Around a Distressed Hotel

The Grandview Hotel, a 250-room property in a

metropolitan area, faced severe financial distress due to declining occupancy rates and mounting debt. After successfully negotiating a workout plan that included reduced monthly payments and a temporary interest rate reduction, the hotel's management team focused on implementing the plan effectively.

Steps Taken:

- Cost-Cutting Measures: The hotel reduced operating costs by renegotiating vendor contracts, reducing energy consumption, and streamlining staffing during off-peak periods.

- Targeted Marketing: The team launched a targeted marketing campaign to attract local leisure travelers, offering discounted weekend rates and special event packages.

- Regular Communication with the Lender: The hotel owner maintained open communication with the lender, providing monthly financial reports and updates on occupancy rates.

Within 18 months, the Grandview Hotel increased its occupancy rate from 55% to 75%, improved cash flow, and met the revised loan obligations. As a result, the lender extended more favorable terms, allowing the hotel to stabilize its financial position and return to profitability.

Key Takeaway: The successful implementation of the workout plan, combined with cost-cutting measures, targeted marketing, and consistent communication with the lender, allowed the Grandview Hotel to overcome financial distress and achieve long-term stability.

Tips for Ensuring Successful Implementation

- Stay Disciplined: Adhering to the workout plan requires discipline and a commitment to making difficult financial decisions. Avoid unnecessary spending and focus on achieving financial stability.

- Engage Staff in the Process: Ensure that staff members understand the importance of the workout plan and how their roles contribute to its success. Involving employees fosters a sense of ownership and commitment to the hotel's recovery.

- Be Proactive: Anticipate potential challenges and address them before they become significant issues. Being proactive helps prevent setbacks and keeps the hotel on track.

Actionable Steps:

- Maintain a disciplined approach to spending and financial management.

- Involve staff in the implementation process to foster commitment.

- Anticipate and address challenges proactively.

Implementing a workout plan requires careful monitoring, disciplined cash flow management, consistent communication with the lender, and a willingness to adapt to changing circumstances. By following these guidelines and learning from real-world examples, distressed hotels can successfully implement their workout plans, regain financial stability, and pave the way for long-term success. With commitment, transparency, and strategic adjustments, the path to recovery becomes achievable, allowing the hotel to emerge stronger and more resilient.

Alternatives to Bank Workouts

While bank workouts are a common path for distressed hotels seeking to regain financial stability, they are not the only option. In some cases, exploring alternatives such as refinancing, asset sales, liquidation, or even bankruptcy might offer a more viable solution. Each alternative comes with its own set of advantages, challenges, and implications, requiring a thorough analysis to determine the best course of action. This section provides an in-depth analysis of these alternatives, practical examples, and actionable steps to help hotel owners make informed decisions.

Exploring Refinancing and Loan Restructuring

Refinancing and loan restructuring involve replacing the existing loan with a new one, typically under more favorable terms, or modifying the existing loan's terms to make it more manageable. These options can help a distressed hotel improve cash flow, reduce monthly payments, or extend the repayment period.

1. Understanding Refinancing: Refinancing involves securing a new loan, often with a lower interest rate or longer repayment term, to pay off the existing loan. This option can significantly reduce monthly payments, freeing up cash flow for hotel operations and improvements.

2. Considering Loan Restructuring: Unlike refinancing, loan restructuring involves modifying the terms of the current loan without replacing it. Restructuring might include extending the repayment period, lowering the interest rate, or temporarily reducing payments.

Practical Example: A hotel in San Francisco, burdened with high-interest debt, successfully refinanced its loan with a new lender at a lower interest rate. The refinancing reduced the hotel's monthly payments by 30%, allowing it to stabilize cash flow and invest in renovations that improved occupancy rates and profitability.

Actionable Steps:

- Assess the current loan terms and identify areas where refinancing or restructuring could offer relief.

- Research lenders that specialize in hotel financing and explore refinancing options.

- Prepare detailed financial statements and projections to present to potential lenders.

Considering Asset Sales and Liquidation

For some distressed hotels, selling assets or liquidating certain parts of the business may be necessary to generate cash and reduce debt. This option can range from selling off non-core assets, such as equipment or land, to selling the entire property.

1. Partial Asset Sales: If the hotel owns valuable assets that are not essential to its core operations, selling them can provide much-needed cash to pay down debt or cover operating expenses. Examples include selling a vacant lot adjacent to the property, excess equipment, or underutilized event space.

2. Full Property Sale or Liquidation: In cases where financial recovery seems unlikely, selling the entire hotel might be the best option to avoid foreclosure and minimize losses. This could involve listing the property for sale with a commercial real estate broker or auctioning it to interested buyers.

Practical Example: A hotel owner in Miami sold an unused banquet hall that was incurring maintenance costs. The sale generated $500,000, which was used to pay off part of the hotel's debt, easing financial pressure and helping the hotel stay afloat.

Actionable Steps:

- Identify non-core assets that could be sold to generate cash.

- Engage a real estate advisor or appraiser to

determine the market value of the assets.

- Consider the long-term impact of asset sales on hotel operations before making a decision.

Evaluating Bankruptcy Options

Bankruptcy is often considered a last resort for distressed hotels, but it can be a viable option for protecting assets and restructuring debt under certain circumstances. There are different types of bankruptcy filings, each with unique implications.

1. Chapter 11 Bankruptcy: Chapter 11 is a reorganization bankruptcy that allows the hotel to continue operating while restructuring its debt. The hotel owner retains control of the property and works with creditors to create a plan to repay the debt over time. This option provides a chance to reorganize finances, renegotiate contracts, and emerge from bankruptcy with a more manageable debt structure.

2. Chapter 7 Bankruptcy: Chapter 7 bankruptcy involves liquidating the hotel's assets to repay creditors. This option typically results in the closure of the hotel and is often pursued when there is little hope of financial recovery.

3. Chapter 13 Bankruptcy: While more commonly used by individuals, Chapter 13 bankruptcy might apply to small hotel owners. It involves creating a repayment plan to pay off debt over three to five years, allowing the owner to keep the property and continue operations.

Practical Example: A boutique hotel in New Orleans filed for Chapter 11 bankruptcy after a series of hurricanes devastated the area. During the bankruptcy process, the hotel was able to renegotiate its contracts with suppliers, restructure its debt, and implement a turnaround plan. Eventually, the hotel emerged from bankruptcy with a healthier financial structure and a clearer path to profitability.

Actionable Steps:

- Consult with a bankruptcy attorney to understand the implications of different bankruptcy options.

- Evaluate whether bankruptcy offers a viable path to financial recovery or if it will result in the closure of the hotel.

- Prepare comprehensive financial documentation to support the bankruptcy filing process.

Working with Professional Advisors

Navigating financial distress can be overwhelming, and working with professional advisors can provide invaluable guidance throughout the process. Advisors can help assess the hotel's financial health, explore alternatives to bank workouts, and negotiate with lenders or potential buyers.

1. Engaging a Financial Advisor: A financial advisor with experience in the hospitality industry can help analyze cash flow, identify cost-saving opportunities,

and create financial projections. They can also assist in exploring refinancing options or developing a plan to present to lenders.

2. Consulting a Bankruptcy Attorney: If bankruptcy is being considered, consulting with an attorney who specializes in bankruptcy law is essential. They can explain the legal implications, guide the filing process, and represent the hotel's interests in court.

3. Working with a Real Estate Broker: If asset sales or liquidation is the chosen path, a commercial real estate broker can help market the property, identify potential buyers, and negotiate favorable terms.

Practical Example: A hotel owner in Chicago facing foreclosure worked with a financial advisor who helped them restructure their debt, improve cash flow, and negotiate a refinancing deal. The advisor's expertise enabled the owner to avoid bankruptcy and stabilize the hotel's finances.

Actionable Steps:

- Identify areas where professional expertise is needed and seek out qualified advisors.

- Be transparent with advisors about the hotel's financial situation to ensure they can provide effective guidance.

- Use the advisor's insights to make informed decisions about the best path forward.

Practical Example: How a Hotel Avoided Foreclosure Through Refinancing

The Sunset Bay Resort, a beachfront property in Florida, faced severe financial distress due to declining tourism and rising operational costs. Unable to meet its monthly loan payments, the resort was on the brink of foreclosure. The owner decided to explore refinancing as an alternative to a bank workout.

After consulting with a financial advisor, the owner approached multiple lenders specializing in hospitality financing. By presenting a detailed turnaround plan, updated financial projections, and proof of improved occupancy rates during the summer season, the resort secured a new loan with a lower interest rate and extended repayment terms. This refinancing deal reduced monthly payments by 40%, allowing the resort to regain financial stability, improve its cash flow, and avoid foreclosure.

Key Takeaway: Proactively exploring refinancing options and working with professional advisors can provide a viable alternative to foreclosure and offer the financial relief needed to turn around a distressed hotel.

Weighing the Pros and Cons of Alternatives

Choosing the right alternative to a bank workout requires carefully weighing the pros and cons of each option:

- Refinancing and Loan Restructuring:

- o Pros: Lower monthly payments, improved cash flow, and the ability to retain control of the property.

- o Cons: May require good credit and additional collateral; possible fees and costs associated with refinancing.

- **Asset Sales and Liquidation:**

  - o Pros: Generates immediate cash flow; can reduce debt burden.

  - o Cons: Loss of assets that could be valuable for future growth; may not generate sufficient funds to cover debt.

- **Bankruptcy:**

  - o Pros: Legal protection from creditors, opportunity to restructure debt, potential to continue operations (Chapter 11).

  - o Cons: Damaging to credit and reputation, high legal costs, risk of losing control of the property (Chapter 7).

Actionable Steps:

- Conduct a comprehensive analysis of each alternative's potential impact on your hotel's financial health.

- Consult with professional advisors to gain insights into the risks and benefits of each option.

- Consider the long-term implications of your choice on the hotel's future operations and growth.

Exploring alternatives to bank workouts requires careful consideration of each option's benefits, challenges, and long-term implications. Whether pursuing refinancing, asset sales, bankruptcy, or working with professional advisors, distressed hotel owners must weigh the pros and cons to determine the best path forward. By taking a proactive approach, leveraging expert guidance, and remaining open to alternative strategies, hotel owners can navigate financial distress and chart a course toward recovery and stability.

Lessons Learned from Bank Workouts

Successfully navigating a bank workout can be a transformative experience for a distressed hotel, but it also presents an opportunity to gain valuable insights into financial management and resilience. Learning from this process can help hotel owners avoid common pitfalls, develop strategies for future financial stability, and ultimately emerge stronger. In this section, we will explore the lessons learned from bank workouts, including common challenges, building resilience, adopting proactive financial management strategies, and applying insights from past experiences. We'll also review a case study of a hotel that emerged stronger from a workout and provide actionable steps to prevent future financial distress.

Common Pitfalls and Challenges

Understanding the common pitfalls that occur during bank workouts can help hotel owners avoid repeating these mistakes in the future. By recognizing these challenges, hotel owners can take proactive steps to address them and navigate the workout process more effectively.

1. Inadequate Preparation and Documentation: One of the most common pitfalls is failing to prepare comprehensive financial documentation before approaching the lender. Inadequate records, incomplete projections, or missing financial statements can undermine credibility and make it difficult to negotiate favorable workout terms.

2. Lack of Clear Communication with Lenders: Failing to maintain open and consistent communication with lenders can lead to misunderstandings, delays, and missed opportunities. Lenders need assurance that the hotel owner is committed to the workout plan and capable of executing it effectively.

3. Overly Optimistic Projections: Presenting overly optimistic cash flow projections or unrealistic financial goals can damage credibility with lenders. When projections are not met, it can lead to increased scrutiny and a lack of confidence in the owner's ability to manage the hotel.

4. Inability to Adapt to Changing Market Conditions:

Many hotel owners fail to adapt their strategies to changing market conditions, resulting in further financial distress. Flexibility and adaptability are crucial for overcoming challenges and maintaining financial stability.

Practical Example: A hotel owner in Los Angeles failed to provide accurate financial statements during the workout process, leading the lender to question the hotel's viability. As a result, the lender imposed stricter terms, making it harder for the hotel to regain financial stability.

Actionable Steps:

- Prepare thorough and accurate financial documentation before approaching lenders.

- Maintain regular communication with lenders throughout the workout process.

- Use realistic, data-driven projections to build credibility.

- Stay informed about market trends and adjust strategies accordingly.

Building Resilience for Future Financial Challenges

The experience of going through a bank workout can be a valuable lesson in building financial resilience. Hotels that emerge successfully from this process are often better equipped to handle future financial challenges and economic downturns.

1. Diversify Revenue Streams: Relying on a single source of revenue can leave a hotel vulnerable to market fluctuations. Explore opportunities to diversify revenue, such as offering additional services (e.g., spa treatments, dining experiences, event hosting), targeting different guest segments (e.g., leisure travelers, corporate clients), or developing partnerships with local businesses.

2. Maintain Healthy Cash Reserves: Having sufficient cash reserves can help weather financial storms and prevent the need for urgent bank workouts in the future. Establish a reserve fund by setting aside a portion of monthly profits, and aim to have enough savings to cover at least three to six months of operating expenses.

3. Regularly Monitor Financial Health: Conduct regular financial reviews to assess the hotel's performance, identify potential issues, and take corrective action early. Monitoring key financial metrics, such as occupancy rates, average daily rate (ADR), and RevPAR (Revenue per Available Room), helps ensure that the hotel remains on track.

Practical Example: After emerging from a workout, a hotel in Chicago implemented new revenue streams, such as offering coworking spaces during weekdays and launching a rooftop bar. These initiatives helped diversify income sources, which provided a financial cushion during seasonal fluctuations.

Actionable Steps:

- Identify and implement opportunities to

diversify revenue streams.

- Build and maintain a cash reserve to handle unexpected financial challenges.

- Regularly monitor financial metrics and review the hotel's financial health.

Developing a Proactive Financial Management Strategy

A proactive financial management strategy is essential for preventing future financial distress. This approach involves anticipating potential risks, managing costs, and making informed decisions based on data and market trends.

1. Create a Detailed Budget: Develop a comprehensive annual budget that includes projected revenue, expenses, and capital expenditures. Regularly compare actual performance against the budget and adjust spending as needed to ensure financial health.

2. Implement Cost Control Measures: Identify areas where costs can be reduced without compromising guest experience. For example, invest in energy-efficient lighting, negotiate bulk discounts with suppliers, or adjust staffing levels based on occupancy rates.

3. Develop Contingency Plans: Prepare for unexpected events by developing contingency plans for various scenarios, such as economic downturns, natural disasters, or sudden drops in occupancy. Having contingency plans in place allows the hotel to respond

quickly and minimize financial impact.

Practical Example: A resort in Florida created a comprehensive financial management strategy that included quarterly financial reviews, regular cost analysis, and contingency plans for hurricane season. This proactive approach helped the resort remain profitable, even during challenging times.

Actionable Steps:

- Create a detailed annual budget and monitor performance against it.

- Implement cost control measures to improve profitability.

- Develop contingency plans for potential risks and disruptions.

Learning from Past Experiences

Experiencing a bank workout provides valuable insights into financial management and decision-making. Applying lessons learned from the process can help hotel owners avoid repeating mistakes and make more informed choices in the future.

1. Analyze the Root Causes of Financial Distress: Conduct a thorough analysis of the factors that led to financial distress, such as poor financial management, overleveraging, or inadequate marketing strategies. Understanding the root causes helps develop strategies to prevent similar issues in the future.

2. Apply Lessons Learned: Use insights gained from the workout process to improve financial management, operational efficiency, and decision-making. For example, if ineffective cost management contributed to financial distress, implement more rigorous expense tracking and budgeting practices.

3. Share Insights with Team Members: Educate your team about the lessons learned from the workout experience. Encourage staff to identify areas for improvement, offer suggestions, and contribute to the hotel's ongoing financial health.

Practical Example: After emerging from a workout, a hotel owner realized that insufficient marketing efforts had contributed to low occupancy rates. By investing in targeted marketing campaigns and improving online visibility, the hotel successfully attracted more guests and increased revenue.

Actionable Steps:

- Analyze the factors that led to financial distress and address them.

- Apply lessons learned to improve financial management and decision-making.

- Educate team members about the importance of financial health and encourage their involvement.

Case Study: How a Hotel Emerged Stronger from a Workout

The Palm Grove Resort, a 200-room beachfront property, faced severe financial distress due to a combination of rising operational costs and declining occupancy rates. After entering a workout agreement with its lender, the resort implemented a comprehensive turnaround plan that focused on cost control, marketing, and diversifying revenue streams.

Steps Taken:

- Cost Reduction: The resort reduced operating expenses by implementing energy-saving measures, renegotiating supplier contracts, and optimizing staff schedules based on occupancy levels.

- Targeted Marketing Campaigns: The management team launched targeted marketing campaigns to attract local guests, offering discounted weekend packages and staycation deals.

- Diversifying Revenue Streams: The resort introduced new revenue streams, such as hosting weddings and corporate events, renting out conference rooms, and offering spa services to both guests and locals.

Within two years, the Palm Grove Resort had increased its occupancy rate by 30%, improved cash flow, and fully met the terms of the workout agreement. As a result, the lender extended more favorable financing terms, and the resort emerged stronger and more resilient.

Key Takeaway: By implementing cost control measures, targeted marketing campaigns, and diversified revenue streams, the Palm Grove Resort transformed its financial health and emerged from the workout stronger than before.

Practical Steps for Preventing Future Financial Distress

- Maintain Strong Relationships with Lenders: Establishing and maintaining positive relationships with lenders can provide flexibility and support during challenging times. Keep lenders informed about the hotel's financial health and performance.

- Regularly Monitor Key Financial Metrics: Track essential financial metrics, such as RevPAR, ADR, and occupancy rates, to identify potential issues early and take corrective action.

- Invest in Staff Training: Equip staff with the skills needed to provide excellent guest service, manage costs, and contribute to the hotel's financial success. Well-trained employees can enhance operational efficiency and guest satisfaction, leading to improved profitability.

- Stay Informed About Market Trends: Continuously monitor industry trends, market conditions, and competitor activities to stay ahead of changes and adapt strategies accordingly.

Actionable Steps:

- Maintain open communication with lenders and stakeholders.

- Monitor financial metrics regularly and take corrective action as needed.

- Invest in ongoing staff training and development.

- Stay informed about market trends and adjust strategies proactively.

The lessons learned from navigating a bank workout provide invaluable insights that can help hotel owners avoid future financial distress and build resilience. By understanding common pitfalls, developing proactive financial management strategies, learning from past experiences, and applying these lessons, hotels can emerge stronger and more prepared for future challenges. With a commitment to financial discipline, adaptability, and ongoing improvement, hotels can not only survive periods of financial difficulty but thrive in the long term.

Chapter 6: Financing Options for Distressed Hotels

Financing a distressed hotel can be a complex challenge, but it's a crucial component of any successful turnaround strategy. Chapter 6 explores the various financing options available to hotel owners and investors, offering a comprehensive guide on how to secure the necessary capital to support renovation, operational improvements, and recovery efforts. Understanding the wide range of financing solutions—ranging from traditional bank loans to innovative crowdfunding platforms—is essential for navigating financial distress and positioning a hotel for long-term success.

The chapter begins by examining traditional bank loans and financing, which, despite being a conventional choice, can still be a viable option for distressed hotels if approached strategically. We'll discuss the requirements that banks typically impose, how loan-to-value (LTV) ratios and interest rates impact financing, and how to negotiate favorable terms with lenders. Through a real-life case study, we'll see how one distressed hotel successfully secured a traditional loan for renovations, offering practical insights into improving the chances of loan approval.

Next, we delve into government programs and SBA loans, which can offer attractive financing alternatives for distressed hotels. These loans, often backed by agencies like the Small Business Administration, provide access to capital with more flexible terms than traditional loans. We'll explore how these government-backed programs can be used to support hotel turnarounds, and a case study will highlight how an SBA loan facilitated a successful recovery for a distressed property.

Private equity and investor funding represent another potential avenue for distressed hotel financing, especially for properties that offer significant upside potential. This section covers how to attract private equity investors, structure partnerships, and negotiate equity stakes. A case study will demonstrate how a hotel leveraged private equity investment to achieve a successful turnaround, offering tips on creating a compelling pitch and understanding investor expectations.

The chapter also covers mezzanine financing and bridge loans, which are specialized financing options that can provide the short-term capital needed during a turnaround. We will discuss how these types of financing work, the associated risks and rewards, and offer practical advice on securing such funding. A case study will illustrate how a bridge loan enabled a hotel to complete critical renovations, highlighting the role these financing options can play in supporting a turnaround.

Crowdfunding and alternative financing have emerged as increasingly popular options for distressed hotels, offering access to a broader pool of investors. This section explores how crowdfunding platforms can be leveraged to raise capital, the different types of crowdfunding available, and how to create a successful campaign. Through a case study, we'll examine a hotel that effectively used crowdfunding to finance its recovery, providing insights into the benefits and drawbacks of this innovative approach.

The chapter concludes by guiding readers on choosing the right financing option for their distressed hotel, weighing the pros and cons of each method, and matching them with the hotel's specific turnaround needs. We'll present a real-life example of a hotel that successfully combined multiple financing options and discuss how to build a financial plan that supports long-term success. This comprehensive overview equips readers with the knowledge to make informed financing decisions, avoid common pitfalls, and present a solid financial plan to potential lenders and investors.

Traditional Bank Loans and Financing

For distressed hotels seeking financial support, traditional bank loans can be a viable option if approached correctly. Despite the challenges that come with securing bank loans, they offer several advantages, including lower interest rates and structured repayment terms. This section provides an in-depth analysis of how distressed hotels can navigate the process of obtaining traditional financing, including understanding loan requirements, evaluating key financial metrics like loan-to-value (LTV) ratios, working with lenders to secure favorable terms, and practical tips for improving loan approval chances. We'll also explore the pros and cons of this financing method through a real-world case study.

Understanding Bank Loan Requirements for Distressed Hotels

Banks are generally cautious when lending to distressed hotels, as they represent a higher risk compared to stable properties. Understanding the requirements and expectations of lenders is essential for hotel owners seeking traditional financing.

1. Financial Documentation: Lenders will require detailed financial statements, including income statements, balance sheets, cash flow statements, and tax returns for the past three to five years. These documents provide a clear picture of the hotel's financial health and ability to repay the loan.

2. Business Plan and Turnaround Strategy: A comprehensive business plan is crucial for distressed hotels seeking bank financing. The plan should outline the turnaround strategy, detailing how the loan will be used to improve operations, increase revenue, and achieve financial stability. This demonstrates to the lender that the hotel owner has a clear plan for returning to profitability.

3. Collateral: Most banks will require collateral to secure the loan, which could be the hotel property itself or other assets. Collateral provides the lender with security in case the borrower defaults on the loan.

4. Debt Service Coverage Ratio (DSCR): The DSCR measures the hotel's ability to cover its debt obligations with its operating income. A DSCR of 1.25 or higher is typically preferred by lenders, as it

indicates that the hotel generates enough income to meet its debt payments.

5. Creditworthiness: The borrower's credit history and credit score play a significant role in determining eligibility for a bank loan. Lenders prefer borrowers with a strong credit history, as it suggests a lower risk of default.

Practical Example: A hotel in Atlanta applied for a bank loan to finance renovations. The hotel owner provided financial statements, a detailed business plan, and a turnaround strategy that demonstrated how the renovations would increase occupancy and revenue. By showing a clear path to profitability, the hotel secured the loan despite its distressed status.

Actionable Steps:

- Prepare comprehensive financial statements and tax returns.

- Develop a detailed business plan that outlines the turnaround strategy.

- Offer collateral to secure the loan and demonstrate commitment.

Evaluating Loan-to-Value (LTV) Ratios and Interest Rates

The loan-to-value (LTV) ratio and interest rate are two critical factors that impact a hotel's ability to secure financing and the overall cost of borrowing.

1. Understanding LTV Ratios: The LTV ratio is the ratio of the loan amount to the appraised value of the property. Lenders use this metric to assess risk, with lower LTV ratios representing lower risk. For distressed hotels, banks typically prefer an LTV ratio of 65% to 75%. This means that if a hotel is valued at $10 million, the bank might be willing to lend up to $6.5 to $7.5 million.

2. Interest Rates: Interest rates for distressed hotels tend to be higher than for stable properties due to the increased risk. Factors that influence interest rates include the borrower's credit score, the hotel's financial health, market conditions, and the overall risk associated with the loan.

3. Fixed vs. Variable Rates: Loans may have fixed or variable interest rates. Fixed rates provide predictable payments, while variable rates can change over time, affecting monthly payments. Distressed hotels should carefully consider which option aligns with their cash flow and long-term financial plans.

Practical Example: A hotel owner in Miami secured a loan with a 70% LTV ratio and a 6% fixed interest rate for five years. By presenting a solid business plan and demonstrating the potential for increased revenue, the owner was able to negotiate a favorable interest rate despite the hotel's distressed condition.

Actionable Steps:

- Determine the hotel's current market value and calculate the LTV ratio.

- Be prepared to negotiate interest rates based on your credit history, DSCR, and turnaround plan.

- Consider both fixed and variable interest rate options based on your financial projections.

Working with Lenders to Secure Favorable Terms

Building a positive relationship with lenders is crucial for securing favorable loan terms. Lenders need assurance that they are making a wise investment, and hotel owners must present themselves as trustworthy, competent borrowers.

1. Present a Detailed Turnaround Plan: Clearly articulate how the loan will be used to improve the hotel's operations and profitability. Provide projections that show how the improvements will increase revenue and cash flow.

2. Negotiate Terms: Be open to negotiating loan terms, such as interest rates, repayment schedules, and covenants. Demonstrating flexibility and a willingness to work with the lender can lead to more favorable terms.

3. Maintain Open Communication: Regularly communicate with the lender, providing updates on the hotel's performance and any progress made on the turnaround plan. This builds trust and shows the lender that you are proactive and committed to the hotel's success.

Practical Example: A hotel owner in Boston successfully negotiated a five-year loan with an interest-only period for the first year, allowing the hotel to stabilize cash flow before making full principal and interest payments. The owner achieved this by demonstrating the expected increase in revenue from planned renovations and marketing efforts.

Actionable Steps:

- Prepare a thorough and convincing turnaround plan.

- Be open to negotiating loan terms and repayment schedules.

- Maintain regular communication with the lender throughout the loan process.

Case Study: How a Distressed Hotel Secured a Traditional Loan for Renovations

The Riverside Hotel, a 150-room property located in a suburban area, experienced financial distress due to declining occupancy rates and outdated facilities. The hotel's management team decided that a renovation was necessary to attract more guests and improve profitability. However, the hotel did not have sufficient funds to finance the renovation internally.

The owner approached a traditional bank and presented a comprehensive business plan that outlined the renovation strategy, targeted marketing campaigns, and projected increases in occupancy and revenue. The plan showed that, with the renovations, the hotel could achieve a 30% increase in RevPAR (Revenue per Available Room) over the next two years. The owner also provided financial statements, a favorable DSCR, and offered the hotel property as collateral.

Impressed with the detailed plan and projected financial improvements, the bank approved a $2 million loan with a 6.5% interest rate, a five-year term, and a 70% LTV ratio. The renovations were completed on time, and within 18 months, the Riverside Hotel saw a significant increase in occupancy rates, allowing it to meet its loan obligations and improve overall profitability.

Key Takeaway: By presenting a well-prepared business plan, realistic financial projections, and securing collateral, the Riverside Hotel was able to obtain traditional financing, complete renovations, and achieve a successful turnaround.

Tips for Improving Your Chances of Loan Approval

- Prepare Comprehensive Documentation: Ensure all financial statements, tax returns, and legal documents are accurate, complete, and up-to-date.

- Develop a Strong Business Plan: A detailed plan that outlines your turnaround strategy, revenue projections, and marketing efforts increases lender confidence.

- Improve Your Credit Score: If possible, take steps to improve your credit score before applying for a loan, as this can lead to better interest rates and loan terms.

- Offer Collateral: Offering collateral, such as the hotel property or other assets, can make lenders more willing to approve the loan.

- Engage with Experienced Financial Advisors: Working with financial advisors or consultants experienced in the hospitality industry can help present your case more effectively.

The Pros and Cons of Traditional Financing for Distressed Assets

Pros:

- Lower Interest Rates: Traditional bank loans typically offer lower interest rates compared to alternative financing options.

- Structured Repayment Terms: Banks provide clear repayment schedules, making it easier to manage cash flow.

- Access to Larger Loan Amounts: Traditional financing can provide substantial capital for renovations or operational improvements.

Cons:

- Stricter Qualification Requirements: Lenders have stringent requirements, making it more challenging for distressed hotels to qualify.

- Collateral Requirements: Banks often require collateral, which puts the hotel property at risk if the loan is not repaid.

- Lengthy Approval Process: The approval process for traditional loans can be time-consuming, which may not be ideal for hotels needing immediate capital.

Traditional bank loans and financing can be a viable option for distressed hotels if approached strategically. By understanding the requirements, preparing comprehensive documentation, evaluating LTV ratios and interest rates, and working closely with lenders, hotel owners can secure the financing needed to support turnaround efforts. Despite the challenges and stringent qualifications, traditional financing offers structured repayment terms and potentially lower interest rates, making it an option worth considering for distressed hotel assets seeking a path to recovery.

Government Programs and SBA Loans

Government-backed loan programs, such as those offered by the Small Business Administration (SBA), provide valuable financing options for distressed hotels seeking to recover and revitalize their operations. These programs offer more flexible terms and lower interest rates than traditional bank loans, making them attractive for hotel owners facing financial challenges. This section provides an in-depth analysis of government-backed loan programs, including eligibility requirements, how these loans can support renovations and improvements, and a step-by-step guide on the application process, illustrated by a case study of a hotel turnaround funded by an SBA loan.

Overview of Government-Backed Loan Programs (e.g., SBA 504, 7(a) Loans)

The SBA offers two primary loan programs that can be particularly beneficial for distressed hotels: the SBA 7(a) loan and the SBA 504 loan.

1. SBA 7(a) Loan Program: The SBA 7(a) loan is the most popular and flexible loan program, providing financing for a variety of business purposes, including working capital, refinancing existing debt, purchasing equipment, or renovating property. Loan amounts can go up to $5 million, and repayment terms can extend up to 25 years for real estate. Interest rates are typically variable and capped, often making them more affordable than traditional bank loans.

2. SBA 504 Loan Program: The SBA 504 loan is designed for long-term, fixed-rate financing and is ideal for purchasing real estate, equipment, or renovating facilities. This loan is structured as a partnership between a Certified Development Company (CDC), a private lender, and the SBA. The typical loan structure involves the bank lending 50% of the project cost, the CDC covering up to 40%, and the borrower contributing 10%. The maximum loan amount can be up to $5.5 million, and repayment terms range from 10 to 25 years.

Key Differences Between SBA 7(a) and 504 Loans:

- SBA 7(a): More flexible, can be used for various purposes, including working capital.

- SBA 504: Focuses on fixed assets like real estate and equipment, with a fixed interest rate.

Practical Example: A hotel owner seeking funds to renovate an aging property could opt for the SBA 504 loan to cover the renovation costs, while a hotel needing both renovations and working capital might choose the SBA 7(a) loan.

Eligibility Requirements for Distressed Hotel Financing

While SBA loans offer more flexible terms than traditional bank loans, distressed hotels must still meet specific eligibility requirements to qualify for these programs:

1. Demonstrating a Need for Funding: The hotel must demonstrate a legitimate need for financing, such as funding renovations, covering operating expenses, or refinancing existing debt.

2. Business Size: The SBA has specific size standards that businesses must meet to qualify. For hotels, eligibility is generally based on the number of employees (typically no more than 500) or average annual revenue.

3. Owner Investment: Owners must demonstrate a willingness to invest in their own business, usually by contributing at least 10% of the total project cost for the SBA 504 loan.

4. Acceptable Credit Score: Although the SBA offers more flexibility than traditional lenders, a reasonable credit score (usually 650 or above) is still required.

5. Ability to Repay the Loan: The hotel must provide financial projections showing its ability to generate sufficient cash flow to meet loan repayments.

Practical Example: A 75-room hotel with annual revenues of $2 million and a credit score of 680 would meet the SBA's eligibility requirements and could apply for an SBA 7(a) loan to finance operational improvements.

Actionable Steps:

- Assess your hotel's eligibility based on the SBA's size standards and credit score requirements.

- Ensure you have a clear need for funding that aligns with the loan's intended use.

- Prepare financial statements demonstrating your ability to repay the loan.

How Government Loans Can Support Renovations and Improvements

Government-backed loans, especially SBA loans, offer

flexible financing that can be used for various purposes, making them ideal for distressed hotels needing capital to fund renovations and improvements.

1. Financing Renovation Projects: The SBA 504 loan can cover up to 90% of renovation costs, making it easier for hotels to invest in upgrades without a significant upfront investment. Renovations can range from room refurbishments and lobby upgrades to infrastructure improvements, such as energy-efficient systems.

2. Purchasing Equipment and Fixtures: Hotels often need to replace outdated equipment or furniture to improve guest experiences. SBA loans can finance the purchase of new kitchen appliances, HVAC systems, furniture, and other fixtures, enhancing the property's appeal.

3. Refinancing Existing Debt: The SBA 7(a) loan allows distressed hotels to refinance existing high-interest debt, which can free up cash flow and make it easier to manage monthly obligations. This option can be particularly beneficial for hotels struggling with debt payments.

Practical Example: A distressed hotel in Dallas used an SBA 504 loan to finance a $1.2 million renovation project, which included upgrading guest rooms, installing energy-efficient lighting, and modernizing the hotel's fitness center. These improvements resulted in increased occupancy rates and higher average daily rates (ADR), ultimately boosting the hotel's profitability.

Case Study: A Hotel Turnaround Funded by an SBA Loan

The Pinewood Inn, a 60-room hotel in a small tourist town, faced declining occupancy rates due to outdated facilities and increased competition from newer properties. The owner sought an SBA 7(a) loan to finance a $750,000 renovation project, which included room refurbishments, lobby upgrades, and exterior improvements.

After securing the SBA loan, the owner implemented the renovation plan, focusing on creating a modern and welcoming atmosphere. Within 12 months of completing the renovations, the Pinewood Inn experienced a 40% increase in occupancy rates, a 20% increase in ADR, and a significant boost in revenue. The hotel's improved financial performance allowed the owner to repay the SBA loan ahead of schedule, transforming the once-distressed property into a profitable and competitive business.

Key Takeaway: By leveraging an SBA 7(a) loan, the Pinewood Inn was able to fund critical renovations, improve its market position, and achieve financial stability.

Steps to Apply for Government-Backed Financing

Applying for an SBA loan involves several steps, and being prepared can streamline the process:

- Determine Loan Type: Identify whether the SBA 7(a) or 504 loan is best suited for your hotel's needs.

- Gather Documentation: Prepare financial statements, tax returns, a detailed business plan, and financial projections.

- Find an SBA-Approved Lender: Work with a lender experienced in hospitality financing and familiar with SBA programs.

- Complete the Loan Application: Fill out the SBA loan application (SBA Form 1919 for the 7(a) loan) and submit it along with the required documentation.

- Work with the Lender and the SBA: The lender will review your application, and if approved, they will submit it to the SBA for final approval.

Actionable Steps:

- Determine which SBA loan is appropriate for your needs.

- Gather all required financial documents and a detailed business plan.

- Find an SBA-approved lender with experience in hotel financing.

Understanding the Application Process and Timeline

The SBA loan application process can be time-consuming, but understanding the timeline helps manage expectations:

- Initial Application (1-2 weeks): Gather documents, find a lender, and submit your application.

- Lender Review (2-4 weeks): The lender reviews the application, assesses risk, and may request additional information.

- SBA Approval (1-3 weeks): The lender submits the application to the SBA for review and approval.

- Loan Closing and Disbursement (2-4 weeks): Once approved, the lender finalizes the loan agreement, and funds are disbursed.

The entire process typically takes 60 to 90 days, so it's important to plan ahead and ensure that your financials and documentation are in order.

Practical Example: A hotel owner who proactively prepared financial statements and identified a suitable lender completed the SBA loan process in just 60 days, allowing them to begin renovations before the peak tourist season.

Actionable Steps:

- Start the application process early to account for potential delays.

- Work closely with the lender to ensure timely responses to requests for additional

information.
- Stay organized and maintain open communication throughout the process.

Government-backed loan programs, particularly SBA loans, provide a valuable financing option for distressed hotels seeking to fund renovations, improvements, or refinance existing debt. By understanding the eligibility requirements, benefits, and application process, hotel owners can leverage these programs to support turnaround efforts and restore financial stability. With careful preparation and strategic use of SBA loans, distressed hotels can achieve the capital needed to implement effective recovery plans and emerge as profitable and competitive businesses.

Private Equity and Investor Funding

Private equity (PE) and investor funding can be powerful solutions for distressed hotels seeking capital for turnaround efforts, renovation projects, or operational improvements. By partnering with private equity investors or forming joint ventures, hotels can access the financial resources, expertise, and strategic guidance needed to recover and thrive. This section provides an in-depth analysis of how to attract private equity investors, structure partnerships, negotiate equity stakes and profit-sharing agreements, and understand investor expectations and exit strategies. We will also explore a real-life case study demonstrating how private equity investment can successfully transform a distressed hotel.

How to Attract Private Equity Investors for Distressed Hotels

Private equity investors are attracted to opportunities with the potential for high returns, and distressed hotels can offer such potential if the turnaround strategy is sound. To attract private equity investors, hotel owners need to present a compelling investment case that demonstrates the property's value, potential for recovery, and profitability.

1. Demonstrate Value and Upside Potential: Investors need to see the potential for significant returns. Highlight aspects of the hotel that present opportunities for growth, such as a prime location, potential for renovations, or untapped market segments. Providing detailed financial projections that show how the investment will result in increased revenue, occupancy rates, and profitability is crucial.

2. Showcase a Strong Turnaround Plan: Investors want assurance that the hotel has a realistic and well-thought-out plan for recovery. Present a detailed turnaround strategy, outlining how the capital will be used, what improvements will be made, and how these changes will drive revenue growth.

3. Highlight Management Expertise: Private equity investors often place great importance on the capabilities of the hotel management team. Demonstrating the experience, expertise, and track record of the management team can increase investor confidence in the property's ability to recover and achieve long-term success.

4. Emphasize Market Trends: Provide data and insights about the hospitality industry, market trends, and the specific niche in which the hotel operates. Demonstrating how the property aligns with emerging trends, such as increased demand for boutique hotels or wellness-focused properties, can make the investment opportunity more attractive.

Practical Example: A distressed beachfront resort in California, facing declining occupancy rates, attracted private equity interest by showcasing its prime location, potential for renovation into a luxury wellness retreat, and the growing demand for wellness tourism. This clear market opportunity, combined with a solid turnaround plan, convinced investors to provide the necessary capital for transformation.

Actionable Steps:

- Highlight the hotel's unique value proposition and potential for growth.

- Develop a comprehensive turnaround plan that demonstrates how investor funding will drive profitability.

- Showcase the expertise and experience of the management team.

Structuring Partnerships and Joint Ventures

When private equity investors fund distressed hotels, they often prefer to structure the investment as a partnership or joint venture. This arrangement allows both parties to share risks, rewards, and responsibilities.

1. Define Roles and Responsibilities: Clearly outline the roles and responsibilities of each party involved in the partnership or joint venture. Define who will manage daily operations, handle financial decisions, and oversee the execution of the turnaround plan. Establishing these parameters upfront helps prevent misunderstandings and ensures smooth collaboration.

2. Determine Ownership Structure: The ownership structure should reflect the level of investment and involvement of each party. For example, the private equity firm might take a 60% equity stake if they are providing the majority of the capital, while the hotel owner retains 40%. Joint ventures can also be structured as 50/50 partnerships, depending on the contributions of both parties.

3. Establish Decision-Making Authority: Determine how decisions will be made within the partnership or joint venture. Will decisions require unanimous consent, or will one party have final authority? Clarifying decision-making authority is essential to avoid conflicts.

Practical Example: A boutique hotel in New York City partnered with a private equity firm to fund a $3 million renovation project. The PE firm provided 70% of the capital, while the hotel owner contributed 30%. The agreement specified that the hotel owner would handle day-to-day operations, while the PE firm would have oversight on major financial decisions, ensuring both parties had a vested interest in the hotel's success.

Actionable Steps:

- Define roles, responsibilities, and ownership structures clearly.

- Establish decision-making processes to prevent conflicts.

- Ensure that both parties have a vested interest in the success of the hotel.

Negotiating Equity Stakes and Profit-Sharing Agreements

Negotiating equity stakes and profit-sharing agreements is a crucial aspect of securing private equity investment. Both parties need to agree on how profits will be distributed and how ownership will be structured.

1. Valuation and Equity Stakes: The hotel's current valuation will play a significant role in determining the equity stake for both the investor and the owner. Consider factors such as the hotel's assets, revenue potential, and market position when negotiating equity terms. An investor providing significant capital may expect a larger equity stake, but this should be balanced against the value the owner brings in terms of management expertise and experience.

2. Profit-Sharing Agreements: Profit-sharing agreements outline how profits will be distributed between the investor and the hotel owner. These agreements can be structured in various ways, such as

a percentage split based on equity ownership or performance-based tiers (e.g., higher profits result in a larger share for the investor).

3. Protecting Ownership Interests: Hotel owners should include clauses that protect their ownership interests, such as buy-back options, anti-dilution provisions, or exit strategies. These clauses can help ensure that owners maintain a degree of control over the property and protect their investment.

Practical Example: A hotel owner in Las Vegas negotiated a profit-sharing agreement with a private equity firm, where the PE firm received 60% of profits until they recouped their initial investment, after which profits were split 50/50. This arrangement incentivized both parties to work towards the hotel's success while ensuring a fair distribution of returns.

Actionable Steps:

- Conduct a thorough valuation of the hotel to inform equity stake negotiations.

- Structure profit-sharing agreements to align with both parties' goals.

- Include protective clauses to safeguard ownership interests.

Case Study: A Successful Private Equity Investment in a Distressed Hotel

The Grand Bay Resort, a 200-room luxury property located in a prime tourist destination, faced financial distress due to increased competition and outdated facilities. The hotel owner sought private equity funding to finance a $5 million renovation project and implement a turnaround strategy.

After presenting a comprehensive business plan that showcased the potential for increased revenue and profitability, the hotel attracted interest from a private equity firm. The two parties formed a joint venture, with the PE firm taking a 65% equity stake and the hotel owner retaining 35%. The PE firm contributed capital for renovations, while the owner leveraged their industry expertise to implement operational improvements.

The renovation and repositioning of the resort as a luxury destination resulted in a 40% increase in occupancy rates and a 25% increase in average daily rates (ADR) within two years. The improved financial performance allowed the PE firm to recoup their investment and realize a 20% return, while the hotel owner regained financial stability and increased the property's value.

Key Takeaway: By partnering with a private equity firm, the Grand Bay Resort accessed the capital needed for renovations, leveraged industry expertise, and achieved a successful turnaround.
Creating a Compelling Pitch for Investors

A compelling pitch is essential for attracting private equity investors. Your pitch should clearly articulate the investment opportunity, potential returns, and how the capital will be used to achieve the desired outcomes.

1. Present a Clear Investment Thesis: Articulate why the investment is an attractive opportunity, highlighting the hotel's value proposition, market potential, and upside potential. Include data on market trends, competitor analysis, and target demographics.

2. Showcase a Strong Turnaround Plan: Present a detailed turnaround strategy that outlines how the funds will be used, projected timelines, and key performance indicators (KPIs) that will measure success. Provide financial projections that demonstrate the potential return on investment (ROI).

3. Highlight the Management Team: Investors want to know that the hotel is in capable hands. Highlight the experience, expertise, and track record of the management team, demonstrating their ability to execute the turnaround plan effectively.

Practical Example: A hotel owner created a compelling pitch by developing a visually engaging presentation that included financial projections, a detailed renovation plan, market analysis, and success stories of similar turnarounds. This well-prepared pitch secured a $2 million investment from a private equity firm.

Actionable Steps:

- Develop a clear and compelling investment thesis.

- Prepare detailed financial projections and a turnaround plan.

- Highlight the strengths and experience of your management team.

Understanding Investor Expectations and Exit Strategies

Private equity investors typically have clear expectations and exit strategies, as they aim to realize returns on their investments within a specific timeframe.

1. Understand the Expected Return on Investment (ROI): Private equity investors generally expect an annual ROI of 15% to 25%. Be transparent about how you plan to achieve this return and how long it will take.

2. Define Exit Strategies: Common exit strategies include selling the hotel, refinancing, or a buyout by the original owner. Ensure that the investor's exit strategy aligns with your long-term goals for the property.

3. Set Realistic Timelines: Discuss realistic timelines for achieving profitability and potential exit strategies. Understanding these timelines helps align expectations and ensures a smoother partnership.

Practical Example: A PE firm invested in a distressed hotel with the expectation of exiting within five years through a sale. The hotel owner and PE firm worked together to improve the property's value, ultimately achieving a successful sale that generated a 30% ROI for the investor.

Actionable Steps:

- Understand the investor's ROI expectations and ensure they align with your projections.

- Discuss potential exit strategies and timelines.

- Maintain transparency about the hotel's progress and financial performance.

Private equity and investor funding offer distressed hotels an opportunity to access the capital, expertise, and strategic guidance needed for a successful turnaround. By attracting the right investors, structuring partnerships effectively, negotiating equity stakes, and understanding investor expectations, hotel owners can leverage private equity to transform their properties and achieve long-term success. With a compelling pitch, transparent communication, and a strong management team, distressed hotels can secure the investment needed to realize their full potential and thrive in a competitive market.

Mezzanine Financing and Bridge Loans

For distressed hotels in need of immediate capital, mezzanine financing and bridge loans can be effective solutions. These financing options provide flexibility and quick access to funds, helping hotels navigate turnaround efforts, renovations, or operational improvements. However, they come with their own set of risks and rewards that hotel owners need to understand before committing. This section delves into how mezzanine financing and bridge loans work, their potential benefits and challenges, and practical examples of how these options can facilitate a successful turnaround.

What is Mezzanine Financing, and How Does It Work?

Mezzanine financing is a hybrid form of financing that combines elements of debt and equity. It is often used by businesses, including hotels, to bridge the gap between traditional senior debt and equity financing. Typically, mezzanine financing is unsecured or subordinated, meaning it ranks below senior debt in terms of priority but above equity in the event of bankruptcy or liquidation.

How Mezzanine Financing Works:

- Debt with Equity Features: Mezzanine financing usually involves a loan that comes with an option for the lender to convert the debt into an equity stake in the business if the borrower defaults. This makes it less risky for lenders than equity investment but riskier than traditional bank loans.

- Flexible Repayment Terms: Interest rates on mezzanine loans are typically higher (ranging from 10% to 20%) than those on senior debt due to the increased risk. However, lenders may offer flexible repayment terms, such as interest-only payments or deferred interest, which can be beneficial for distressed hotels with cash flow constraints.

- Non-Dilutive Financing: While mezzanine financing may include equity-like features, it doesn't dilute ownership as much as issuing new shares. This allows hotel owners to retain more control over their property.

Practical Example: A hotel owner needed $3 million to complete a renovation project but had already exhausted their traditional bank loan options. By securing mezzanine financing, the owner was able to access the additional funds needed to finish the renovations without relinquishing significant equity or ownership control.

Actionable Steps:

- Assess whether mezzanine financing fits your hotel's capital needs, especially if you have exhausted traditional lending options.

- Prepare a detailed business plan, financial projections, and turnaround strategy to present to potential mezzanine lenders.

- Understand the terms and potential equity conversion clauses included in the mezzanine loan agreement.

How Bridge Loans Can Provide Short-Term Capital During a Turnaround

Bridge loans are short-term, high-interest loans designed to "bridge" the gap between a hotel's immediate capital needs and longer-term financing solutions. They are typically used to address short-term liquidity issues, finance renovations, or cover operational expenses until more permanent financing is secured.

Characteristics of Bridge Loans:

- Short-Term Duration: Bridge loans are designed to be repaid within 6 to 24 months, making them suitable for urgent capital needs during a turnaround process.

- Quick Access to Funds: One of the primary advantages of bridge loans is their rapid approval and funding process, which can be completed in weeks rather than months, making them ideal for hotels facing time-sensitive financial challenges.

- Higher Interest Rates: Due to their short-term nature and increased risk, bridge loans carry higher interest rates, often ranging from 8% to 15%. Some loans may include additional fees, such as origination fees or exit fees, which should be factored into the overall cost.

Practical Example: A hotel owner in Miami needed $1.5 million to complete a renovation project before the peak tourist season. By securing a bridge loan, the owner was able to access the funds quickly, complete the renovations on time, and significantly increase occupancy rates, allowing them to refinance the bridge loan with long-term financing at a lower interest rate.

Actionable Steps:

- Identify a reputable lender with experience in hospitality bridge financing.

- Prepare financial statements, cash flow projections, and a clear repayment plan to present to potential bridge loan lenders.

- Have a clear exit strategy for repaying or refinancing the bridge loan before it matures.

The Risks and Rewards of Mezzanine and Bridge Financing

While mezzanine financing and bridge loans offer advantages, they also come with inherent risks that hotel owners must carefully evaluate.

Rewards:

- Quick Access to Capital: Both mezzanine financing and bridge loans provide rapid access to funds, enabling hotels to address immediate financial needs, complete renovations, or support turnaround strategies.

- Flexibility: These financing options offer more flexible terms than traditional bank loans, which can be particularly valuable for distressed hotels with cash flow challenges.

- Non-Dilutive Ownership: Mezzanine financing allows owners to access capital without significantly diluting their ownership stake, while bridge loans provide short-term funding without impacting equity.

Risks:

- Higher Interest Rates: The cost of mezzanine and bridge financing is significantly higher than traditional loans, increasing the financial burden on the hotel. Failure to manage these higher costs can exacerbate financial distress.

- Repayment Pressure: Both financing options require strict adherence to repayment terms. Missing payments can lead to penalties, foreclosure, or equity conversion (in the case of mezzanine financing).

- Potential for Equity Loss: If a mezzanine loan is not repaid, the lender may convert the debt into equity, potentially resulting in loss of ownership or control for the hotel owner.

Actionable Steps:

- Carefully assess the total cost of mezzanine and bridge financing, including interest rates, fees, and potential equity loss.

- Ensure you have a solid repayment or refinancing strategy before committing to these financing options.

- Consult with financial advisors or attorneys to fully understand the risks and implications of these financing arrangements.

Case Study: How a Bridge Loan Helped a Hotel Complete Renovations

The Sunset Beach Resort, a 120-room hotel in a popular tourist destination, faced financial difficulties due to outdated facilities and declining occupancy rates. The hotel owner identified an opportunity to revitalize the property through renovations but lacked the necessary capital. After exploring financing options, the owner secured a $2 million bridge loan with a 12-month term to cover the renovation costs.

The bridge loan allowed the owner to complete the renovations just before the peak tourist season, resulting in a 50% increase in occupancy rates and a significant boost in average daily rates (ADR). With improved cash flow and revenue, the hotel owner refinanced the bridge loan with a longer-term, lower-interest loan, ensuring financial stability and profitability.

Key Takeaway: The strategic use of a bridge loan enabled the Sunset Beach Resort to complete essential renovations, increase revenue, and secure more favorable long-term financing, ultimately transforming the distressed property into a profitable asset.

Tips for Securing Mezzanine Financing

- Present a Strong Business Plan: Lenders will assess your hotel's turnaround potential and ability to generate sufficient cash flow. Prepare a detailed business plan that outlines your renovation or growth strategy, market analysis, and financial projections.

- Demonstrate Management Expertise: Mezzanine lenders want assurance that the management team has the experience and capability to execute the turnaround strategy successfully. Highlight your team's track record and industry expertise.

- Show Existing Equity Investment: Mezzanine lenders prefer borrowers with a significant equity investment in their property, as it demonstrates commitment and reduces their risk. Ensure you can demonstrate your financial stake in the hotel.

- Establish a Clear Exit Strategy: Lenders need to know how you plan to repay the mezzanine loan. Present a clear exit strategy, such as refinancing, selling the property, or generating increased cash flow through operational improvements.

Actionable Steps:

- Develop a comprehensive business plan with financial projections.

- Highlight the experience and expertise of your management team.

- Demonstrate your existing equity investment and commitment to the hotel's success.

Managing Repayment Obligations During a Turnaround

Effective management of repayment obligations is critical to avoid defaulting on mezzanine or bridge financing. Failure to meet repayment terms can lead to penalties, loss of equity, or even foreclosure.

1. Maintain a Detailed Cash Flow Forecast: Create a cash flow forecast that accounts for all revenue and expenses, ensuring you can meet repayment obligations. Update this forecast regularly to anticipate potential shortfalls and take corrective action.

2. Prioritize Loan Repayments: Ensure that loan repayments are prioritized in your financial planning. If cash flow becomes tight, identify non-essential expenses that can be reduced or deferred to meet your obligations.

3. Communicate with Lenders: Maintain open communication with lenders, especially if you anticipate difficulties in meeting repayment terms. Being proactive can help you negotiate temporary relief, such as deferred payments or modified terms, to avoid default.

4. Consider Refinancing Options: Explore refinancing options before the mezzanine or bridge loan matures. Refinancing with a longer-term, lower-interest loan can reduce monthly payments and ease financial pressure.

Practical Example: A hotel owner with a mezzanine

loan used a cash flow management tool to track monthly expenses and revenue, ensuring timely loan repayments. When facing a temporary cash flow shortfall, the owner proactively communicated with the lender, who agreed to a three-month interest-only period, providing the hotel with much-needed relief.

Actionable Steps:

- Maintain an updated cash flow forecast to anticipate repayment challenges.

- Prioritize loan repayments in your financial planning.

- Communicate proactively with lenders and explore refinancing options.

Mezzanine financing and bridge loans can be valuable tools for distressed hotels seeking short-term capital to support turnaround efforts, renovations, or operational improvements. While these financing options offer quick access to funds and flexible terms, they come with higher costs and risks that require careful management. By understanding how mezzanine and bridge financing work, developing a solid repayment strategy, and demonstrating the hotel's turnaround potential, hotel owners can leverage these financing solutions to transform their properties and achieve long-term success.

Crowdfunding and Alternative Financing

Crowdfunding and alternative financing have emerged as innovative options for distressed hotels seeking to raise capital for turnaround efforts, renovations, or operational improvements. By leveraging the power of the crowd, hotel owners can access a diverse pool of investors, bypassing traditional financing channels like banks or private equity firms. In this section, we will explore how crowdfunding platforms can be used to finance distressed hotels, the different types of crowdfunding available, strategies for creating a compelling campaign, a case study demonstrating successful crowdfunding, tips for marketing your campaign, and the benefits and drawbacks of this alternative financing method.

How Crowdfunding Platforms Can Be Used to Finance Distressed Hotels

Crowdfunding platforms enable hotel owners to raise funds from a large group of individual investors, each contributing a small amount toward a funding goal. By reaching out to a broad audience, hotel owners can tap into the collective capital of investors who are interested in real estate, hospitality, or alternative investment opportunities.

1. Access to a Large Pool of Investors: Crowdfunding platforms allow distressed hotels to reach potential investors worldwide, many of whom may be looking for opportunities to diversify their investment portfolios. This approach can be particularly advantageous for hotels in need of substantial capital that may be difficult to secure through traditional financing methods.

2. Transparency and Engagement: Crowdfunding

platforms typically provide transparency, allowing investors to track the progress of their investments. This transparency fosters a sense of community and engagement, with investors often feeling more connected to the project, which can be beneficial for hotels seeking to build a loyal customer base.

3. Flexibility in Financing: Crowdfunding offers flexible financing options, enabling hotel owners to raise funds for various purposes, including renovations, marketing campaigns, debt refinancing, or expanding services. It is especially valuable for distressed hotels that may not qualify for bank loans or other traditional financing due to financial instability.

Practical Example: A hotel owner in Los Angeles used a crowdfunding platform to raise $500,000 to upgrade outdated guest rooms and renovate the lobby. By reaching out to a global audience, the campaign attracted 250 individual investors, each contributing between $1,000 and $10,000, allowing the hotel to complete the renovations and improve guest satisfaction.

Actionable Steps:

- Research crowdfunding platforms that cater to real estate and hospitality investments.

- Develop a detailed plan for how the funds will be used and the potential returns for investors.

- Prepare to engage with investors by providing regular updates on the project's progress.

Understanding the Different Types of Crowdfunding (Equity vs. Debt)

There are two main types of crowdfunding that hotels can use to raise capital: equity crowdfunding and debt crowdfunding. Each has its own set of advantages and considerations.

1. Equity Crowdfunding: In equity crowdfunding, investors provide capital in exchange for ownership shares in the hotel. This means that investors become partial owners of the property and may receive dividends or profit-sharing based on the hotel's performance. Equity crowdfunding is ideal for hotels looking to raise substantial capital without the pressure of monthly repayments.

Key Characteristics of Equity Crowdfunding:

- Investors gain equity ownership in the hotel.

- There is no requirement for monthly repayments, reducing immediate financial pressure.

- Investors share in the profits or losses, which can be a strong motivator for supporting the hotel's success.

2. Debt Crowdfunding: In debt crowdfunding, investors provide a loan to the hotel, and the owner agrees to repay the principal amount with interest over a specified period. This model is similar to traditional bank loans but often offers more flexible terms and lower interest rates.

Key Characteristics of Debt Crowdfunding:

- Investors act as lenders, and the hotel owner is obligated to repay the loan with interest.

- There is a fixed repayment schedule, making it important to ensure consistent cash flow.

- Suitable for hotels that prefer not to give up ownership or equity stakes.

Practical Example: A boutique hotel in Chicago used equity crowdfunding to raise $1 million from 500 investors, each contributing $2,000. In exchange, the investors received a 10% collective equity stake in the hotel, allowing them to share in future profits.

Actionable Steps:

- Determine whether equity or debt crowdfunding aligns with your financial goals and the hotel's turnaround strategy.

- Understand the implications of giving up equity versus taking on debt to make an informed decision.

Creating a Compelling Campaign to Attract Investors

To attract investors through crowdfunding, hotel owners need to create a compelling campaign that stands out and clearly communicates the investment opportunity. This involves presenting a well-thought-out strategy, showcasing the potential returns, and building trust with potential investors.

1. Develop a Strong Value Proposition: Clearly articulate why the hotel represents a good investment opportunity. Highlight its location, market potential, competitive advantages, and the planned improvements that will drive profitability. Provide financial projections and explain how the funds will be used to achieve the desired outcomes.

2. Use High-Quality Visuals and Storytelling: Investors are more likely to engage with campaigns that include high-quality images, videos, and storytelling. Showcase the hotel's current state, the envisioned changes, and how the investment will transform the property.

3. Offer Attractive Incentives: Provide incentives to encourage investment, such as discounted stays, exclusive access to hotel amenities, or profit-sharing arrangements. These perks can motivate potential investors and create a sense of excitement around the project.

Practical Example: A hotel owner in Miami created a crowdfunding campaign that included a video tour of the property, interviews with the management team, and testimonials from guests. The campaign offered investors a 15% discount on future stays, which helped generate interest and raise $600,000 for renovations.

Actionable Steps:

- Create a detailed campaign plan with a strong value proposition and financial projections.

- Use high-quality visuals and storytelling to engage potential investors.

- Offer attractive incentives that add value to the investment opportunity.

Case Study: A Hotel That Raised Capital Through Crowdfunding

The Ocean View Inn, a 50-room hotel located in a coastal town, faced financial distress due to declining tourism and outdated facilities. The owner decided to use an equity crowdfunding platform to raise $750,000 for renovations and marketing initiatives. By presenting a detailed turnaround plan and leveraging high-quality visuals of the hotel and surrounding area, the campaign quickly gained traction.

The owner offered investors an equity stake in the hotel, along with a 20% discount on future bookings. Within 90 days, the Ocean View Inn successfully raised the full amount from 300 individual investors. The funds were used to upgrade the guest rooms, renovate common areas, and launch a targeted marketing campaign. As a result, occupancy rates increased by 35%, and the hotel's revenue grew by 50% within the first year after the renovations.

Key Takeaway: By leveraging the power of equity crowdfunding, the Ocean View Inn raised the capital needed for a successful turnaround, demonstrating that crowdfunding can be a viable financing option for distressed hotels.

Tips for Marketing Your Crowdfunding Campaign

Marketing is crucial to the success of a crowdfunding campaign. To reach a broad audience and attract investors, hotel owners should employ multiple marketing strategies:

1. Leverage Social Media: Use platforms like Facebook, Instagram, LinkedIn, and Twitter to share campaign updates, success stories, and visuals. Engage with followers and encourage them to share the campaign with their networks.

2. Reach Out to Existing Customers and Supporters: Tap into your existing customer base, loyalty program members, and email subscribers. Encourage them to invest in the hotel or share the campaign with others who might be interested.

3. Collaborate with Influencers: Partner with travel bloggers, influencers, or real estate experts who can promote the campaign to their followers. This can help increase visibility and reach a wider audience.

4. Use Paid Advertising: Invest in targeted online advertising on platforms like Google Ads, Facebook Ads, and LinkedIn to reach potential investors who may be interested in hospitality investments.

Practical Example: A hotel owner in New York City used social media influencers to promote their crowdfunding campaign, which resulted in a 200% increase in traffic to the campaign page and helped raise $300,000 in just 60 days.

Actionable Steps:

- Develop a comprehensive marketing plan that includes social media, email marketing, and influencer partnerships.

- Regularly update your campaign with progress reports and success stories to maintain interest.

- Invest in targeted advertising to reach potential investors beyond your immediate network.

The Benefits and Drawbacks of Alternative Financing

While crowdfunding and alternative financing offer unique advantages, they also come with potential challenges that hotel owners should consider.

Benefits:

- Access to Capital: Crowdfunding provides access to a broad pool of investors, allowing hotels to raise substantial funds without relying on traditional financing.

- Market Validation: A successful crowdfunding campaign demonstrates demand and interest in the project, validating the hotel's potential for recovery.

- Flexible Funding Options: Hotels can choose

between equity and debt crowdfunding based on their financial goals and preferences.

Drawbacks:

- Time-Consuming: Creating and marketing a crowdfunding campaign requires significant time and effort, which can be challenging for distressed hotels with limited resources.

- No Guarantee of Success: Crowdfunding campaigns can fail if they do not reach their funding goals, which may result in wasted time and resources.

- Investor Expectations: Managing a large group of investors can be demanding, as they will expect regular updates and transparent communication.

Actionable Steps:

- Weigh the benefits and drawbacks of crowdfunding before deciding if it's the right option for your hotel.

- Prepare to invest time and resources into creating a compelling campaign and engaging with potential investors.

- Be ready to manage investor relationships and expectations throughout the process.

Crowdfunding and alternative financing offer distressed hotels an innovative way to raise capital, engage with investors, and execute turnaround strategies. By understanding the different types of crowdfunding, creating a compelling campaign, and effectively marketing it to attract investors, hotel owners can leverage this financing method to achieve their goals. While crowdfunding presents unique challenges, its potential to provide much-needed capital, validate the hotel's market potential, and build a loyal customer base makes it an option worth considering for hotels seeking a path to recovery.

Choosing the Right Financing Option

Selecting the most suitable financing option is a critical decision for distressed hotels undergoing a turnaround. Given the variety of financing methods available—ranging from traditional bank loans to private equity, mezzanine financing, bridge loans, crowdfunding, and government-backed programs—it's essential to evaluate the pros and cons of each, align them with your hotel's specific needs, and develop a solid financial plan to ensure long-term success. This section provides an in-depth analysis of these aspects, including real-world examples and actionable steps for presenting your financial plan to lenders and investors while avoiding common pitfalls.

Evaluating the Pros and Cons of Each Financing Method

Each financing option comes with its unique advantages and challenges. Understanding the pros and cons of each method helps in selecting the right approach for your hotel's needs.

1. Traditional Bank Loans:

- Pros: Lower interest rates, structured repayment schedules, and the potential for long-term financing.

- Cons: Strict eligibility requirements, lengthy approval process, and the need for substantial collateral.

2. Private Equity and Investor Funding:

- Pros: Access to significant capital, strategic guidance, and operational expertise from experienced investors.

- Cons: Loss of ownership or control, profit-sharing requirements, and the need to meet investor expectations.

3. Mezzanine Financing and Bridge Loans:

- Pros: Quick access to capital, flexible repayment terms, and non-dilutive financing.

- Cons: High-interest rates, potential for equity loss if repayment terms are not met, and short repayment periods (for bridge loans).

4. Government Programs and SBA Loans:

- Pros: Lower interest rates, longer repayment terms, and support for renovations and operational improvements.

- Cons: Lengthy application process, strict eligibility requirements, and the need for a detailed business plan.

5. Crowdfunding and Alternative Financing:

- Pros: Access to a broad pool of investors, flexible funding options, and potential for marketing exposure.

- Cons: Time-consuming campaign setup and marketing, no guarantee of success, and managing multiple investor relationships.

Practical Example: A boutique hotel in Denver considered various options and ultimately chose a combination of mezzanine financing and an SBA 504 loan. The mezzanine financing provided quick access to capital for immediate renovations, while the SBA loan offered longer-term funding with favorable terms to support the hotel's ongoing recovery.

Actionable Steps:

- Create a detailed list of your hotel's financing needs and match them with the pros and cons of each option.

- Consider factors like the urgency of funds, repayment flexibility, interest rates, and control over your hotel when evaluating options.

- Consult with financial advisors or experts to gain insights into the best financing strategy for your situation.

Matching Financing Options with Your Hotel's Turnaround Needs

Matching the right financing option to your hotel's specific needs is crucial for a successful turnaround. Consider your hotel's financial health, operational challenges, and growth potential when selecting a financing method.

1. Urgency of Funds: If your hotel requires immediate capital for renovations or operational expenses, bridge loans or mezzanine financing might be the most appropriate option. For longer-term funding needs, traditional bank loans or SBA loans could be a better fit.

2. Financial Stability: For hotels with a relatively stable cash flow but needing capital to expand or renovate, government-backed loans or private equity funding may provide the required support. In contrast, highly distressed hotels may benefit more from equity crowdfunding or mezzanine financing due to the flexibility and risk tolerance offered by these options.

3. Ownership and Control: If maintaining ownership and control is a priority, avoid equity financing options such as private equity or equity crowdfunding. Instead, explore debt options like SBA loans, mezzanine financing, or bridge loans.

Practical Example: A hotel owner in Orlando needed $2 million for a comprehensive renovation project but wanted to retain ownership. The owner opted for a mix of debt crowdfunding and an SBA loan, which allowed them to secure the funds without sacrificing equity or control.

Actionable Steps:

- Identify your hotel's most pressing turnaround needs, such as capital for renovations, working capital, or refinancing.

- Match these needs with financing options that align with your goals, whether it's quick access to funds, maintaining control, or minimizing interest expenses.

- Use financial projections to determine which financing option offers the most sustainable solution.

Building a Financial Plan that Supports Long-Term Success

A robust financial plan is essential for ensuring the success of your hotel's turnaround. This plan should outline your strategy for using the funds, achieving profitability, and repaying any borrowed capital.

1. Detailed Budgeting: Create a comprehensive budget that covers all aspects of your hotel's turnaround, including renovation costs, marketing expenses, operational improvements, and debt repayments. This budget should include realistic revenue projections and expense forecasts.

2. Cash Flow Management: Develop a cash flow projection that shows how the hotel will generate sufficient revenue to cover expenses and meet financing obligations. Regularly review and update this projection to ensure the hotel remains on track.

3. Debt Management Strategy: If using debt financing, develop a strategy for managing and repaying loans. Consider refinancing options, consolidating debt, or using revenue from improved operations to pay down loans more quickly.

Practical Example: A hotel in San Diego developed a financial plan that included a detailed renovation budget, monthly cash flow projections, and a repayment schedule for a combination of an SBA loan and mezzanine financing. This plan helped the hotel maintain financial discipline, complete renovations on time, and meet loan repayment obligations.

Actionable Steps:

- Create a detailed budget that outlines all expenses, revenue sources, and projected profits.

- Develop a cash flow projection that ensures you can meet financing obligations.

- Establish a debt management strategy that supports timely repayments and minimizes interest expenses.

Real-Life Example: A Hotel That Combined Multiple Financing Options

The Harbor View Inn, a 150-room hotel located in a coastal town, faced financial distress due to outdated facilities and declining occupancy rates. The owner decided to pursue a multi-faceted financing approach, combining an SBA 504 loan, mezzanine financing, and equity crowdfunding to raise $3 million for renovations and marketing initiatives.

1. The SBA 504 Loan: Provided $1.5 million for long-term renovation financing with a low-interest rate and extended repayment period.

2. Mezzanine Financing: Secured $1 million in mezzanine financing, which provided quick access to capital for immediate renovation needs.

3. Equity Crowdfunding: Raised an additional $500,000 from 200 investors, allowing the owner to finance marketing efforts without taking on additional debt.

The combination of these financing methods enabled the Harbor View Inn to complete renovations, launch a targeted marketing campaign, and improve occupancy rates. Within two years, the hotel's revenue increased by 40%, and the owner successfully repaid the mezzanine loan while continuing to benefit from the SBA loan's favorable terms.

Key Takeaway: By combining multiple financing options, the Harbor View Inn accessed the necessary capital for a successful turnaround while balancing

debt obligations and maintaining ownership.
How to Present a Solid Financial Plan to Lenders and Investors

Presenting a solid financial plan is essential for gaining the confidence of lenders and investors. This plan should be comprehensive, transparent, and demonstrate your ability to execute the turnaround strategy successfully.

1. Provide Detailed Financial Projections: Include profit and loss statements, cash flow projections, and balance sheets for at least three years. Ensure these projections are realistic and aligned with your turnaround strategy.

2. Highlight Your Turnaround Plan: Clearly explain how the funds will be used, the expected impact on revenue and profitability, and the timeline for achieving financial stability. Include key performance indicators (KPIs) that demonstrate progress.

3. Showcase Your Management Team: Highlight the experience and expertise of your management team, demonstrating their ability to execute the turnaround plan effectively.

Practical Example: A hotel owner seeking private equity funding presented a comprehensive financial plan that included detailed projections, a breakdown of renovation costs, and a marketing strategy. The plan demonstrated how the funding would increase occupancy rates by 30%, resulting in a successful $2 million investment.

Actionable Steps:

- Prepare detailed financial projections that show the potential return on investment.

- Clearly outline your turnaround plan and how the funds will be used.

- Emphasize the strengths of your management team.

Avoiding Common Financing Pitfalls

Financing pitfalls can derail your hotel's turnaround if not managed properly. Be aware of these common challenges and take steps to avoid them:

1. Overleveraging: Taking on too much debt can strain cash flow and hinder your ability to repay loans. Carefully assess your debt capacity and avoid overburdening the hotel with excessive financing.

2. Lack of Financial Discipline: Failing to manage funds effectively can lead to financial instability. Stick to your budget, monitor cash flow, and adjust spending as needed to avoid unnecessary expenses.

3. Inadequate Planning: Entering into a financing agreement without a clear plan for repayment or long-term growth can result in financial difficulties. Always have a comprehensive financial plan in place before securing financing.

Practical Example: A hotel in Atlanta overleveraged itself by taking on multiple high-interest loans, leading to cash flow issues and missed payments. To avoid this pitfall, the owner should have consolidated debts or sought financing with lower interest rates to maintain financial stability.

Actionable Steps:

- Assess your debt capacity before taking on additional financing.

- Maintain financial discipline by adhering to your budget and cash flow projections.

- Develop a repayment strategy before securing financing.

Choosing the right financing option is crucial for a successful hotel turnaround. By carefully evaluating the pros and cons of each financing method, aligning them with your hotel's specific needs, and developing a comprehensive financial plan, you can secure the capital needed to transform your distressed hotel into a thriving business. By presenting a solid financial plan to lenders and investors and avoiding common pitfalls, you can navigate the complexities of hotel financing and achieve long-term financial success.

Chapter 7: Disposition and Sale of Distressed Hotels

The process of disposing of or selling a distressed hotel can be complex, requiring strategic planning and a deep understanding of the market to achieve the best possible outcome. In this chapter, we will explore the critical elements involved in selling a distressed hotel, offering practical guidance on how to maximize value and navigate the intricacies of the sale process. Whether an owner is seeking to minimize losses, capitalize on market opportunities, or transition to a new venture, this chapter provides a comprehensive roadmap for making informed decisions.

We begin by examining the factors that influence the decision to sell a distressed hotel, including how to evaluate whether to hold, sell, or refinance. Understanding market conditions, timing, and the hotel's current and potential value is essential for determining the right moment to initiate a sale. Through a case study of a successful hotel sale at peak value, we'll explore the importance of timing and preparation in achieving a favorable outcome. Practical tips on preparing for a sale will also be discussed, offering insights into how to assess potential buyer interest and position the property for maximum appeal.

Next, we delve into the steps required to prepare a distressed hotel for sale. This includes conducting a pre-sale audit and due diligence to identify potential issues, enhancing the hotel's curb appeal, and ensuring all financial records, legal documents, and operational data are in order. We'll explore how even small renovations can significantly increase a hotel's sale price, as demonstrated in a case study, and provide guidance on creating an effective marketing strategy. The chapter also emphasizes the value of working with experienced brokers and real estate agents who can help navigate the complexities of the sale process.

Marketing a distressed hotel asset is a crucial component of a successful sale. We will discuss how to utilize online and offline marketing channels to target the right buyer audience, highlighting the hotel's unique selling points to attract interest. A case study of a marketing campaign that resulted in multiple offers will illustrate the effectiveness of leveraging industry contacts and distribution networks. Additionally, strategies for handling sensitive information during the sale will be covered, ensuring that confidentiality is maintained while reaching the right potential buyers.

Negotiating offers and sale terms is often the most challenging aspect of selling a distressed hotel. This chapter offers insights into handling offers, counteroffers, and due diligence requests, as well as addressing buyer concerns and objections. Through a case study of a hotel owner who secured a premium sale price, we'll explore negotiation techniques and the role of legal and financial advisors in achieving favorable terms. We will also discuss how to structure the sale for tax efficiency, ensuring that the transaction is as financially advantageous as possible.

The chapter will then guide you through the closing process, covering the final steps needed to finalize legal and financial documents, transition ownership, and manage post-sale tasks. A case study highlighting a smooth transition that minimized operational disruption will demonstrate best practices for ensuring a seamless handover. Effective communication with stakeholders about the sale and reflecting on lessons learned are also emphasized as essential components of a successful disposition.

Finally, we conclude by examining the lessons learned from hotel dispositions, including common pitfalls to avoid and strategies for maximizing sale value. We'll explore how building a successful exit strategy can lead to future investment opportunities and provide insights into developing the skills needed for future hotel investments. By the end of this chapter, readers will be well-equipped with the knowledge and strategies necessary to navigate the disposition process and prepare for the next opportunity in the hospitality market.

Deciding When to Sell a Distressed Hotel

Deciding when to sell a distressed hotel is one of the most critical decisions an owner or investor can make. The right timing and strategy can significantly impact the sale's outcome, influencing whether the transaction minimizes losses or achieves a successful turnaround. This section explores how to evaluate whether to hold, sell, or refinance, understand market conditions, assess the hotel's market value, and identify factors that influence the decision to sell. It also includes a case study of a successful hotel sale and practical tips for preparing a distressed hotel for sale.

Evaluating Whether to Hold, Sell, or Refinance

Before deciding to sell, hotel owners must first consider whether holding the property, selling it, or refinancing represents the best course of action. This evaluation requires a thorough understanding of the hotel's financial health, the broader market environment, and long-term investment goals.

1. Holding the Hotel:

- Pros: Holding allows owners to retain control and gives more time for market conditions to improve, potentially increasing the hotel's value. This strategy might be ideal if the property is located in a market expected to rebound or if the owner has the resources to implement a successful turnaround plan.

- Cons: Continuing to operate a distressed hotel can be financially draining, especially if cash flow remains negative or if the property's condition continues to deteriorate.

2. Selling the Hotel:

- Pros: Selling can provide immediate cash flow, helping owners avoid further financial losses. It may be the best option if the hotel is struggling to generate revenue or if market conditions suggest that it is the right time to exit.

- Cons: Selling at the wrong time or in a buyer's market may result in a lower sale price, potentially leading to financial losses.

3. Refinancing:

- Pros: Refinancing can provide access to capital to cover renovations or operational improvements, offering a chance to reposition the hotel and increase its value. It's a viable option if the hotel has the potential to recover and grow in value over time.

- Cons: Refinancing may be challenging if the hotel's financials are weak, and it could lead to increased debt obligations.

Practical Example: A 100-room hotel in Miami faced declining occupancy rates due to outdated facilities and increased competition. After evaluating their options, the owner decided to refinance, using the funds to renovate guest rooms and upgrade amenities. Within 18 months, occupancy rates improved, allowing the owner to sell the hotel at a significantly higher price than initially estimated.

Actionable Steps:

- Analyze your hotel's financial health, including cash flow, debt obligations, and potential for recovery.

- Assess market trends and forecast future demand to determine whether holding, selling, or refinancing aligns with your goals.

- Consult with financial advisors or real estate experts to gain insights into the best course of action.

Understanding Market Conditions and Timing the Sale

Timing plays a crucial role in the successful sale of a distressed hotel. Understanding market conditions helps owners determine the optimal moment to sell and maximize value.

1. Analyzing Market Trends:

- Monitor local and national hospitality trends, such as occupancy rates, average daily rates (ADR), and revenue per available room (RevPAR). These indicators provide insights into demand and potential buyer interest.

- Assess broader economic factors, such as interest rates, tourism trends, and regional economic growth, as these can impact hotel valuations and buyer sentiment.

2. Identifying a Seller's Market vs. Buyer's Market:

- In a seller's market, demand for hotels exceeds supply, leading to higher sale prices and increased competition among buyers.

- In a buyer's market, there is an oversupply of properties, resulting in lower sale prices. Understanding these dynamics helps determine whether it's the right time to list your hotel.

Practical Example: A hotel owner in New York City decided to sell during a period of high tourism and strong ADR growth, resulting in a quick sale at a premium price. By waiting for the market to peak, the owner maximized the value of the transaction.

Actionable Steps:

- Regularly track market indicators, such as occupancy rates, ADR, and RevPAR, to gauge demand.

- Research regional economic trends and tourism forecasts to predict future market conditions.

- Consider working with a real estate advisor who specializes in hospitality assets to gain insights into market timing.

Assessing the Hotel's Market Value and Potential Buyer Interest

Accurately assessing your hotel's market value is essential for setting a realistic asking price and attracting potential buyers. This process involves evaluating both the hotel's intrinsic value and its potential for growth.

1. Conducting a Property Valuation:

- Obtain a professional appraisal to determine the hotel's current market value, considering factors such as location, condition, revenue performance, and competitive positioning.

- Compare your hotel to similar properties that have recently sold to gauge its market value relative to comparable sales.

2. Identifying Potential Buyers:

- Analyze the types of buyers who may be interested in your hotel, such as institutional investors, private equity firms, or individual buyers. Each buyer type has different investment goals and criteria.

- Determine whether your hotel's location, brand, or unique features will appeal to specific buyer segments.

Practical Example: A hotel owner in Los Angeles worked with a real estate broker to assess the property's market value, identifying that it was undervalued compared to recent sales of similar hotels. By pricing the hotel competitively, the owner attracted multiple offers and sold at a higher price than expected.

Actionable Steps:

- Hire a professional appraiser to conduct a valuation of your hotel.

- Identify potential buyer segments and tailor your marketing strategy to their preferences.
- Research comparable sales in your market to

establish a realistic asking price.

Case Study: A Successful Sale of a Distressed Hotel at Peak Value

The Lakeside Resort, a 200-room property in a popular tourist destination, faced financial difficulties due to declining occupancy rates and mounting debt. The owner considered holding the hotel, but market conditions indicated that it was an optimal time to sell, as tourism was booming and investors were actively seeking hospitality assets.

The owner took several steps to prepare for the sale:

- Conducted a valuation, which identified the property's potential worth after minor renovations.
- Invested in targeted renovations, such as updating guest rooms and improving curb appeal.

- Engaged a real estate broker experienced in hospitality sales to market the hotel to institutional investors.

The result was a successful sale that generated 20% more than the original valuation, as the owner timed the sale to coincide with peak tourism demand and presented the hotel as an attractive investment opportunity.

Key Takeaway: By understanding market conditions, investing in strategic improvements, and working with experienced professionals, the Lakeside Resort owner maximized the property's value and achieved a successful sale.

Factors That Influence the Decision to Sell

Several factors influence the decision to sell a distressed hotel, including:

- Financial Performance: Consistent negative cash flow or mounting debt may signal that it's time to sell.

- Market Conditions: Favorable market trends, such as increased demand or rising hotel valuations, can create an opportunity to sell at a premium.

- Personal Circumstances: Changes in personal circumstances, such as retirement, health issues, or a desire to invest in other opportunities, may drive the decision to sell.

- Renovation Costs: If renovation costs exceed the potential return on investment, selling may be a more viable option.

Practical Example: A hotel owner in Texas decided to sell after realizing that the cost of renovating the property was too high to justify the potential return. By selling, the owner avoided further financial strain and was able to invest in a more profitable venture.

Actionable Steps:

- Evaluate your hotel's financial performance and potential for improvement.

- Consider market conditions, personal circumstances, and renovation costs when deciding to sell.

- Consult with financial advisors to weigh the pros and cons of selling versus holding or refinancing.

Practical Tips for Preparing for a Sale

- Conduct a Pre-Sale Audit: Identify any operational, financial, or legal issues that may affect the sale process. Address these issues before listing the hotel to avoid complications.

- Enhance Curb Appeal: Invest in minor renovations, landscaping, and cosmetic improvements to make the hotel more attractive to buyers.

- Organize Financial Records: Gather all financial documents, such as income statements, tax returns, and occupancy reports, to present a clear picture of the hotel's performance.

- Work with Experienced Professionals: Engage a real estate broker or advisor with experience in hospitality sales to guide you through the process.

Practical Example: A distressed hotel owner in Florida invested $50,000 in renovations, which led to a 15% increase in the final sale price. By enhancing curb appeal and organizing financial records, the owner attracted more buyers and achieved a successful sale.

Actionable Steps:

- Conduct a pre-sale audit to identify and address potential issues.

- Invest in improvements that enhance the hotel's curb appeal and value.

- Gather financial records and work with experienced professionals to prepare for the sale.

Deciding when to sell a distressed hotel involves careful consideration of multiple factors, including market conditions, the hotel's financial health, and potential buyer interest. By evaluating whether to hold, sell, or refinance, understanding market trends, accurately assessing the hotel's value, and preparing the property for sale, hotel owners can maximize their chances of achieving a successful transaction. With the right strategy, timing, and preparation, even a distressed hotel can be sold at peak value, turning a challenging situation into a rewarding opportunity.

Preparing for the Sale Process

Preparing a distressed hotel for sale is a critical step that can significantly impact its final sale price and attractiveness to potential buyers. A well-prepared sale process not only demonstrates the hotel's potential value but also instills confidence in buyers, reducing uncertainties and facilitating smoother negotiations. This section provides a comprehensive guide to conducting a pre-sale audit, enhancing the hotel's marketability, organizing essential documents, implementing renovations, creating a marketing strategy, and working with professional brokers or real estate agents.

Conducting a Pre-Sale Audit and Due Diligence

Before listing a distressed hotel for sale, conducting a thorough pre-sale audit and due diligence process is essential. This involves assessing the hotel's financial health, operational efficiency, legal compliance, and physical condition.

1. Financial Audit:

- Review all financial records, including income statements, balance sheets, and cash flow statements, to identify any discrepancies or areas that require improvement.

- Analyze the hotel's revenue sources, expenses, and profitability to understand its financial performance and potential value.

- Identify outstanding debts, liens, or other financial obligations that may impact the sale process.

2. Operational Audit:

- Evaluate the hotel's operational efficiency, including staffing levels, guest service quality, and maintenance procedures.

- Identify areas where operational improvements can increase the hotel's profitability and appeal to potential buyers.

3. Legal and Compliance Audit:

- Ensure that all permits, licenses, and regulatory requirements are up to date. Address any legal issues, such as zoning violations, environmental concerns, or pending lawsuits, before the sale process.

- Review existing contracts with vendors, suppliers, and service providers to ensure they can be transferred or renegotiated with the new owner.

4. Physical Condition Audit:

- Inspect the hotel's physical condition, including the building structure, guest rooms, amenities, and common areas. Identify any maintenance issues, repairs, or upgrades needed to enhance the hotel's appeal.

Practical Example: A hotel owner in Chicago conducted a pre-sale audit and discovered that the property's HVAC system was outdated and inefficient.

By replacing the system, the owner not only reduced operational expenses but also improved the hotel's energy efficiency, making it more attractive to potential buyers.

Actionable Steps:

- Hire professionals to conduct a thorough financial, operational, legal, and physical audit.

- Address any issues identified during the audit to improve the hotel's overall value and marketability.

- Ensure all permits, licenses, and contracts are in good standing before listing the property.

Enhancing the Hotel's Curb Appeal and Marketability

First impressions matter, especially when selling a distressed hotel. Enhancing the property's curb appeal and marketability can significantly impact buyer interest and the final sale price.

1. Focus on Exterior Improvements:

- Invest in landscaping, painting, and signage to create a welcoming entrance. Ensure that the parking lot, walkways, and exterior lighting are well-maintained.

- Repair or replace any damaged exterior

features, such as windows, doors, or roofing, to improve the hotel's overall appearance.

2. Upgrade Guest Rooms and Amenities:

- Renovate guest rooms to create a modern and comfortable environment. This may include updating furnishings, replacing worn carpets, or repainting walls.

- Ensure that amenities, such as the lobby, fitness center, or pool area, are clean, functional, and visually appealing.

3. Highlight Unique Selling Points (USPs):

- Identify and enhance the hotel's unique features, such as a scenic view, historical architecture, or proximity to popular attractions. Emphasizing these USPs can differentiate the property from competitors and attract more buyers.

Practical Example: A distressed hotel in Miami invested $100,000 in landscaping, repainting, and upgrading the lobby area. These improvements not only increased the property's curb appeal but also contributed to a 20% increase in the final sale price.

Actionable Steps:

- Invest in exterior and interior improvements that enhance the hotel's visual appeal.

- Emphasize unique features and amenities

that make the hotel stand out from competitors.
- Set a budget for renovations to ensure you achieve a positive return on investment.

Gathering Financial Records, Legal Documents, and Operational Data

Organizing and presenting accurate financial records, legal documents, and operational data is crucial for gaining buyer confidence and expediting the sale process.

1. Financial Records:

- Collect income statements, balance sheets, cash flow statements, and tax returns for the past three to five years. Ensure that these documents are accurate, up to date, and professionally prepared.

- Prepare a summary of the hotel's revenue streams, expenses, and profitability to provide potential buyers with a clear financial overview.

2. Legal Documents:

- Compile all legal documents, including property deeds, permits, licenses, zoning certificates, and any pending legal matters. Ensure that all documents are organized, complete, and accessible.

- Review existing contracts with suppliers,

service providers, and employees to identify any agreements that may need to be transferred or renegotiated.

3. Operational Data:

- Gather data on occupancy rates, average daily rate (ADR), revenue per available room (RevPAR), and guest demographics. This information provides valuable insights into the hotel's performance and potential for growth.

- Include details on the hotel's staffing levels, maintenance procedures, and marketing strategies to give buyers a comprehensive understanding of the hotel's operations.

Practical Example: A hotel owner in Los Angeles who provided organized financial records, legal documents, and operational data was able to streamline the due diligence process, leading to a quicker sale and a more favorable purchase price.

Actionable Steps:

- Work with financial advisors, accountants, and legal professionals to organize and verify all documents.
- Ensure that all records are complete, accurate, and ready to present to potential buyers.

- Create an operational data summary to highlight the hotel's performance and growth potential.

Case Study: How a Distressed Hotel Increased Its Sale Price Through Renovations

The Oceanfront Hotel, a 150-room property in a coastal town, was experiencing financial difficulties due to outdated facilities and declining occupancy rates. The owner decided to invest in strategic renovations to increase the hotel's marketability and sale price.

Steps Taken:

- Renovations: The owner invested $200,000 in renovating the lobby, guest rooms, and common areas, focusing on creating a modern, welcoming atmosphere.

- Enhanced Amenities: The hotel upgraded its pool area, added a small fitness center, and introduced complimentary breakfast for guests.

- Curb Appeal: Landscaping improvements and exterior painting were made to enhance the hotel's visual appeal.

Outcome: The renovations resulted in a 30% increase in occupancy rates, allowing the hotel to raise its ADR and overall revenue. When the property was listed for sale, the increased profitability and enhanced appearance attracted multiple offers, ultimately leading to a sale at 25% above the original asking price.

Key Takeaway: Strategic renovations can significantly increase a distressed hotel's market value, making it

more appealing to potential buyers and improving the final sale price.
Creating a Marketing Strategy to Attract Buyers

A well-executed marketing strategy is essential for reaching the right buyers and generating interest in your distressed hotel.

1. Develop a Compelling Marketing Package:

- Create a marketing package that includes high-quality photos, videos, floor plans, and a detailed property description. Highlight the hotel's features, amenities, and USPs.

- Include financial performance data, occupancy rates, and recent renovations to showcase the hotel's potential.

2. Utilize Multiple Marketing Channels:

- Leverage online platforms such as LoopNet, CoStar, and commercial real estate websites to reach a broad audience.

- Promote the hotel through industry publications, trade shows, and hospitality networks to connect with potential buyers.

3. Target the Right Buyer Audience:

- Identify potential buyer segments, such as institutional investors, private equity firms, hotel management companies, or individual investors. Tailor your marketing approach to each segment's preferences and investment criteria.

Practical Example: A distressed hotel in Las Vegas used a combination of online listings, direct mail campaigns, and industry networking events to generate interest from multiple buyers, resulting in a competitive bidding process and a higher sale price.

Actionable Steps:

- Develop a comprehensive marketing package that showcases the hotel's value and potential.

- Use a mix of online and offline marketing channels to reach potential buyers.

- Tailor your marketing approach to target the most likely buyer segments.

Working with Brokers and Real Estate Agents

Engaging experienced brokers or real estate agents who specialize in hotel sales can help navigate the complexities of the sale process and maximize the property's value.

1. Selecting the Right Broker/Agent:

- Choose a broker or agent with experience in selling distressed hotels and a strong network of industry contacts.

- Look for professionals who understand the

local market and have a track record of successful hotel sales.

2. Leveraging Broker Expertise:

- Brokers can provide valuable insights into pricing strategies, market trends, and buyer behavior, helping you position your hotel for a successful sale.

- They can handle negotiations, due diligence, and the closing process, ensuring a smooth transaction.

Practical Example: A hotel owner in New York worked with a broker specializing in distressed properties, who used their industry connections to find an institutional investor interested in acquiring the hotel. The broker's expertise and network contributed to a swift sale at an attractive price.

Actionable Steps:

- Research and interview brokers or agents with experience in the hospitality industry.

- Evaluate their track record, network, and marketing strategies before making a selection.

- Collaborate closely with your broker to develop a sales strategy that aligns with your goals.

Preparing a distressed hotel for sale requires a strategic approach, thorough planning, and attention to detail. By conducting a pre-sale audit, enhancing the property's curb appeal, organizing financial and legal documents, implementing a targeted marketing strategy, and working with experienced brokers, hotel owners can significantly improve their chances of attracting buyers and achieving a successful sale. With the right preparation, even a distressed hotel can be transformed into a valuable investment opportunity, resulting in a more favorable outcome for the seller.

Marketing the Distressed Hotel Asset

Effectively marketing a distressed hotel asset is crucial to attracting the right buyers, generating interest, and achieving a favorable sale outcome. A well-executed marketing strategy can turn a potentially challenging sale into a competitive process, driving up the sale price and ensuring a smoother transaction. In this section, we'll explore how to utilize online and offline marketing channels, target the right buyer audience, highlight the hotel's unique selling points (USPs), and leverage industry contacts and distribution networks. We'll also provide a case study of a successful marketing campaign and discuss strategies for handling sensitive information during the sale process.

Utilizing Online and Offline Marketing Channels

To maximize exposure and reach a diverse pool of potential buyers, it's essential to use a combination of online and offline marketing channels. Each channel offers unique advantages, and a multi-faceted approach ensures that your distressed hotel reaches the right audience.

1. Online Marketing Channels:

- Commercial Real Estate Websites: List your property on well-known platforms like LoopNet, CoStar, CREXi, and Ten-X. These websites are frequented by real estate investors, brokers, and institutional buyers looking for hotel assets.

- Social Media Platforms: Utilize LinkedIn, Facebook, and Twitter to promote the hotel. Sharing high-quality images, videos, and articles about the property can attract potential buyers, especially those who follow hospitality or real estate investment pages.

- Email Marketing: Create a targeted email campaign directed at your existing database of potential buyers, industry contacts, and investors. Include key details about the hotel, such as its location, features, and potential for turnaround, to pique their interest.

2. Offline Marketing Channels:

- Industry Publications and Magazines: Advertise in trade publications such as Hotel Business, Hotel Management, and Hospitality Net. These publications reach a targeted audience of hotel owners, operators, and investors.

- Trade Shows and Conferences: Attend hospitality industry events, such as the Hunter

Hotel Investment Conference or the Lodging Conference, to network with potential buyers and promote your distressed hotel asset.

- Direct Mail Campaigns: Send marketing materials, brochures, and information packets to potential buyers, brokers, and investors. This personalized approach can make a lasting impression and generate interest.

Practical Example: A distressed hotel owner in San Francisco utilized both online (listing on LoopNet and social media campaigns) and offline (advertising in Hotel Management magazine and attending a hotel investment conference) channels, which resulted in a surge of inquiries from qualified buyers.

Actionable Steps:

- Create a comprehensive marketing plan that includes a mix of online and offline channels.

- Develop high-quality marketing materials, including photos, videos, brochures, and fact sheets, to share across different platforms.

- Track the performance of each marketing channel to determine which ones generate the most interest and adjust your strategy accordingly.

Targeting the Right Buyer Audience (Institutional Investors, Individuals, etc.)

Identifying and targeting the right buyer audience is

crucial for a successful sale. Different types of buyers have varying investment criteria, financial capabilities, and levels of experience, so tailoring your marketing strategy to each group is essential.

1. Institutional Investors:

- Institutional investors, such as real estate investment trusts (REITs), private equity firms, and hedge funds, typically have significant capital and are experienced in acquiring hotel assets. These buyers often look for properties with the potential for repositioning or those located in prime markets.

- To attract institutional investors, emphasize the hotel's potential return on investment (ROI), revenue projections, and potential for value enhancement.

2. High-Net-Worth Individuals and Family Offices:

- High-net-worth individuals and family offices may be interested in acquiring hotels as part of their investment portfolio. These buyers may be more flexible in their investment criteria and may be attracted to properties with strong cash flow or unique features.

- Highlight the hotel's potential for passive income, capital appreciation, and lifestyle benefits, such as ownership of a prestigious or luxury property.

3. Hotel Operators and Management Companies:

- Hotel operators and management companies may seek to acquire distressed hotels as part of their expansion strategy. They may be attracted to properties that align with their brand standards or offer opportunities for operational improvements.

- Emphasize the potential for operational efficiencies, brand repositioning, and revenue growth when targeting this audience.

Practical Example: A distressed hotel in Chicago focused its marketing efforts on targeting private equity firms with experience in hospitality turnarounds. By emphasizing the hotel's strong location and potential for renovation, the owner attracted multiple offers from institutional buyers.

Actionable Steps:

- Identify your target buyer audience based on the hotel's characteristics, location, and potential for growth.

- Tailor your marketing materials and messaging to highlight the features most relevant to each buyer group.

- Use industry databases and networking platforms to reach potential buyers within each target audience segment.

Highlighting the Hotel's Unique Selling Points (USPs)

To differentiate your distressed hotel from others on the market, it's essential to highlight its unique selling points (USPs). USPs are the features, amenities, or advantages that make the property stand out and attract potential buyers.

1. Location: Emphasize the hotel's proximity to popular attractions, business districts, transportation hubs, or tourist destinations. A prime location can significantly enhance the hotel's appeal, even if it's distressed.

2. Architectural Features and Design: If the hotel has unique architectural elements, historical significance, or a distinctive design, highlight these features to appeal to buyers interested in properties with character or heritage.

3. Potential for Value-Add Improvements: Showcase opportunities for value-add improvements, such as renovation potential, expansion possibilities, or the ability to reposition the property within a different market segment. Buyers are often attracted to hotels with untapped potential.

Practical Example: A distressed hotel in New Orleans highlighted its historic architecture, proximity to the French Quarter, and potential for conversion into a boutique luxury property. This approach attracted buyers interested in the value-add potential, resulting in a successful sale.

Actionable Steps:

- Identify and emphasize your hotel's most compelling USPs in all marketing materials.

- Use high-quality images and videos to showcase the property's unique features.

- Provide data or examples demonstrating how the USPs can translate into increased revenue or profitability.

Case Study: A Marketing Campaign That Attracted Multiple Offers

The Sunset Bay Resort, a 100-room distressed hotel located in a popular tourist destination, needed a strategic marketing campaign to attract potential buyers. The owner developed a comprehensive marketing strategy that included:

- Listing the property on commercial real estate websites and social media platforms.

- Advertising in trade publications and attending hospitality investment conferences.

- Highlighting the resort's oceanfront location, potential for renovation, and untapped revenue opportunities (such as converting unused space into a spa or restaurant).

By targeting institutional investors, high-net-worth individuals, and hotel management companies, the campaign generated significant interest, resulting in multiple offers within three months. The competitive bidding process led to a final sale price 15% above the initial asking price.

Key Takeaway: A well-executed marketing campaign that effectively combines online and offline channels, targets the right audience, and highlights the hotel's USPs can generate multiple offers and drive up the sale price.

Leveraging Industry Contacts and Distribution Networks

Leveraging industry contacts and distribution networks can significantly increase exposure for your distressed hotel asset, reaching potential buyers who may not be actively searching for properties.

1. Engage with Brokers and Real Estate Agents:

- Collaborate with brokers and agents who specialize in hotel sales and have an extensive network of potential buyers. These professionals can provide valuable insights and introduce your property to qualified prospects.

2. Utilize Industry Associations and Networks:

- Join hospitality associations, such as the American Hotel & Lodging Association (AHLA) or the Hotel Sales & Marketing Association International (HSMAI). These organizations offer access to a network of industry professionals, investors, and buyers.

3. Reach Out to Existing Contacts:

- Engage with your existing contacts, such as past investors, industry colleagues, or suppliers, who may be interested in acquiring the hotel or know someone who is.

Practical Example: A hotel owner in Orlando worked with a broker who had extensive contacts in the hospitality industry. By leveraging the broker's network, the owner was able to connect with several interested buyers, resulting in a successful sale within 60 days.

Actionable Steps:

- Partner with brokers or agents who have a strong track record in hotel sales.

- Attend industry events and join associations to expand your network.

- Engage with existing contacts and inform them about the hotel's availability.

Strategies for Handling Sensitive Information During a Sale

During the sale of a distressed hotel, it's important to manage sensitive information carefully to avoid jeopardizing the transaction or damaging the hotel's reputation.

1. Use Confidentiality Agreements: Require potential buyers to sign a confidentiality agreement (non-

disclosure agreement) before providing access to detailed financial, operational, or legal information.

2. Limit Access to Sensitive Information: Only share sensitive information with serious, qualified buyers who have demonstrated genuine interest and financial capability. Use a secure data room to control access and monitor who views your documents.

3. Maintain Discretion During Marketing: Avoid publicly disclosing that the hotel is distressed or undergoing a sale. This can help prevent negative perceptions among customers, employees, and competitors.

Practical Example: A distressed hotel owner in Dallas used a secure online data room to share financial information with qualified buyers, ensuring that sensitive data remained confidential throughout the sale process.

Actionable Steps:

- Require confidentiality agreements from all potential buyers.

- Use a secure data room to share sensitive documents with qualified buyers.

- Maintain discretion and control the flow of information throughout the sale process.

Marketing a distressed hotel asset requires a strategic approach that combines online and offline channels, targets the right buyer audience, highlights the property's unique selling points, and leverages industry contacts. By creating a comprehensive marketing campaign and managing sensitive information effectively, hotel owners can generate interest, attract multiple offers, and achieve a successful sale. A well-executed marketing strategy can transform a distressed hotel into a valuable investment opportunity, ultimately leading to a more favorable sale outcome.

Negotiating Offers and Sale Terms

The negotiation phase is a crucial step in the sale process of a distressed hotel, and it can significantly impact the final outcome in terms of price and conditions. Effective negotiation requires preparation, flexibility, and the ability to address buyer concerns while protecting your interests. In this section, we'll explore the key aspects of negotiating offers and sale terms, including handling offers and counteroffers, addressing buyer objections, negotiating favorable terms, and the role of legal and financial advisors. We'll also present a case study demonstrating how a hotel owner secured a premium sale price and provide insights into structuring the sale for tax efficiency.

Handling Offers, Counteroffers, and Due Diligence Requests

When a potential buyer submits an offer, the negotiation process officially begins. It's essential to handle offers, counteroffers, and due diligence requests effectively to ensure the sale progresses smoothly.

1. Reviewing Initial Offers:

- Evaluate the offer based on the proposed price, terms, contingencies, and financing arrangements. Compare the offer with your valuation of the property and your desired sale outcome.

- Consider the buyer's financial capability and experience in the hospitality industry, as this can impact the likelihood of a successful transaction.

2. Crafting Counteroffers:

- If the initial offer doesn't meet your expectations, consider submitting a counteroffer. Adjust the price, terms, or contingencies to align with your goals.

- Be prepared to negotiate multiple times, as buyers may respond with their own counteroffers. Maintain a flexible but firm stance to protect your interests.

3. Managing Due Diligence Requests:

- Buyers will likely request access to financial records, operational data, legal documents, and property inspections as part of the due diligence process. Be prepared to provide accurate and comprehensive information.

- Address any discrepancies or concerns promptly to avoid delays in the negotiation process.

Practical Example: A hotel owner in Atlanta received an initial offer that was 20% below the asking price. After reviewing the buyer's financial capability and intentions, the owner submitted a counteroffer with a 10% reduction in price, along with a condition that the buyer closes within 60 days. The buyer accepted the terms, leading to a successful sale.

Actionable Steps:

- Review all offers thoroughly, considering both price and terms.

- Develop a strategy for counteroffers that align with your goals and market value.

- Be prepared to provide detailed information to buyers during the due diligence process.

Addressing Buyer Concerns and Objections

During negotiations, buyers may raise concerns or objections related to the hotel's financial performance, physical condition, or market potential. Successfully addressing these concerns can build trust and help move the negotiation process forward.

1. Be Transparent:

- Provide honest and accurate information about the hotel's financials, occupancy rates, and operational challenges. Buyers appreciate transparency and are more likely to proceed with the sale if they feel informed.

2. Offer Solutions:

- Address concerns by offering solutions, such as providing a credit for necessary repairs, offering a detailed renovation plan, or including operational improvement strategies. Demonstrating how the hotel can be improved or repositioned can alleviate buyer concerns.

3. Highlight Opportunities:

- Emphasize the potential for value-add improvements, such as renovation opportunities, revenue growth, or expansion possibilities. Help buyers see the long-term potential of the hotel beyond its current challenges.

Practical Example: A buyer expressed concerns about the condition of a distressed hotel's plumbing system, which required repairs. The seller offered a $50,000 credit toward repairs at closing, which satisfied the buyer's concerns and helped secure the deal.

Actionable Steps:

- Anticipate potential buyer concerns and prepare responses in advance.

- Be transparent and proactive in addressing objections.

- Emphasize the hotel's potential for future growth and profitability.

Negotiating Favorable Terms and Conditions

Negotiating favorable terms goes beyond the sale price; it involves addressing the various conditions, contingencies, and contractual details that impact the sale's outcome.

1. Contingencies:

- Common contingencies include financing, property inspections, and due diligence. Aim to limit the number and duration of contingencies to reduce the risk of the deal falling through.

- Consider negotiating a non-refundable deposit if the buyer requests extensive contingencies, as this demonstrates their commitment to the purchase.

2. Payment Terms:

- Negotiate payment terms that align with your financial goals, such as a lump-sum payment, installment payments, or seller financing. Evaluate the buyer's ability to meet these terms and any potential risks involved.

3. Closing Timeline:

- Establish a realistic but firm closing timeline. The sooner the transaction is completed, the less risk there is of market changes or buyer withdrawal.

Practical Example: A hotel owner in New York negotiated a deal where the buyer agreed to a 30-day due diligence period with a $100,000 non-refundable deposit. This commitment encouraged the buyer to complete the process quickly, resulting in a swift and successful sale.

Actionable Steps:

- Identify key terms that are most important to you, such as contingencies, payment structure, and closing timeline.

- Be willing to negotiate, but remain firm on terms that protect your interests.

- Consider offering incentives, such as a credit for repairs, to expedite the deal.

Case Study: How a Hotel Owner Secured a Premium Sale Price

The Riverside Hotel, a 150-room property in a suburban area, faced declining revenue and increasing competition. Despite the hotel's distressed status, the owner aimed to secure a premium sale price by implementing a strategic negotiation approach.

Steps Taken:

- The owner conducted minor renovations to enhance the hotel's appearance, positioning it as an attractive investment opportunity.

- The marketing campaign targeted institutional investors and high-net-worth individuals, emphasizing the hotel's potential for repositioning and revenue growth.

- During negotiations, the owner addressed buyer concerns about occupancy rates by providing detailed financial projections and a clear turnaround plan.

- The owner received multiple offers and used the competitive bidding process to negotiate favorable terms, including a higher sale price and a shortened closing period.

Outcome: The Riverside Hotel was sold for 15% above the initial asking price, with the buyer agreeing to a 45-day closing period and a $250,000 non-refundable deposit.

Key Takeaway: Strategic renovations, effective marketing, and skillful negotiation can help distressed hotel owners secure a premium sale price, even in challenging market conditions.

The Role of Legal and Financial Advisors in Negotiations

Legal and financial advisors play a vital role in ensuring that negotiations proceed smoothly and that the final sale terms are favorable and legally sound.

1. Legal Advisors:

- Review all contracts, purchase agreements, and due diligence documents to ensure compliance with local laws and regulations.

- Assist in negotiating complex terms, such as contingencies, warranties, and indemnifications, to protect your interests.

2. Financial Advisors:

- Provide insights into the hotel's valuation, financial projections, and potential tax implications of the sale.

- Help structure the deal in a way that maximizes your financial outcome, whether through payment terms, financing arrangements, or tax-efficient strategies.

Practical Example: A hotel owner in Miami worked with a legal advisor who identified a clause in the purchase agreement that could have resulted in a significant financial penalty if the sale fell through. By renegotiating the clause, the advisor protected the owner's interests and ensured a smoother transaction.

Actionable Steps:

- Engage experienced legal and financial advisors early in the sale process.

- Involve advisors in all negotiations to ensure that contracts are favorable and legally compliant.

- Use their expertise to navigate complex terms, contingencies, and financial implications.

Structuring the Sale for Tax Efficiency

Tax implications can have a significant impact on the financial outcome of a hotel sale. Structuring the deal for tax efficiency can help you retain more of the sale proceeds.

1. Capital Gains Tax:

- Consult with a tax advisor to determine whether the sale will be subject to short-term or long-term capital gains tax. Long-term capital gains (for assets held over a year) are typically taxed at a lower rate.

2. 1031 Exchange:

- Consider a 1031 exchange, which allows you to defer capital gains taxes by reinvesting the proceeds into a similar property. This strategy can be particularly beneficial if you plan to reinvest in another hotel or real estate asset.

3. Installment Sale:

- An installment sale allows you to spread the sale proceeds over multiple years, reducing the immediate tax burden. This approach can be advantageous if you prefer steady income over a lump-sum payment.

Practical Example: A hotel owner in Los Angeles structured the sale as a 1031 exchange, reinvesting the proceeds into a new property. This allowed the owner to defer capital gains taxes and leverage the funds for future investment opportunities.

Actionable Steps:

- Consult with a tax advisor to understand the tax implications of the sale.

- Explore options like 1031 exchanges or installment sales to minimize tax liabilities.

- Structure the sale agreement to ensure that tax-efficient strategies are legally implemented.

Successfully negotiating offers and sale terms is a critical step in selling a distressed hotel. By handling offers and counteroffers effectively, addressing buyer concerns, negotiating favorable terms, and leveraging the expertise of legal and financial advisors, hotel owners can achieve a sale that maximizes value and minimizes risks. Additionally, structuring the deal for tax efficiency can significantly impact the financial outcome, ensuring that you retain more of your hard-earned proceeds. With the right approach and preparation, even a distressed hotel can be sold at a premium, turning a challenging situation into a rewarding opportunity.

Closing the Sale

The closing phase of selling a distressed hotel is the

final step in the transaction process, but it's also one of the most critical. Ensuring that all legal and financial documents are finalized, transitioning ownership smoothly, and managing post-sale tasks and obligations are key components that can make or break the success of the sale. This section provides an in-depth analysis of how to effectively close a sale, transition ownership and management, communicate with stakeholders, and learn from the experience. We'll also look at a case study illustrating a smooth transition that minimized disruption.

Finalizing Legal and Financial Documents

The first step in closing a sale is to finalize all legal and financial documents. This ensures that both the buyer and seller have fulfilled their obligations and that the transaction is legally binding and enforceable.

1. The Purchase and Sale Agreement (PSA):

- The PSA outlines the terms and conditions of the sale, including the purchase price, closing date, contingencies, warranties, and representations. Ensure that all negotiated terms are accurately reflected in the agreement.

- It's important to review the PSA carefully with your legal advisor to avoid any potential misunderstandings or disputes. This document serves as the foundation of the sale, so accuracy is crucial.

2. Transfer of Title and Deed:

- The transfer of the title and deed is a crucial step in legally transferring ownership of the hotel to the buyer. Work with your attorney to ensure that all necessary documents are correctly prepared and recorded with the appropriate government agency.

- Any liens, encumbrances, or outstanding debts must be resolved before the transfer of title can be completed.

3. Settling Financial Obligations:

- Settle any outstanding debts, taxes, or liens on the property before closing. This includes paying off mortgages, utility bills, property taxes, and vendor invoices.

- Coordinate with the buyer's legal and financial team to ensure that funds are transferred according to the agreed-upon payment terms.

Practical Example: A hotel owner in Dallas worked with their attorney to ensure all legal documents were accurately prepared and signed before the closing date. By proactively addressing liens and financial obligations, the owner avoided delays and completed the transaction on time.

Actionable Steps:

- Collaborate closely with legal and financial advisors to review and finalize all documents.

- Resolve any outstanding debts or liens before

the closing date.
- Ensure all documents are signed, notarized, and recorded as required by law.

Transitioning Ownership and Management

Transitioning ownership and management is a delicate process that requires careful planning to minimize disruption to operations, guests, and employees. A smooth handover helps ensure that the new owner can take over seamlessly and continue running the hotel effectively.

1. Preparing for the Handover:

- Create a transition plan that outlines the steps required to transfer ownership, including the transfer of licenses, permits, contracts, and vendor agreements.

- Organize and hand over all operational documents, such as employee records, maintenance schedules, service contracts, and vendor contact information.

2. Communicating with Staff and Guests:

- Inform employees about the transition and introduce the new owner to ensure a smooth changeover. Address any concerns they may have and provide clarity on how the change will affect them.

- Communicate with guests, especially those with upcoming reservations or events, to reassure them that service levels will remain consistent.

3. Training and Support:

- Offer to provide training and support to the new owner's management team to help them understand the hotel's operations, systems, and procedures. This can include introducing them to key staff members, vendors, and service providers.

Practical Example: The owner of a distressed hotel in Miami worked closely with the buyer to create a detailed transition plan that included a week-long training program for the new management team. This helped the buyer's team become familiar with the hotel's systems, leading to a smooth transfer of responsibilities.

Actionable Steps:

- Develop a detailed transition plan to guide the transfer of ownership and management.

- Communicate openly with staff and guests about the upcoming change.

- Offer training and support to help the new owner's team get up to speed.

Managing Post-Sale Tasks and Obligations

Even after the sale is complete, there are several post-sale tasks and obligations that must be managed to ensure a successful transition.

1. Finalizing Financial Settlements:

- Settle any outstanding financial obligations, such as paying brokers' fees, legal fees, and taxes. Ensure that all financial accounts related to the hotel are closed or transferred as required.

- Provide the buyer with any final financial documents, such as utility bills, vendor invoices, and payroll records.

2. Transfer of Licenses and Permits:

- Work with the buyer to transfer all necessary licenses and permits, such as liquor licenses, health department permits, and business licenses. This process can be time-consuming, so it's essential to start early.

3. Notification of Sale:

- Notify stakeholders, including vendors, suppliers, utility companies, and regulatory agencies, of the change in ownership. Update all contact information and ensure that all accounts and contracts are transferred to the new owner.

Practical Example: A hotel owner in Los Angeles worked with their legal team to ensure that all necessary permits were transferred to the new owner within 30 days of the sale. This proactive approach helped avoid operational disruptions and ensured the hotel remained compliant with regulations.

Actionable Steps:

- Finalize all financial settlements and provide the buyer with any necessary financial documents.
- Begin the process of transferring licenses and permits as early as possible.

- Notify all stakeholders of the change in ownership and update contact information.

Case Study: A Smooth Transition that Minimized Disruption

The Harborfront Hotel, a 120-room property located in a tourist destination, was sold to a private equity firm after experiencing financial difficulties. The previous owner was committed to ensuring a smooth transition, so they took the following steps:

- Developed a comprehensive transition plan that included a timeline for transferring ownership, training the new management team, and updating operational documents.

- Scheduled regular meetings with the buyer's team to address any questions or concerns and provide guidance on the hotel's operations.

- Communicated with employees and guests well in advance of the sale to minimize uncertainty and maintain morale.

Outcome: The transition was completed within 60 days, with minimal disruption to operations. The new management team was fully prepared to take over, and the hotel experienced a seamless handover, resulting in positive feedback from both employees and guests.

Key Takeaway: A well-organized transition plan, open communication, and collaboration between the buyer and seller can lead to a smooth transfer of ownership and minimize operational disruptions.

Communicating with Stakeholders About the Sale

Effective communication with stakeholders is essential for a successful transition. Properly informing employees, guests, vendors, and investors about the sale ensures that they remain informed and engaged throughout the process.

1. Communicating with Employees:

- Hold a staff meeting to announce the sale and introduce the new owner. Provide clarity on how the sale will impact their roles and address any concerns they may have.

- Offer reassurance about job security and emphasize the positive aspects of the transition, such as new opportunities for growth.

2. Communicating with Guests:

- Notify guests, especially those with upcoming reservations, about the change in ownership. Assure them that their bookings will be honored and that service quality will remain consistent.

- Update the hotel's website, social media profiles, and booking platforms to reflect the change in ownership.

3. Communicating with Vendors and Suppliers:

- Contact all vendors and suppliers to inform them of the sale and provide updated contact information for the new owner. Ensure that all existing contracts and agreements are transferred smoothly.

Practical Example: A hotel owner in Chicago sent personalized emails to key stakeholders, including employees, guests, and suppliers, informing them of the sale and introducing the new owner. This proactive approach helped maintain confidence and trust among stakeholders.

Actionable Steps:

- Develop a communication plan to inform employees, guests, vendors, and other stakeholders about the sale.

- Use multiple communication channels, such as emails, meetings, and announcements, to reach all stakeholders.

- Provide contact information for the new owner to facilitate a smooth transition.

Reflecting on Lessons Learned from the Sale Process

After closing the sale, it's essential to take time to reflect on the process and identify lessons learned. This reflection can provide valuable insights for future transactions and help you improve your approach to hotel sales.

1. Evaluate What Worked Well:

- Identify the strategies and tactics that were most effective in achieving a successful sale. This could include marketing efforts, negotiation techniques, or the transition plan.

2. Analyze Challenges and Obstacles:

- Reflect on any challenges encountered during the sale process, such as legal issues, financing hurdles, or buyer concerns. Consider how these challenges were addressed and what could be done differently in the future.

3. Document Key Takeaways:

- Create a summary of key lessons learned from the sale process. This can serve as a valuable resource for future transactions and help you refine your approach.

Practical Example: A hotel owner in New York documented the entire sale process, including challenges faced and strategies used. This documentation provided a blueprint for future sales and helped the owner improve their approach to selling distressed properties.

Actionable Steps:

- Set aside time after the sale to reflect on the process and identify lessons learned.

- Document your reflections and share them with your team or advisors.

- Use the insights gained to improve your approach to future hotel sales.

Closing the sale of a distressed hotel is a complex process that requires careful planning, effective communication, and diligent management of legal and financial details. By finalizing all documents, ensuring a smooth transition of ownership and management, and communicating effectively with stakeholders, hotel owners can complete the sale process successfully. Reflecting on the experience and learning from the challenges and successes encountered during the sale will provide valuable insights for future transactions, ensuring that each sale becomes a stepping stone toward greater expertise and success in the hospitality industry.

Lessons Learned from Hotel Dispositions

The process of selling a distressed hotel offers

valuable insights into the complexities of the hospitality market, revealing both the common pitfalls that can derail a sale and the strategies that can maximize value and lead to future opportunities. By reflecting on the lessons learned, hotel owners and investors can build a more successful exit strategy, enhance their investment skills, and prepare for the next opportunity in the hospitality market. This section delves into these lessons, providing practical examples, case studies, and actionable steps to guide future dispositions and investments.

Common Pitfalls to Avoid During the Sale Process

The sale process of a distressed hotel is often fraught with challenges that can result in financial losses, delays, or failed transactions if not properly managed. Recognizing and avoiding these common pitfalls is essential for a successful sale.

1. Inadequate Preparation:

- Failing to conduct thorough due diligence, organize financial records, or address legal issues before listing the hotel can lead to complications during the sale process. Buyers may be deterred by missing documentation, undisclosed liabilities, or operational inefficiencies, resulting in reduced offers or failed negotiations.

Practical Example: A hotel owner in Miami lost a potential buyer because the property's financial records were incomplete and disorganized, making it difficult for the buyer to assess the hotel's profitability. As a result, the deal fell through, and the owner had to spend additional time and resources preparing the property for another sale attempt.

2. Overvaluing the Property:

- Overestimating the hotel's value can result in unrealistic expectations, deterring potential buyers and prolonging the sale process. It's crucial to conduct an accurate valuation based on market conditions, the hotel's financial performance, and comparable sales.

- Practical Example: An owner in Los Angeles set an asking price significantly above market value, believing that the hotel's location would attract a premium. However, buyers perceived the price as unreasonable, and the hotel remained on the market for over a year, ultimately selling for 20% less than the original asking price.

3. Poor Communication with Stakeholders:

- Ineffective communication with employees, vendors, guests, and buyers can create uncertainty and erode trust. This can lead to operational disruptions, reduced employee morale, and potential deal collapses.

- Practical Example: A hotel sale in Chicago was delayed because the owner failed to communicate the sale process to key stakeholders, leading to confusion and resistance from staff and suppliers, which complicated negotiations with the buyer.

Actionable Steps:

- Conduct thorough due diligence and prepare all necessary documentation before listing the hotel.

- Obtain a professional appraisal to set a realistic asking price based on market trends and comparable sales.

- Maintain open and transparent communication with all stakeholders throughout the sale process.

Strategies for Maximizing Sale Value

To achieve the highest possible sale price for a distressed hotel, owners must implement strategies that enhance the property's appeal and value. These strategies can significantly impact buyer perceptions and lead to more favorable outcomes.

1. Enhance Curb Appeal and Marketability:

- Simple upgrades, such as fresh paint, landscaping, and lobby renovations, can make a significant difference in a buyer's perception of the hotel's value. Enhancing curb appeal can lead to higher offers and a quicker sale.

- Practical Example: A distressed hotel in Orlando invested $50,000 in exterior improvements, including new signage, landscaping, and lighting. The improvements attracted more interest from buyers, resulting in a sale that was $300,000 above the initial offers.

2. Provide Detailed Financial Projections:

- Buyers want to understand the potential return on investment. Providing detailed financial projections, including projected occupancy rates, average daily rates (ADR), and revenue growth, can demonstrate the hotel's potential profitability.

- Practical Example: A hotel owner in Dallas presented a comprehensive financial forecast showing how a planned renovation could increase RevPAR by 25% within two years. This data convinced the buyer to pay a premium price for the property.

3. Create a Competitive Bidding Environment:

- Attract multiple buyers by marketing the hotel through various channels and emphasizing its unique selling points. A competitive bidding environment often leads to higher offers and better terms.

- Practical Example: An owner in New York created a sense of urgency by setting a deadline for offers and promoting the property through multiple real estate platforms. The resulting competition among buyers led to a final sale price 15% above the initial asking price.

Actionable Steps:

- Invest in cost-effective improvements to enhance the hotel's appearance and marketability.

- Prepare detailed financial projections to demonstrate the property's potential for growth and profitability.

- Use targeted marketing strategies to create a competitive bidding environment.

Building a Successful Exit Strategy

A successful exit strategy involves planning for the sale well in advance and aligning it with your financial goals and market conditions. A well-executed exit strategy ensures a smoother sale process and maximizes financial returns.

1. Define Your Exit Goals:

- Clearly outline your objectives for the sale, such as achieving a specific sale price, reducing debt, or freeing up capital for other investments. These goals will guide your decision-making throughout the sale process.

- Practical Example: A hotel owner in Atlanta set a clear goal to sell the property within 12 months to reinvest in a new development project. This goal motivated the owner to make strategic improvements and price the hotel competitively, resulting in a timely and profitable sale.

2. Monitor Market Trends:

- Stay informed about market trends, interest rates, and buyer demand in the hospitality industry. Timing your sale to coincide with favorable market conditions can significantly impact the outcome.

- Practical Example: An owner in Las Vegas sold their hotel just as the market rebounded from a downturn, resulting in multiple offers and a sale price that exceeded expectations.

3. Prepare for Different Scenarios:

- Be prepared to adjust your exit strategy if market conditions change or if unexpected challenges arise. Flexibility is essential for navigating the complexities of a distressed hotel sale.

- Practical Example: A hotel owner in Denver originally planned to hold the property for another year but decided to sell early after receiving an unsolicited offer from a private equity firm. This adaptability allowed the owner to capitalize on a favorable opportunity.

Actionable Steps:

- Define your exit goals and create a timeline for

achieving them.

- Regularly monitor market trends to identify the optimal time to sell.

- Be flexible and open to adjusting your strategy as needed.

Case Study: How a Hotel Sale Led to Future Investment Opportunities

The Seaside Resort, a distressed hotel located in a coastal town, was sold to a savvy investor who recognized the property's potential for turnaround. The seller had initially purchased the hotel at a significant discount during a market downturn but decided to sell after improving its financial performance and enhancing its marketability.

Key Steps Taken:

- The seller invested in strategic renovations, including updating guest rooms and adding new amenities, which increased occupancy rates and revenue.

- By effectively marketing the hotel's turnaround story, the seller attracted multiple buyers and ultimately secured a sale price that was double the original purchase price.

- The proceeds from the sale were reinvested in a new hospitality venture, allowing the seller to acquire a larger, more profitable hotel.

Outcome: The successful sale of the Seaside Resort provided the seller with the capital and confidence to pursue more ambitious hotel investments. The experience gained from this transaction enabled the seller to identify and capitalize on future opportunities in the hospitality market.

Key Takeaway: A successful hotel sale can serve as a springboard for future investment opportunities, providing both the financial resources and experience needed to pursue more significant ventures.
Developing Skills for Future Hotel Investments

The skills developed during a hotel sale can be invaluable for future investments. These skills include financial analysis, negotiation, marketing, and project management.

1. Financial Analysis and Valuation:

- Understanding how to analyze financial statements, assess property values, and forecast revenue potential is essential for making informed investment decisions.

- Practical Example: A hotel investor in Boston used their financial analysis skills to identify a distressed property with strong turnaround potential. After purchasing the hotel and implementing improvements, they sold it for a substantial profit.

2. Negotiation and Deal-Making:

- Effective negotiation skills are critical for

securing favorable sale terms and conditions. These skills are equally important when acquiring new properties or negotiating with lenders, vendors, and partners.

- Practical Example: An investor who successfully negotiated favorable financing terms for a hotel acquisition in San Francisco was able to maximize their return on investment upon resale.

3. Marketing and Branding:

- Developing the ability to market and position a hotel effectively can enhance its perceived value and attract more buyers or guests. These skills are crucial for both selling and operating hotels.

- Practical Example: A hotel owner in Austin who used creative marketing strategies to sell their property at a premium later applied these skills to build a successful brand for their next hotel investment.

Actionable Steps:

- Invest time in learning financial analysis, valuation, and negotiation techniques.

- Attend industry seminars, workshops, and networking events to develop your skills and expand your knowledge.

- Apply the lessons learned from previous sales

to future hotel investments.

Preparing for the Next Opportunity in the Hospitality Market

To succeed in future hotel investments, it's essential to stay informed about market trends, emerging technologies, and shifts in consumer preferences. Being prepared for the next opportunity involves continuous learning, networking, and adapting to changes in the industry.

1. Stay Informed:

- Keep up with industry news, market reports, and hospitality trends to identify potential investment opportunities early.

- Practical Example: An investor who closely monitored the rise of experiential travel was able to acquire and transform a boutique hotel into a unique experience-focused property, attracting a new wave of guests.

2. Build Relationships:

- Develop a network of industry professionals, including brokers, investors, operators, and lenders. These relationships can provide valuable insights and access to off-market deals.

- Practical Example: A hotel investor in Chicago leveraged their network to gain access to a distressed property before it was publicly listed, allowing them to negotiate favorable purchase terms.

3. Continuously Improve Your Skills:

- Attend industry conferences, take online courses, and participate in workshops to stay ahead of the curve and improve your investment skills.

- Practical Example: A hotel owner who participated in a financial modeling course gained a deeper understanding of hotel valuation, which enabled them to make more informed investment decisions.

Actionable Steps:

- Regularly read industry publications and reports to stay informed about market trends.

- Attend networking events and build relationships with industry professionals.

- Continuously invest in your education and skills to prepare for future opportunities.

The process of selling a distressed hotel provides valuable lessons that can guide future investment decisions. By avoiding common pitfalls, implementing strategies to maximize sale value, building a successful exit strategy, and developing skills for future investments, hotel owners and investors can position themselves for long-term success in the hospitality market. Each sale offers an opportunity to learn, grow, and prepare for the next investment, turning challenges into stepping stones toward greater profitability and achievement in the hospitality industry.

Chapter 8: Bankruptcy for Distressed Hotels

Navigating bankruptcy proceedings can be one of the most daunting challenges for distressed hotels, yet it also presents an opportunity for financial renewal and strategic reinvention. This chapter delves into the complexities of the bankruptcy process, offering insights into how hotel owners can emerge from it stronger and more financially stable. Understanding the different types of bankruptcy, such as Chapter 11 and Chapter 7, is crucial, as each path carries its own set of implications for hotel operations, finances, and future prospects. By examining the impact of bankruptcy on day-to-day operations and evaluating potential alternatives like restructuring or workouts, hotel owners can make informed decisions about their next steps. Through real-world examples, such as a hotel that successfully navigated Chapter 11, this chapter provides a comprehensive look at the practical and legal considerations involved in choosing the right bankruptcy path.

Preparation is key to managing bankruptcy proceedings effectively, and this chapter outlines the steps involved in engaging legal and financial advisors, filing the necessary paperwork, and communicating with creditors and stakeholders. Protecting hotel assets and maintaining operations during this period is critical, and we'll examine how a hotel owner successfully managed the filing process while minimizing disruptions. The chapter also addresses the unique challenges of operating a hotel during bankruptcy, focusing on maintaining guest satisfaction, managing cash flow, and working with bankruptcy trustees and court officials. Through case studies and actionable strategies, we'll explore how hotels can implement cost-saving measures without compromising quality and keep employees motivated despite financial uncertainties.

Developing a comprehensive reorganization plan is essential for hotels seeking to emerge from bankruptcy on solid footing. This chapter provides guidance on creating a detailed financial and operational restructuring plan, gaining creditor approval, and executing necessary changes. By sharing the journey of a hotel that successfully reorganized, we highlight the importance of tracking progress and making adjustments as needed to ensure long-term success. We'll also explore the steps required to rebuild credit, rebrand the hotel, and establish sustainable growth strategies once bankruptcy proceedings are complete.

Emerging from bankruptcy is just the beginning of a hotel's journey toward financial recovery. This chapter outlines how hotels can rebuild credit, rebrand, and reposition themselves in the market to regain competitiveness. By learning from a case study of a hotel that rebounded successfully after bankruptcy, readers will gain insights into avoiding common post-bankruptcy pitfalls and preparing for future challenges. Finally, the chapter emphasizes the importance of proactive financial management to prevent future financial distress, with practical advice on building cash reserves, implementing risk management practices, and maintaining profitability.

Through the story of a hotel that achieved financial resilience, readers will learn valuable strategies for maintaining stability and avoiding the mistakes that led to bankruptcy in the first place.

Ultimately, this chapter aims to provide hotel owners with a comprehensive understanding of the bankruptcy process, equipping them with the knowledge and tools needed to navigate these challenging circumstances and emerge stronger, more resilient, and better prepared for future success.

Understanding the Different Types of Bankruptcy

When a hotel faces severe financial distress, bankruptcy can serve as a potential pathway to resolve overwhelming debts and provide a chance to reorganize or liquidate the business. Understanding the differences between Chapter 11 and Chapter 7 bankruptcy, their impact on hotel operations, and the alternatives available is crucial for hotel owners seeking the best solution for their situation. In this section, we'll provide an in-depth analysis of these bankruptcy types, explore their implications, examine a case study of a hotel that successfully emerged from Chapter 11, and outline practical steps for choosing the right bankruptcy path.

Chapter 11 vs. Chapter 7 Bankruptcy Explained

Chapter 11 Bankruptcy: Reorganization Chapter 11 bankruptcy is often referred to as "reorganization bankruptcy." It allows a hotel to remain operational while restructuring its debts, giving the business an opportunity to negotiate new terms with creditors and implement a plan to restore profitability.

Key Features of Chapter 11:

- Operational Continuity: The hotel can continue to operate while working through its financial difficulties. This means the business retains control over day-to-day operations, albeit with oversight from the bankruptcy court.

- Debt Restructuring: Chapter 11 provides the chance to renegotiate debt terms, such as lowering interest rates, extending repayment periods, or reducing the total amount owed.

- Reorganization Plan: The hotel owner must develop a reorganization plan detailing how debts will be repaid, restructured, or discharged. This plan requires approval from creditors and the bankruptcy court.

Pros of Chapter 11:

- Allows the hotel to maintain operations and generate revenue during bankruptcy.

- Provides time to implement operational and financial improvements.

- Offers flexibility in restructuring debt obligations.

Cons of Chapter 11:

- The process can be lengthy, complex, and expensive.

- Requires significant oversight and reporting to the bankruptcy court.

Chapter 7 Bankruptcy: Liquidation Chapter 7 bankruptcy is a liquidation process where the hotel's assets are sold to repay creditors. In most cases, the business ceases operations, and any remaining debts are discharged.

Key Features of Chapter 7:

- Asset Liquidation: A trustee is appointed to oversee the sale of the hotel's assets, such as furniture, equipment, and property, to repay creditors.

- Debt Discharge: Once assets are liquidated, any remaining debts are typically discharged, relieving the owner of further obligations.

Pros of Chapter 7:

- Provides a clean break from unmanageable debts.

- The process is usually faster than Chapter 11.

Cons of Chapter 7:

- The hotel ceases operations, and the business is

dissolved.

- Owners lose control over the assets and the liquidation process.

Practical Example: A 200-room hotel in New York faced severe financial challenges due to declining occupancy rates and rising debt. The owner opted for Chapter 11 bankruptcy, allowing the hotel to continue operating while renegotiating debt with creditors. Over two years, the hotel successfully restructured its debt and emerged from bankruptcy, ultimately improving its profitability.

The Impact of Bankruptcy on Hotel Operations

Declaring bankruptcy has significant implications for hotel operations, regardless of whether the process follows Chapter 11 or Chapter 7.

1. Impact on Employees:

- Chapter 11 allows the hotel to retain employees, but there may be changes in staffing levels, wages, or benefits to reduce costs. Employee morale may be affected, so communication is vital.

- In Chapter 7, employees are often laid off as the hotel ceases operations.

2. Impact on Guest Services:

- Maintaining guest satisfaction is a challenge

during Chapter 11 bankruptcy. It's essential to ensure that service quality remains consistent to retain guests and revenue.

- In Chapter 7, operations halt, and all guest reservations are canceled.

3. Impact on Vendor and Supplier Relationships:

- During Chapter 11, the hotel must negotiate with vendors and suppliers to continue providing goods and services. Some may require upfront payments or renegotiated terms.

- In Chapter 7, contracts with suppliers are terminated, and any outstanding invoices are managed by the appointed trustee.

Practical Example: A hotel undergoing Chapter 11 bankruptcy in Los Angeles implemented a cost-saving initiative by renegotiating contracts with suppliers and reducing non-essential expenses. This allowed the hotel to maintain service quality and avoid significant disruptions to operations during the bankruptcy process.

Evaluating Alternatives to Bankruptcy (e.g., Restructuring, Workouts)

Before resorting to bankruptcy, distressed hotels should explore alternative solutions that might offer a less drastic resolution to financial challenges.

1. Debt Restructuring:

- Debt restructuring involves negotiating new terms with creditors, such as extending repayment periods, lowering interest rates, or reducing the total debt amount. This can provide immediate relief without the need for bankruptcy.

- Practical Example: A boutique hotel in Miami successfully restructured its debt by negotiating with its primary lender, reducing monthly payments by 30% and avoiding bankruptcy.

2. Workouts:

- A workout is a negotiated agreement between the hotel and its creditors to modify debt terms. This often involves the assistance of financial advisors or consultants who can help reach a mutually beneficial arrangement.

- Practical Example: A hotel in Chicago entered into a workout agreement with its creditors, allowing it to repay debt over a more extended period, maintain operations, and avoid bankruptcy.

3. Asset Sales or Refinancing:

- Selling non-core assets or refinancing existing loans can provide the cash flow needed to address financial distress. This strategy can help avoid bankruptcy by injecting liquidity into the business.

- Practical Example: A hotel owner in Las Vegas sold an adjacent parking lot to generate funds for debt repayment, allowing the hotel to continue operations without declaring bankruptcy.

Actionable Steps:

- Consult with financial advisors to assess the feasibility of debt restructuring, workouts, or asset sales.

- Engage with creditors early to negotiate terms and explore alternatives to bankruptcy.

- Evaluate the potential impact of each option on the hotel's operations, finances, and long-term viability.

Case Study: A Hotel That Emerged from Chapter 11 Successfully

The Riverside Resort, a 300-room hotel located in a popular tourist destination, faced mounting debt and declining revenues due to market changes and increased competition. The owner chose to file for Chapter 11 bankruptcy, allowing the hotel to continue operating while developing a reorganization plan.

Key Steps Taken:

- Engaged a team of legal and financial advisors to develop a comprehensive reorganization plan, which included cost-cutting measures,

renegotiating vendor contracts, and implementing marketing initiatives to increase occupancy rates.
- Presented the plan to creditors and obtained approval for reduced debt payments over five years.

- Improved operational efficiency by implementing energy-saving measures and streamlining the hotel's workforce.

Outcome: The Riverside Resort successfully emerged from Chapter 11 bankruptcy after two years, with a 25% reduction in debt and a 15% increase in occupancy rates. The hotel was able to regain profitability, and the owner retained control of the property.

Key Takeaway: By proactively developing a reorganization plan, engaging with creditors, and maintaining operational efficiency, the Riverside Resort emerged from Chapter 11 stronger and more financially stable.

Practical Steps for Choosing the Right Bankruptcy Path

- Choosing between Chapter 11, Chapter 7, or an alternative solution requires careful consideration of the hotel's financial situation, long-term goals, and potential impact on operations.

- Assess Financial Viability: Evaluate whether the hotel has the potential to recover with restructuring or whether liquidation is the only viable option.

- Engage Professional Advisors: Consult with legal and financial experts who specialize in hospitality bankruptcy to assess your options and develop a plan.

- Consider Operational Impact: Determine the impact of each option on employees, guests, and daily operations. Chapter 11 may be more suitable if you want to maintain operations, while Chapter 7 may be necessary if the hotel is beyond recovery.

- Evaluate Long-Term Goals: Consider how each option aligns with your long-term goals, such as retaining ownership, minimizing debt, or transitioning to a new venture.

Practical Example: A hotel owner in San Diego consulted with a bankruptcy attorney and financial advisor to assess the hotel's financial health and explore options. After evaluating the hotel's cash flow, debt obligations, and market conditions, the owner chose Chapter 11, allowing the hotel to restructure debt and eventually regain profitability.

Understanding the Legal Implications of Bankruptcy

Filing for bankruptcy has significant legal implications, and understanding these is essential for navigating the process effectively.

- Automatic Stay: Filing for bankruptcy initiates an automatic stay, which halts creditor actions, such as foreclosure or lawsuits, providing temporary relief while the bankruptcy process unfolds.

- Creditor Involvement: Creditors have the right to participate in the bankruptcy process, and their approval is often required for the reorganization plan (in Chapter 11).

- Legal Obligations: Hotel owners must adhere to strict reporting requirements, court oversight, and compliance with bankruptcy laws. Failing to comply can result in penalties or dismissal of the case.

Practical Example: A hotel owner in Boston who filed for Chapter 11 bankruptcy was required to submit monthly operating reports and attend court hearings, ensuring transparency and compliance with legal obligations throughout the process.

Actionable Steps:

- Hire an experienced bankruptcy attorney to guide you through the legal process.

- Understand the reporting requirements, court involvement, and legal obligations associated with bankruptcy.

- Communicate regularly with creditors and the bankruptcy court to ensure compliance.

Understanding the different types of bankruptcy and their implications is crucial for distressed hotel owners seeking to navigate financial challenges effectively. By evaluating the pros and cons of Chapter 11 and Chapter 7, exploring alternatives such as restructuring and workouts, and considering the impact on operations, owners can make informed decisions about the best path forward. Engaging professional advisors, developing a comprehensive plan, and understanding the legal implications will help hotel owners emerge from bankruptcy stronger and more financially stable, positioning them for future success in the hospitality industry.

Preparing for Bankruptcy Proceedings

Preparing for bankruptcy proceedings is a crucial step that can determine the success of a distressed hotel's journey through financial hardship. Proper preparation involves engaging the right legal and financial advisors, ensuring all necessary paperwork is in order, communicating effectively with creditors and stakeholders, and protecting assets while maintaining guest service and operations. In this section, we will delve into these aspects, provide practical examples, and share a case study of a hotel owner who effectively managed the bankruptcy filing process.

Engaging Legal and Financial Advisors

Hiring experienced legal and financial advisors is the foundation of any successful bankruptcy process. These experts will guide you through the complexities of bankruptcy laws, help protect your interests, and develop strategies for a successful reorganization or liquidation.

1. The Role of a Bankruptcy Attorney:

- A bankruptcy attorney is essential for navigating the legal aspects of the process, ensuring compliance with bankruptcy laws, and representing your hotel in court. They will help you decide which type of bankruptcy to file (Chapter 11 or Chapter 7) and guide you through every step of the process.

- Practical Example: A hotel owner in Las Vegas hired a bankruptcy attorney who specialized in the hospitality industry. The attorney helped the owner understand the implications of Chapter 11 and assisted in drafting the reorganization plan, which ultimately enabled the hotel to emerge from bankruptcy successfully.

2. Engaging Financial Advisors:

- Financial advisors can assess your hotel's financial health, develop a plan to manage debts, and create strategies for restructuring. They will assist in preparing financial statements, forecasts, and cash flow analyses that are critical for the bankruptcy process.

- Practical Example: A hotel in Miami engaged a financial consultant to create a detailed cash flow analysis, which was instrumental in demonstrating to creditors that the hotel could continue operating profitably under a reorganization plan.

Actionable Steps:

- Research and select an attorney and financial advisor with experience in hospitality bankruptcies.

- Arrange an initial consultation to discuss your situation, objectives, and options.

- Ensure that your advisors work together to create a cohesive strategy for navigating bankruptcy proceedings.

Filing the Necessary Paperwork and Documentation

Bankruptcy involves a significant amount of paperwork, and filing accurate, comprehensive documents is crucial for avoiding delays, penalties, or even dismissal of your case.

1. Preparing Financial Documents:

- Gather all financial records, including profit and loss statements, balance sheets, tax returns, bank statements, and accounts payable/receivable reports. This information will be used to prepare the bankruptcy petition and present a clear picture of your hotel's financial status.

- Practical Example: A hotel owner in Atlanta compiled three years of financial records, including monthly cash flow statements and annual tax returns, to support their Chapter 11 bankruptcy petition. This thorough documentation helped build credibility with the bankruptcy court and creditors.

2. Completing the Bankruptcy Petition:

- The bankruptcy petition is a detailed legal document that includes information about the hotel's assets, liabilities, income, expenses, and creditor details. It's essential to work closely with your attorney to ensure that this document is accurate and complete.

- Practical Example: A hotel owner in Chicago worked with their attorney to prepare a bankruptcy petition that outlined all debts, including secured loans, vendor invoices, and outstanding taxes. This transparency facilitated smoother interactions with the bankruptcy court.

Actionable Steps:

- Collect and organize all financial records well in advance of filing.

- Work with your advisors to ensure the bankruptcy petition is accurate and complete.

- Submit all required paperwork promptly to avoid delays in the bankruptcy process.

Communicating with Creditors and Stakeholders

Effective communication with creditors, employees, guests, and other stakeholders is essential during bankruptcy proceedings to maintain relationships, manage expectations, and ensure operational continuity.

1. Engaging with Creditors:

- Proactive communication with creditors can foster goodwill and cooperation, which is vital when negotiating payment terms or seeking approval for a reorganization plan. Keeping creditors informed about your intentions and progress demonstrates transparency and builds trust.

- Practical Example: A hotel in New York maintained regular communication with its largest creditor, providing monthly financial updates and progress reports. This transparency helped the creditor understand the hotel's challenges and ultimately led to more favorable repayment terms.

2. Communicating with Employees and Guests:

- Employees and guests may become concerned upon learning about bankruptcy proceedings, fearing job loss or service disruptions. It's crucial to reassure employees about job security and explain how the bankruptcy will affect daily operations.

- Practical Example: A hotel owner in Los Angeles held an all-staff meeting to explain the Chapter 11 bankruptcy filing and assured employees that the hotel would continue operating. This approach helped maintain employee morale and prevented turnover.

Actionable Steps:

- Create a communication plan that includes regular updates to creditors, employees, and guests.

- Be transparent and honest about the bankruptcy process and its potential impact on stakeholders.

- Provide employees with opportunities to ask questions and express concerns.

Case Study: How a Hotel Owner Managed the Bankruptcy Filing Process

The Palm Coast Resort, a 150-room beachfront hotel in Florida, faced financial difficulties due to declining tourism and rising operational costs. The owner decided to file for Chapter 11 bankruptcy to restructure the hotel's debts and regain profitability.

Key Actions Taken:

- Engaged a bankruptcy attorney and financial advisor who specialized in the hospitality industry. These experts helped the owner develop a reorganization plan that included cost-cutting measures, renegotiated contracts with suppliers, and a marketing strategy to attract more guests.

- Compiled comprehensive financial records, including detailed profit and loss statements, cash flow projections, and a list of all creditors. The owner worked closely with the attorney to ensure that the bankruptcy petition was complete and accurate.

- Communicated with creditors, employees, and stakeholders throughout the process, explaining the bankruptcy's purpose and how it would allow the hotel to continue operating and eventually return to profitability.

Outcome: By preparing thoroughly and engaging experienced advisors, the Palm Coast Resort emerged from bankruptcy within 18 months. The hotel's occupancy rates increased by 20%, and the owner successfully renegotiated debt terms, allowing the business to regain financial stability.

Key Takeaway: Engaging the right advisors, preparing accurate documentation, and communicating effectively with stakeholders are critical factors in successfully navigating the bankruptcy process. Protecting Hotel Assets During Bankruptcy

One of the most significant concerns during bankruptcy is protecting the hotel's assets from seizure or liquidation. This requires strategic planning and an understanding of the legal protections available.

1. Automatic Stay Protection:

- Filing for bankruptcy triggers an automatic stay, which temporarily prevents creditors from taking legal action against the hotel or seizing its assets. This gives the hotel time to reorganize and develop a plan to repay debts.

- Practical Example: A hotel owner in Houston used the automatic stay to halt foreclosure proceedings on the property, allowing time to negotiate with the lender and develop a reorganization plan.

2. Asset Valuation and Inventory:

- Conduct a detailed inventory and valuation of all hotel assets, such as furnishings, equipment, and property. This information will be used during bankruptcy proceedings to determine asset values and repayment plans.

- Practical Example: A hotel in San Francisco completed an inventory of all assets, which helped the owner demonstrate to the bankruptcy court that selling certain non-essential items could generate cash flow to fund operations during the bankruptcy process.

Actionable Steps:

- Take advantage of the automatic stay to protect your hotel's assets.

- Conduct a thorough inventory and valuation of assets to support your reorganization plan.

- Work with your advisors to develop strategies for asset protection throughout the bankruptcy process.

Tips for Maintaining Guest Service and Operations

Maintaining high levels of guest service and operational efficiency during bankruptcy is crucial for generating revenue and preserving the hotel's reputation.

1. Focus on Core Services:

- Concentrate on delivering the essential services that guests expect, such as clean rooms, prompt service, and well-maintained facilities. Reduce non-essential amenities to cut costs without compromising guest satisfaction.

- Practical Example: A hotel in Chicago undergoing Chapter 11 bankruptcy focused on maintaining its core services, such as housekeeping and front desk operations, while temporarily suspending non-essential amenities like spa services. This helped the hotel maintain guest satisfaction despite financial challenges.

2. Motivate and Support Employees:

- Employee morale is vital to maintaining service

quality. Keep staff informed about the bankruptcy process and involve them in finding ways to reduce costs and improve efficiency.

- Practical Example: A hotel in Denver implemented an employee incentive program that rewarded staff for suggesting cost-saving measures, which helped reduce expenses and maintain morale during bankruptcy.

Actionable Steps:

- Prioritize essential services that contribute to guest satisfaction.

- Communicate with employees about the bankruptcy process and encourage their involvement in cost-saving initiatives.

- Monitor guest feedback to identify areas for improvement and maintain service quality.

Preparing for bankruptcy proceedings requires meticulous planning, effective communication, and the support of experienced advisors. By engaging legal and financial experts, filing the necessary paperwork, communicating transparently with stakeholders, and protecting hotel assets, owners can navigate the bankruptcy process more effectively. Additionally, maintaining guest service and operational efficiency during bankruptcy can help preserve the hotel's reputation and improve the chances of emerging from bankruptcy stronger and more financially stable. Through careful preparation and strategic action, distressed hotel owners can turn bankruptcy into an opportunity for recovery and long-term success.

Operating a Hotel During Bankruptcy

Operating a hotel during bankruptcy presents unique challenges, requiring careful management to maintain guest satisfaction, control expenses, and navigate the legal requirements of bankruptcy proceedings. While the situation may seem daunting, maintaining operations and providing high-quality service is crucial to generating revenue and improving the likelihood of a successful financial turnaround. This section explores how to manage these aspects, with practical examples, a case study, and actionable steps to guide hotel owners through this challenging period. Maintaining Guest Satisfaction and Service Quality

Maintaining guest satisfaction and service quality is essential for generating revenue and preserving the hotel's reputation, even during bankruptcy. Guests are often unaware of the hotel's financial difficulties, and any decline in service quality could lead to negative reviews, decreased bookings, and long-term damage to the brand.

1. Prioritize Core Services:

- Focus on delivering the fundamental services that guests expect, such as clean and comfortable rooms, prompt check-in/check-out processes, and responsive customer service. Temporarily reduce or eliminate non-essential amenities that do not significantly impact the guest experience.

- Practical Example: A distressed hotel in Miami continued to prioritize housekeeping, front desk operations, and room service, ensuring that guests received a high-quality experience despite financial constraints. By maintaining these core services, the hotel retained loyal customers and minimized the impact of bankruptcy on guest satisfaction.

2. Communicate with Guests:

- Transparency with guests can build trust and understanding. While it's not necessary to disclose bankruptcy details, reassure guests that their experience remains a top priority. Respond to any concerns promptly and professionally.

- Practical Example: A hotel in Las Vegas provided regular updates to guests about ongoing renovations and service improvements, assuring them that the changes were part of efforts to enhance their stay.

Actionable Steps:

- Identify and prioritize core services that contribute most to guest satisfaction.

- Train staff to focus on delivering exceptional service in these key areas.

- Communicate regularly with guests, addressing any concerns or service disruptions proactively.

Managing Cash Flow and Expenses During Bankruptcy

Maintaining positive cash flow and reducing expenses are critical for sustaining operations during bankruptcy. Effective financial management ensures that the hotel can cover essential expenses, such as payroll, utilities, and supplier payments, while navigating the bankruptcy process.

1. Monitor Cash Flow Closely:

- Regularly track cash inflows and outflows to understand the hotel's financial position and identify potential shortfalls. Implement a cash flow forecast to project future revenues and expenses, allowing you to make informed decisions about budgeting and cost control.

- Practical Example: A hotel in New York implemented a weekly cash flow analysis, which helped the owner identify periods of low cash availability and adjust spending accordingly, ensuring that essential expenses were covered.

2. Negotiate with Vendors and Suppliers:

- Reach out to vendors and suppliers to negotiate more favorable payment terms, discounts, or deferred payments. Many suppliers are willing to accommodate temporary adjustments to maintain a long-term business relationship.

- Practical Example: A hotel in Los Angeles

successfully negotiated a 30-day extension on payments to its food and beverage supplier, easing cash flow pressures during a period of low occupancy.

Actionable Steps:

- Create a detailed cash flow forecast to monitor and project cash availability.

- Identify non-essential expenses that can be reduced or eliminated.

- Contact vendors and suppliers to negotiate payment terms and reduce immediate financial obligations.

Working with Bankruptcy Trustees and Court Officials

During bankruptcy proceedings, hotels are required to work closely with bankruptcy trustees and court officials, who oversee the process and ensure compliance with legal requirements. Effective communication and cooperation with these parties can help ensure a smoother process and minimize disruptions to operations.

1. Understand the Role of the Bankruptcy Trustee:

- The bankruptcy trustee's role is to protect the interests of creditors and ensure that the hotel adheres to bankruptcy laws. They may request financial documents, monitor operations, and review the reorganization plan (in Chapter 11 cases).

- Practical Example: A hotel in Atlanta maintained open communication with the bankruptcy trustee, providing monthly financial reports and updates on operational changes. This transparency helped build trust and facilitated a more efficient bankruptcy process.

2. Comply with Reporting Requirements:

- Bankruptcy proceedings require regular reporting, such as submitting monthly operating reports, financial statements, and updates on the hotel's cash flow and expenses. Adhering to these requirements is essential for avoiding legal complications or delays.

- Practical Example: A hotel in Chicago submitted all required documentation on time, which helped expedite the bankruptcy process and avoid court-imposed penalties.

Actionable Steps:

- Familiarize yourself with the role and responsibilities of the bankruptcy trustee.

- Maintain organized financial records and submit reports as required.

- Communicate regularly with the trustee and court officials, addressing any concerns or questions promptly.

Case Study: How a Hotel Maintained Operations and Guest Satisfaction

The Crescent Bay Inn, a 120-room hotel located in a popular coastal destination, faced severe financial challenges due to a decline in tourism and rising operational costs. The owner filed for Chapter 11 bankruptcy to restructure debts while continuing operations.

Key Actions Taken:

- The hotel owner focused on maintaining guest satisfaction by ensuring that core services, such as housekeeping, front desk operations, and dining, remained unaffected. This helped retain repeat guests and maintain occupancy rates.

- The owner implemented a cost-saving plan that included negotiating with suppliers, reducing energy consumption, and temporarily closing low-demand amenities, such as the hotel spa.

- The hotel provided ongoing training to staff, emphasizing the importance of excellent customer service despite financial challenges. This kept employees motivated and ensured consistent service quality.

Outcome: Over 18 months, the Crescent Bay Inn successfully emerged from bankruptcy with improved cash flow and increased occupancy rates. Guest satisfaction remained high, resulting in positive online reviews and an influx of new bookings once the hotel's financial position stabilized.

Key Takeaway: By prioritizing core services, managing expenses effectively, and keeping employees motivated, the Crescent Bay Inn maintained operations and guest satisfaction throughout the bankruptcy process.

Implementing Cost-Saving Measures Without Compromising Quality

Implementing cost-saving measures is essential for managing expenses during bankruptcy, but it's important to do so in a way that doesn't compromise the guest experience or overall service quality.

1. Optimize Energy Usage:

- Implement energy-saving practices, such as using energy-efficient lighting, adjusting thermostat settings, and installing motion sensors to reduce electricity costs. These measures can lead to significant savings without affecting guest comfort.

- Practical Example: A hotel in San Francisco installed energy-efficient LED lighting throughout the property, resulting in a 20% reduction in electricity costs without affecting service quality.

2. Streamline Staffing Levels:

- Evaluate staffing levels to identify areas where

schedules can be adjusted based on occupancy rates. Cross-train employees to handle multiple roles, reducing the need for additional staff during low-demand periods.

- Practical Example: A hotel in Denver cross-trained front desk staff to assist with housekeeping duties during off-peak hours, reducing labor costs while maintaining service quality.

3. Renegotiate Contracts and Supplier Agreements:

- Review existing contracts with suppliers and service providers to identify opportunities for cost savings. Negotiate discounts, bulk purchase rates, or deferred payment options to reduce expenses.

- Practical Example: A hotel in Orlando negotiated a 15% discount on laundry services by agreeing to a long-term contract, reducing operational costs while maintaining service standards.

Actionable Steps:

- Implement energy-saving practices to reduce utility expenses.

- Cross-train employees to handle multiple roles and optimize staffing levels.

- Review and renegotiate contracts with suppliers to obtain more favorable terms.

Strategies for Keeping Employees Motivated During Bankruptcy

Maintaining employee morale is critical for delivering high-quality service during bankruptcy. Engaged and motivated employees are more likely to provide excellent service, contributing to positive guest experiences and the hotel's long-term recovery.

1. Communicate Openly and Honestly:

- Keep employees informed about the bankruptcy process, the hotel's goals, and the steps being taken to address financial challenges. Transparent communication helps reduce uncertainty and builds trust.

- Practical Example: A hotel owner in Dallas held regular staff meetings to update employees on the bankruptcy process, address concerns, and provide reassurance about job security. This transparency helped maintain morale and minimize turnover.

2. Recognize and Reward Employee Efforts:

- Acknowledge and reward employees for their hard work and dedication, even if financial constraints limit monetary rewards. Recognition programs, certificates of appreciation, or additional time off can boost morale.

- Practical Example: A hotel in Boston

implemented an employee recognition program that rewarded staff with gift cards for going above and beyond in providing exceptional service during the bankruptcy process.

3. Involve Employees in Cost-Saving Initiatives:

- Encourage employees to contribute ideas for cost-saving measures and efficiency improvements. Involving staff in decision-making gives them a sense of ownership and investment in the hotel's success.

- Practical Example: A hotel in Seattle created a "cost-saving challenge," encouraging employees to submit suggestions for reducing expenses. The winning idea resulted in a 10% reduction in supply costs.

Actionable Steps:

- Communicate regularly with employees about the bankruptcy process and provide updates.
- Recognize and reward employees for their contributions and dedication.

- Involve employees in brainstorming and implementing cost-saving measures.

Operating a hotel during bankruptcy requires a balanced approach that prioritizes guest satisfaction, manages cash flow effectively, and maintains employee motivation. By focusing on core services, implementing cost-saving measures without compromising quality, and working closely with bankruptcy trustees and court officials, hotel owners can navigate the complexities of bankruptcy while maintaining operations. As demonstrated by the Crescent Bay Inn, it is possible to emerge from bankruptcy with a stronger, more financially stable business that continues to deliver excellent guest experiences. With careful planning, transparent communication, and a commitment to service, hotel owners can successfully manage their operations during this challenging period and position themselves for future recovery and growth.

Developing a Reorganization Plan

Developing a reorganization plan is the cornerstone of successfully emerging from bankruptcy under Chapter 11. This process requires crafting a detailed strategy for financial and operational restructuring, gaining creditor approval, implementing changes, and continually tracking progress. A well-executed reorganization plan can help a distressed hotel not only survive but also emerge stronger and more competitive. In this section, we'll explore how to create and implement an effective reorganization plan, illustrated with practical examples, a case study, and actionable steps.

Creating a Detailed Plan for Financial and Operational Restructuring

The first step in developing a reorganization plan is to create a comprehensive blueprint for how the hotel will address its financial challenges and optimize operations to become profitable. This plan must be detailed, realistic, and tailored to the hotel's unique circumstances.

1. Assess the Current Financial Situation:

- Conduct a thorough analysis of the hotel's financial health, including revenue streams, expenses, debt obligations, cash flow, and profitability. Identify which areas contribute to financial distress and which offer opportunities for improvement.

- Practical Example: A 200-room hotel in Miami facing financial difficulties discovered that high operational costs, particularly in utilities and staffing, were contributing to its cash flow problems. The reorganization plan focused on reducing these expenses through energy-efficient upgrades and optimized staffing schedules.

2. Identify Areas for Operational Restructuring:

- Evaluate the hotel's operations, including staffing, marketing, guest services, maintenance, and procurement. Identify inefficiencies or areas where costs can be reduced without compromising service quality.

- Practical Example: A hotel in Chicago restructured its housekeeping department by cross-training employees to handle multiple roles, reducing labor costs without sacrificing service standards.

3. Develop Strategies for Revenue Enhancement:

- Create initiatives to boost revenue, such as introducing dynamic pricing strategies, launching targeted marketing campaigns, or expanding service offerings (e.g., food and beverage, events, or wellness services).

- Practical Example: A hotel in New Orleans implemented a new marketing campaign targeting leisure travelers and business groups, resulting in a 15% increase in bookings within six months.

Actionable Steps:

- Conduct a comprehensive financial and operational analysis to identify areas of improvement.

- Develop strategies for reducing costs, enhancing revenue, and improving efficiency.

- Create a detailed plan outlining specific actions, timelines, and targets for financial and operational restructuring.

Gaining Creditor Approval for the Reorganization Plan

Once the reorganization plan is developed, gaining approval from creditors is a critical step. Creditors must be convinced that the plan offers the best chance for debt repayment and that it is a viable solution for the hotel's financial recovery.

1. Present a Clear and Compelling Plan:

- The reorganization plan should be presented to creditors clearly and professionally, highlighting how it will improve the hotel's financial performance, increase revenue, and enable debt repayment. Include detailed financial projections, cash flow forecasts, and timelines for implementation.

- Practical Example: A hotel in San Francisco provided creditors with a comprehensive plan showing how cost-cutting measures and a revamped marketing strategy would generate enough cash flow to meet restructured debt obligations over the next five years.

2. Demonstrate Credibility and Commitment:

- Establish credibility by demonstrating your commitment to the plan and willingness to make necessary changes. This can include implementing some of the restructuring measures before the plan is approved, showing that you're serious about turning the business around.

- Practical Example: A hotel owner in Dallas implemented energy-saving measures and negotiated reduced rates with suppliers before presenting the plan to creditors, showcasing the owner's commitment to improving the hotel's financial health.

3. Engage in Negotiations and Be Open to Adjustments:

- Be prepared to negotiate with creditors and make adjustments to the plan if needed. Creditors may request changes to repayment terms, interest rates, or timelines.

- Practical Example: A hotel in Denver modified its reorganization plan to include a higher interest rate on restructured debt after negotiations with creditors, ensuring the plan was approved while still maintaining feasible repayment terms.

Actionable Steps:

- Prepare a detailed and persuasive presentation of the reorganization plan for creditors.

- Demonstrate your commitment to the plan by implementing initial changes.

- Engage in negotiations with creditors and be open to adjusting the plan as needed.

Executing Operational and Financial Changes

Execution is the most challenging yet crucial part of the reorganization process. Implementing operational and financial changes as outlined in the plan requires dedication, monitoring, and adaptability.

1. Implement Cost-Saving Measures:

- Execute the cost-saving initiatives identified in the reorganization plan, such as reducing energy consumption, renegotiating supplier contracts, or optimizing staffing levels.

- Practical Example: A hotel in Atlanta saved over $50,000 annually by switching to energy-efficient lighting and implementing water-saving practices in guest rooms.

2. Drive Revenue Growth:

- Launch marketing campaigns, adjust pricing strategies, and introduce new revenue streams as planned. Track the effectiveness of these initiatives and adjust as needed.

- Practical Example: A hotel in Los Angeles increased its ADR (average daily rate) by introducing a dynamic pricing model that adjusted rates based on demand, leading to a 10% increase in revenue.

3. Monitor Progress and Performance:

- Establish key performance indicators (KPIs) to track progress, such as occupancy rates, RevPAR (revenue per available room), cash flow, and cost savings. Regularly monitor these metrics to ensure the plan is on track.

- Practical Example: A hotel in Orlando monitored its KPIs weekly, allowing the management team to make quick adjustments to marketing and operational strategies as needed.

Actionable Steps:

- Implement cost-saving and revenue-enhancing initiatives as outlined in the reorganization plan.

- Track KPIs to monitor progress and identify areas that need adjustment.

- Stay committed to the plan, even when faced with challenges or setbacks.

Case Study: A Hotel's Successful Reorganization Journey

The Riverside Hotel, a 150-room property in a bustling downtown area, faced declining revenues and rising operational costs, leading to severe financial distress. The hotel filed for Chapter 11 bankruptcy and developed a comprehensive reorganization plan.

Key Actions Taken:

- Operational Restructuring: The hotel owner identified staffing inefficiencies and implemented cross-training programs, reducing labor costs by 15%. Additionally, the hotel switched to a cloud-based property management system, which streamlined operations and improved guest experience.

- Revenue Enhancement: A targeted marketing campaign focused on corporate travelers and weekend leisure guests. The hotel introduced bundled packages, including dining and spa services, which increased bookings by 20% within six months.

- Cost-Cutting Measures: The hotel implemented energy-efficient lighting and water-saving initiatives, reducing utility costs by 25%. Negotiating with suppliers led to a 10% reduction in monthly expenses.

Outcome: Within 18 months, the Riverside Hotel emerged from bankruptcy with improved cash flow, increased occupancy rates, and a more sustainable cost structure. The reorganization plan not only saved the hotel but also positioned it for long-term profitability.

Key Takeaway: A well-executed reorganization plan, combined with strategic cost-saving measures and revenue enhancement initiatives, can help a distressed hotel emerge from bankruptcy stronger and more financially stable.
Tracking Progress and Adjusting the Plan as Needed

Tracking progress is essential to ensure that the reorganization plan is achieving its intended goals. Regularly monitoring key metrics and being willing to adjust the plan based on results is crucial for long-term success.

1. Monitor Key Performance Indicators (KPIs):

- Regularly track KPIs such as cash flow, occupancy rates, ADR, RevPAR, and expenses.

These metrics provide insights into the hotel's financial health and the effectiveness of the reorganization plan.

- Practical Example: A hotel in Seattle monitored its cash flow weekly, allowing management to quickly identify and address any shortfalls, ensuring that the reorganization plan stayed on track.

2. Adjust the Plan as Needed:

- Be prepared to adapt the reorganization plan based on changing market conditions or operational challenges. Flexibility is crucial for addressing unforeseen issues and seizing new opportunities.

- Practical Example: A hotel in New York adjusted its marketing strategy to target local guests during a travel downturn, resulting in a steady stream of weekend bookings that helped maintain cash flow.

Actionable Steps:

- Establish regular intervals for monitoring KPIs and reviewing progress.

- Be proactive in adjusting the plan based on performance data and market conditions.

- Communicate any adjustments to the plan with key stakeholders, including creditors and staff.

Tips for Emerging from Bankruptcy Stronger

Emerging from bankruptcy is just the beginning of the journey toward financial recovery. The following tips can help hotels build a solid foundation for long-term success:

- Continue Monitoring Financial Health: Maintain rigorous financial oversight, even after emerging from bankruptcy, to avoid falling back into financial distress. Implement regular financial reviews and adjust strategies as needed.

- Focus on Rebuilding Credit: Work to rebuild the hotel's credit by consistently paying debts on time and establishing a positive credit history. This will improve access to financing for future projects.

- Invest in Staff Training and Development: Invest in staff training programs to enhance service quality, improve efficiency, and create a positive guest experience. Engaged and skilled employees contribute to long-term success.

- Leverage Marketing and Branding: Reinvest in marketing and branding efforts to regain market share and attract guests. Highlight any improvements or renovations made during the reorganization process to create a positive image.

Practical Example: After emerging from bankruptcy, a hotel in San Diego reinvested in marketing, targeting travelers with a refreshed brand identity. This effort led to a 30% increase in bookings within a year, demonstrating the importance of proactive marketing in driving growth.

Actionable Steps:

- Implement financial controls and regularly review financial performance.

- Focus on rebuilding the hotel's creditworthiness and reputation.

- Invest in marketing, branding, and employee training to support long-term growth.

Developing a comprehensive reorganization plan is a critical step in successfully navigating bankruptcy and emerging as a stronger, more financially stable business. By creating a detailed plan for financial and operational restructuring, gaining creditor approval, executing changes, and tracking progress, hotels can transform financial challenges into opportunities for growth. The journey of the Riverside Hotel demonstrates that with a strategic approach, careful execution, and ongoing commitment, even distressed hotels can achieve a successful turnaround and build a foundation for long-term profitability and success.

Emerging from Bankruptcy

Emerging from bankruptcy marks a significant milestone for a distressed hotel, but it is just the beginning of a journey toward renewed financial health, brand revitalization, and long-term growth.

Successfully rebuilding credit, rebranding, establishing growth strategies, and preparing for future challenges are crucial steps to ensure the hotel remains on a sustainable path. This section will provide in-depth analysis, practical examples, a case study, and actionable steps on how to navigate this critical phase.

Rebuilding Credit and Financial Stability

Rebuilding credit and achieving financial stability are top priorities for any hotel emerging from bankruptcy. Lenders, vendors, and potential investors will evaluate the hotel's creditworthiness, making it essential to restore financial credibility.

1. Establishing Consistent Payment Habits:

- Regularly pay all debts and expenses on time, including utility bills, supplier invoices, loan repayments, and tax obligations. Timely payments demonstrate financial responsibility and help rebuild your credit score.

- Practical Example: A hotel in New York City emerged from Chapter 11 bankruptcy and set up automatic payments for all recurring bills, ensuring that no payments were missed. This practice helped improve the hotel's credit score over the following year.

2. Building Relationships with Lenders and Creditors:

- Re-establish trust with creditors by maintaining open communication and transparency. Provide regular financial updates to lenders and creditors, demonstrating that the hotel is on a stable path to recovery.

- Practical Example: A hotel in San Francisco provided quarterly financial reports to its primary lender, showcasing improved cash flow and profitability. This transparency encouraged the lender to extend additional credit when the hotel needed to finance renovations.

3. Gradual Expansion of Credit:

- Start by securing small lines of credit or business credit cards with manageable limits. Use these responsibly and pay off balances in full each month to build a positive credit history.

- Practical Example: A hotel in Miami obtained a small line of credit post-bankruptcy and used it exclusively for purchasing supplies. By consistently paying off the balance, the hotel improved its credit rating within six months.

Actionable Steps:

- Set up automatic payments for all bills to avoid missing due dates.

- Maintain regular communication with creditors and lenders, sharing financial updates.

- Apply for small lines of credit and use them

responsibly to build a positive credit history.

Rebranding and Repositioning the Hotel

Bankruptcy often leaves a negative impression, making it essential to rebrand and reposition the hotel to attract guests, investors, and partners. A fresh image can signal a new beginning and help the hotel regain market share.

1. Refresh the Hotel's Visual Identity:

- Update the hotel's logo, website, signage, and marketing materials to create a modern and appealing image. Consider a new color scheme, tagline, or design elements that reflect the hotel's renewed vision.

- Practical Example: A hotel in Atlanta changed its logo, redesigned its website, and updated its social media profiles after emerging from bankruptcy. The new branding emphasized the hotel's commitment to providing a fresh, high-quality guest experience, attracting a surge of bookings.

2. Implement a Targeted Marketing Campaign:

- Launch a marketing campaign to reintroduce the hotel to the market. Highlight any renovations, service improvements, or unique experiences that guests can expect. Use social media, email marketing, and online travel agencies (OTAs) to reach your target audience.

- Practical Example: A hotel in Las Vegas ran a "Grand Reopening" campaign that offered discounted rates, complimentary breakfast, and free parking. The campaign generated significant interest, resulting in a 30% increase in occupancy within three months.

3. Enhance Guest Experience and Services:

- Reposition the hotel by improving guest services, amenities, and overall experience. Consider adding new amenities, upgrading existing facilities, or introducing special events and packages.

- Practical Example: A boutique hotel in Chicago introduced a rooftop bar and live music events as part of its rebranding efforts, differentiating itself from competitors and attracting a new demographic of guests.

Actionable Steps:

- Redesign the hotel's branding elements, such as the logo and website, to reflect a fresh start.

- Launch a marketing campaign that showcases the hotel's renewed image and offerings.

- Improve guest services and amenities to create a memorable experience that aligns with the new brand.

Establishing Long-Term Growth Strategies

Emerging from bankruptcy provides an opportunity to develop strategies that ensure long-term growth and financial resilience. By focusing on revenue diversification, cost management, and strategic partnerships, hotels can build a strong foundation for the future.

1. Diversify Revenue Streams:

- Expand revenue sources by offering additional services, such as catering, events, spa treatments, or wellness programs. Diversifying income helps protect the hotel from market fluctuations and increases overall profitability.

- Practical Example: A hotel in Denver introduced corporate event packages, generating an additional $150,000 in revenue within the first year after emerging from bankruptcy.

2. Invest in Technology and Efficiency:

- Implement technology solutions to streamline operations, improve guest experiences, and reduce costs. Consider adopting property management systems, revenue management software, or mobile check-in/check-out services.

- Practical Example: A hotel in Seattle invested in a cloud-based property management system, which improved operational efficiency, reduced manual errors, and enhanced guest satisfaction.

3. Form Strategic Partnerships:

- Collaborate with local businesses, travel agencies, tour operators, and online travel agencies (OTAs) to increase visibility and attract new guests. Partnering with complementary businesses can also lead to cross-promotion and shared marketing opportunities.

- Practical Example: A hotel in Orlando partnered with a nearby theme park, offering discounted tickets to guests. This partnership led to a 25% increase in bookings during the peak tourist season.

Actionable Steps:

- Identify opportunities to diversify revenue streams by offering new services or amenities.

- Invest in technology to improve operational efficiency and guest experience.

- Form strategic partnerships to expand your reach and attract more guests.

Case Study: How a Hotel Rebounded After Bankruptcy

The Sunset Bay Resort, a 150-room beachfront hotel, faced financial challenges due to declining tourism and rising operational costs, eventually filing for

Chapter 11 bankruptcy. However, through a well-executed reorganization plan, the resort successfully emerged from bankruptcy and experienced a remarkable turnaround.

Key Actions Taken:

- Rebuilding Credit: The resort made timely payments on all restructured debts, improved financial management, and established a positive credit history within a year.

- Rebranding and Marketing: The resort invested in a rebranding campaign, updating its website, logo, and marketing materials to emphasize a new luxury experience. A "Grand Reopening" campaign offered special discounts and attracted new guests.

- Revenue Diversification: The resort introduced wedding packages, spa services, and water sports activities, generating additional revenue streams.

- Technology Investment: Implementing a new property management system and revenue management software helped optimize pricing and improve operational efficiency.

Outcome: Within two years, the Sunset Bay Resort's occupancy rate increased by 35%, and annual revenue grew by 40%. The resort not only emerged from bankruptcy but also became a top choice for travelers in the region.

Key Takeaway: A strategic approach to rebuilding credit, rebranding, and diversifying revenue streams can lead to a successful rebound after bankruptcy. Avoiding Common Post-Bankruptcy Pitfalls

After emerging from bankruptcy, many hotels face the risk of falling back into financial distress. Avoiding common pitfalls is essential for maintaining financial stability and growth.

1. Overextending Financial Commitments:

- Avoid taking on excessive debt or financial obligations, even if credit becomes more accessible. Focus on building financial reserves and maintaining a healthy debt-to-equity ratio.

- Practical Example: A hotel in Miami maintained strict financial discipline after bankruptcy, only taking on debt that could be supported by projected cash flows, ensuring long-term stability.

2. Neglecting Financial Monitoring:

- Regularly monitor financial performance, including cash flow, expenses, and profitability. Implement financial controls to identify potential issues early and take corrective action.

- Practical Example: A hotel in San Diego conducted monthly financial reviews, enabling management to address revenue shortfalls and reduce unnecessary expenses.

Actionable Steps:

- Avoid taking on excessive debt, even if credit is available.

- Establish regular financial monitoring practices to identify and address potential problems early.

Preparing for Future Challenges

To ensure long-term success, hotels must be prepared for future challenges, whether economic downturns, shifts in market demand, or unexpected events.

1. Build Financial Reserves:

- Establish a cash reserve or contingency fund to provide a financial cushion during periods of low occupancy or unexpected expenses.

- Practical Example: A hotel in Los Angeles built a reserve fund equivalent to three months of operating expenses, which helped it weather a temporary drop in bookings due to a regional natural disaster.

2. Stay Agile and Adaptable:

- Continuously monitor market trends, guest preferences, and industry developments. Be ready to adapt your services, pricing strategies, and marketing efforts to remain competitive.

- Practical Example: A hotel in Boston quickly

shifted its marketing focus to target local travelers during an economic downturn, resulting in a steady stream of bookings despite reduced international travel.

Actionable Steps:

- Build a financial reserve to protect against future uncertainties.

- Stay informed about industry trends and be prepared to adapt your business model as needed.

Emerging from bankruptcy is a challenging journey that requires strategic planning, disciplined financial management, and a commitment to rebuilding the hotel's brand and market presence. By focusing on rebuilding credit, rebranding, establishing long-term growth strategies, and preparing for future challenges, a hotel can transform bankruptcy into an opportunity for renewed success. The experience of the Sunset Bay Resort illustrates that with the right approach, hotels can rebound from financial distress and thrive in the hospitality market, emerging stronger and more competitive than ever before.

Preventing Future Financial Distress

Preventing future financial distress is a critical goal for any hotel that has emerged from bankruptcy or financial difficulties. Establishing robust financial management strategies, building cash reserves, implementing risk management practices, and learning from past experiences are essential to ensure long-term stability and profitability. This section will provide in-depth analysis, practical examples, and a case study demonstrating how a hotel achieved financial resilience, offering actionable steps to guide hotel owners in safeguarding their businesses against future challenges.

Developing Proactive Financial Management Strategies

Proactive financial management is the foundation of preventing financial distress. By closely monitoring finances, optimizing cash flow, and making data-driven decisions, hotel owners can identify potential problems early and take corrective action before they escalate.

1. Create and Maintain a Detailed Financial Plan:

- Develop a comprehensive financial plan that outlines revenue targets, expense projections, debt repayment schedules, and investment goals. Regularly review and update this plan to reflect changes in market conditions, occupancy rates, or operational expenses.

- Practical Example: A hotel in Miami developed a detailed financial plan that included monthly revenue and expense projections. By tracking performance against this plan, the hotel quickly identified an unexpected increase in utility costs and implemented energy-saving measures to address the issue.

2. Implement Robust Financial Monitoring Systems:

- Use accounting software or financial management tools to monitor income, expenses, cash flow, and key financial metrics (e.g., RevPAR, ADR, occupancy rates). Regularly reviewing these metrics helps identify trends and potential risks early.

- Practical Example: A boutique hotel in San Francisco used cloud-based financial software to track daily revenue and expenses. This enabled the hotel to spot a decline in occupancy rates during the off-season and adjust marketing strategies to attract more guests.

3. Regularly Review Financial Performance:

- Schedule monthly or quarterly financial reviews to assess the hotel's financial health. Compare actual performance against budgeted targets and investigate any variances to understand their causes and take corrective action.

- Practical Example: A hotel in New Orleans conducted monthly financial reviews with its management team, allowing it to identify and address overspending in the food and beverage department. By renegotiating supplier contracts, the hotel reduced costs by 15%.

Actionable Steps:

- Create a detailed financial plan with clear

revenue and expense projections.

- Use financial management software to track income, expenses, and key performance metrics.

- Conduct regular financial reviews to identify and address potential issues.

Building Cash Reserves and Contingency Plans

Having sufficient cash reserves and contingency plans is crucial for weathering unexpected challenges, such as economic downturns, natural disasters, or sudden drops in occupancy rates.

1. Establish a Cash Reserve Fund:

- Set aside a portion of monthly profits to build a cash reserve fund. Aim to accumulate enough cash to cover at least three to six months of operating expenses. This reserve can provide a financial cushion during periods of low revenue or emergencies.

- Practical Example: A hotel in Boston established a cash reserve fund by setting aside 5% of its monthly revenue. When the hotel experienced a temporary closure due to a severe winter storm, the reserve fund covered payroll and essential expenses until operations resumed.

2. Develop a Contingency Plan for Unexpected Events:

- Create a contingency plan that outlines steps to take in response to various scenarios, such as a sudden decline in occupancy, a natural disaster, or an economic recession. Include strategies for reducing expenses, securing emergency financing, and communicating with stakeholders.

- Practical Example: A hotel in Denver developed a contingency plan that included a list of cost-saving measures (e.g., reducing non-essential services, implementing hiring freezes) and pre-established lines of credit with local banks. When occupancy rates dropped due to a downturn in tourism, the hotel implemented the plan and avoided financial distress.

Actionable Steps:

- Build a cash reserve fund by setting aside a percentage of monthly profits.

- Develop a contingency plan that addresses potential financial challenges and outlines steps for responding to them.

- Regularly review and update your contingency plan to ensure it remains relevant.

Case Study: A Hotel's Journey to Financial Resilience

The Seaside Retreat Hotel, a 120-room property located in a coastal tourist destination, experienced severe financial distress due to declining bookings and rising operational costs. After emerging from bankruptcy, the hotel implemented proactive financial management strategies and established cash reserves to build financial resilience.

Key Actions Taken:

- Developing a Financial Plan: The hotel owner worked with a financial advisor to create a detailed plan that included revenue goals, expense projections, and a debt repayment schedule. Regular financial reviews allowed the hotel to identify potential issues early.

- Building Cash Reserves: The hotel set aside 10% of monthly profits to build a cash reserve fund. Within two years, the fund grew to cover six months of operating expenses, providing a safety net during off-peak seasons.

- Implementing Cost Controls: The hotel reduced utility expenses by installing energy-efficient lighting and water-saving devices. It also renegotiated supplier contracts, resulting in a 20% reduction in monthly expenses.

Outcome: When the COVID-19 pandemic led to a significant drop in bookings, the Seaside Retreat Hotel used its cash reserves to cover essential expenses and avoid layoffs. The hotel's financial resilience allowed it to weather the crisis and emerge stronger, with improved profitability and stability.

Key Takeaway: Building cash reserves, developing a financial plan, and implementing cost controls can help hotels achieve financial resilience and navigate unexpected challenges successfully.

Implementing Risk Management Practices

Risk management is an essential aspect of preventing future financial distress. Identifying potential risks and developing strategies to mitigate them can protect the hotel from financial shocks and disruptions.

1. Identify Potential Risks:

- Conduct a risk assessment to identify potential threats to the hotel's financial stability, such as market fluctuations, natural disasters, legal issues, or changes in consumer behavior. Evaluate the likelihood and potential impact of each risk.

- Practical Example: A hotel in Orlando identified its reliance on seasonal tourism as a significant risk. To mitigate this, the hotel diversified its marketing efforts to target corporate travelers and local events during off-peak seasons.

2. Develop Risk Mitigation Strategies:

- Create strategies to mitigate identified risks, such as obtaining insurance coverage, diversifying revenue streams, or establishing contracts with suppliers that allow for flexibility during downturns.

- Practical Example: A hotel in Los Angeles obtained business interruption insurance, which provided financial support during an unexpected closure due to a fire. This insurance coverage helped the hotel recover quickly and minimize financial losses.

3. Monitor and Update Risk Management Plans:

- Regularly review and update risk management plans to address new threats or changes in the business environment. Engage with key stakeholders, such as insurance providers and legal advisors, to stay informed about potential risks.

- Practical Example: A hotel in Seattle conducted annual risk assessments to identify emerging threats, such as changes in local regulations or economic trends. This proactive approach allowed the hotel to adjust its strategies and avoid potential pitfalls.

Actionable Steps:

- Conduct a comprehensive risk assessment to identify potential threats to your hotel.

- Develop and implement strategies to mitigate identified risks.

- Regularly review and update your risk management plan.

Tips for Maintaining Profitability and Stability

Maintaining profitability and financial stability

requires a combination of disciplined financial management, strategic planning, and ongoing investment in guest experiences.

1. Focus on Revenue Management:

- Implement dynamic pricing strategies that adjust room rates based on demand, occupancy levels, and market conditions. Use revenue management software to optimize pricing and maximize revenue.

- Practical Example: A hotel in Las Vegas implemented a dynamic pricing strategy, adjusting rates during high-demand periods, such as conventions and holidays. This resulted in a 12% increase in annual revenue.

2. Invest in Guest Experience:

- Continuously invest in improving guest experiences, as satisfied guests are more likely to return and recommend the hotel to others. This can lead to increased bookings, higher occupancy rates, and greater profitability.

- Practical Example: A hotel in Austin invested in upgrading its amenities, such as adding a rooftop bar and renovating guest rooms. These improvements led to a 20% increase in repeat bookings and positive online reviews.

3. Diversify Marketing Efforts:

- Use a mix of online and offline marketing

channels to reach a broader audience. Target different market segments, such as leisure travelers, corporate groups, or local events, to increase occupancy throughout the year.

- Practical Example: A hotel in Chicago partnered with a local theater group to offer package deals for guests attending performances. This collaboration attracted a new segment of guests and boosted occupancy during slower months.

Actionable Steps:

- Implement a dynamic pricing strategy to maximize revenue.

- Invest in guest experience improvements to encourage repeat bookings.

- Diversify marketing efforts to reach different target audiences.

Learning from Past Experiences

Learning from past financial challenges is essential for preventing future distress. Reflecting on previous mistakes and successes helps hotel owners develop strategies to avoid similar issues in the future.

1. Conduct a Post-Mortem Analysis:

- After emerging from financial distress, conduct a thorough analysis of what went wrong, what was done well, and what could have been improved. Use this analysis to inform future decisions and strategies.

- Practical Example: A hotel in Denver conducted a post-mortem analysis after emerging from bankruptcy, identifying that poor cash flow management was a primary cause of its financial problems. As a result, the hotel implemented strict cash flow monitoring and improved financial planning practices.

2. Implement Lessons Learned:

- Apply the lessons learned from past experiences to improve financial management, operational efficiency, and decision-making processes. Share these lessons with management teams and employees to create a culture of continuous improvement.

- Practical Example: A hotel in San Francisco developed a training program for its management team, focusing on financial literacy and cash flow management. This program helped prevent future financial mismanagement and improved overall performance.

Actionable Steps:

- Conduct a post-mortem analysis to identify lessons learned from past financial distress.

- Implement changes based on the insights gained to prevent future challenges.

- Create a culture of continuous improvement by sharing lessons learned with your team.

Preventing future financial distress requires proactive financial management, building cash reserves, implementing risk management practices, and learning from past experiences. By developing and maintaining a detailed financial plan, establishing contingency funds, and adopting strategies to mitigate risks, hotels can protect themselves against potential challenges and build a foundation for long-term profitability and stability. The journey of the Seaside Retreat Hotel demonstrates that with the right strategies and a commitment to financial resilience, hotels can not only recover from financial difficulties but also thrive in an ever-changing hospitality market.

Chapter 9: Receivership for Distressed Hotels

The receivership process plays a crucial role in addressing financial distress for hotels facing significant operational and financial challenges. This chapter explores the intricacies of receivership, offering insights into how it functions, its implications for distressed hotels, and how owners and stakeholders can navigate this often-complex process. Receivership is a legal mechanism whereby a court appoints a neutral third party, known as a receiver, to manage a distressed hotel's operations, finances, and assets. This step is typically taken when the hotel's financial condition has deteriorated to the point where lenders or creditors seek intervention to protect their interests. Understanding how receivership works and when it is necessary is the first step in effectively navigating this process.

Once a hotel enters receivership, the appointed receiver assumes control over the property's day-to-day operations, addressing both financial and operational challenges. This chapter examines the receiver's role and responsibilities in detail, focusing on how they can implement turnaround strategies to stabilize the hotel and enhance its performance. We will analyze a case study demonstrating how a receiver successfully improved a hotel's financial health and operational efficiency, showcasing the potential benefits of receivership when managed effectively. It is essential to maintain compliance with court orders during this process and ensure clear communication with stakeholders, including creditors, employees, and guests.

Exiting receivership is another critical aspect addressed in this chapter, as it involves preparing the hotel for sale, transfer, or a return to ownership. The transition requires completing all legal and financial obligations, and ensuring a smooth handover to new management or ownership. By exploring a case study of a hotel that successfully exited receivership, we will highlight the key factors that contribute to a seamless transition, along with actionable tips to prevent future financial distress and build resilience.

In addition to exploring the process itself, this chapter delves into the lessons learned from receivership experiences. Many hotels emerge from receivership stronger, having undergone significant changes that pave the way for a successful turnaround. Understanding common pitfalls and challenges can help hotel owners and stakeholders develop a post-receivership action plan that sets the stage for long-term success.

The role of professional advisors is another crucial element covered in this chapter, as legal, financial, and operational experts play a significant role in guiding the receivership process. Building a team of skilled advisors and effectively managing these relationships can make a substantial difference in navigating the complexities of receivership. By examining how advisors have helped hotels manage the process successfully, this chapter provides practical guidance on selecting the right experts and maintaining effective communication.

Finally, the chapter addresses how to rebuild the hotel's brand and reputation following receivership. Emerging from receivership presents an opportunity to restore trust with guests, re-engage with travel agents and distribution networks, and launch marketing campaigns that highlight the hotel's renewed commitment to quality and service. A case study of a successful rebranding effort demonstrates how a hotel can transform its image and regain market share post-receivership, offering valuable insights and tips for leveraging guest feedback to create a positive brand perception.

Overall, this chapter provides a comprehensive guide to understanding, navigating, and emerging successfully from receivership, equipping hotel owners, managers, and stakeholders with the knowledge and strategies needed to manage this challenging process and position their property for long-term success.

Understanding the Receivership Process

Receivership is a legal process often employed when a distressed hotel is unable to meet its financial obligations, and creditors seek intervention to protect their interests. This section explores the receivership process in-depth, examining how it works, the role and responsibilities of a receiver, and the legal and practical aspects of working with courts and professionals. We will analyze a real-world case study of a hotel that benefited from receivership and provide actionable steps for navigating this complex process.

What is Receivership, and How Does it Work?

Receivership is a legal remedy used when a hotel faces severe financial distress and is unable to fulfill its debt obligations. In such cases, a court appoints a receiver—an impartial third party—to take temporary control of the hotel's assets and operations. The receiver's primary role is to manage the property, stabilize its finances, and work toward maximizing the value of the assets for the benefit of creditors, stakeholders, and sometimes, the hotel owner.

Key Features of Receivership:

- Court Appointment: A receiver is appointed by the court at the request of creditors, typically lenders, who are concerned about the hotel's ability to repay debts. The receiver operates under the court's supervision.

- Temporary Control: Receivership is not a permanent solution. It is a temporary measure designed to protect the interests of creditors, stabilize the hotel's operations, and explore options for recovery, restructuring, or sale.

- Operational Management: The receiver takes full control of the hotel's day-to-day operations, including managing staff, overseeing finances, addressing maintenance issues, and implementing strategies to improve profitability.

Practical Example: A hotel in New York with mounting debt was unable to make loan payments.

The lender petitioned the court to place the hotel in receivership, and a court-appointed receiver took over operations. This intervention stabilized the hotel's finances and operations, allowing for an eventual sale that benefited both the lender and the hotel owner. The Role and Responsibilities of a Hotel Receiver

The receiver's role is multifaceted and requires a high level of expertise in hospitality management, finance, and legal compliance. Once appointed, the receiver assumes responsibility for managing all aspects of the hotel's operations and finances.

1. Stabilizing Operations:

- The receiver assesses the hotel's operational challenges, including staffing, guest services, maintenance, and supply chain issues. They implement measures to improve efficiency and ensure the hotel continues to operate smoothly.

- Practical Example: At a hotel in Miami placed under receivership, the receiver identified inefficiencies in the housekeeping department and implemented a new scheduling system, resulting in a 20% reduction in labor costs without compromising service quality.

2. Managing Finances and Cash Flow:

- The receiver takes control of the hotel's finances, including bank accounts, revenue management, and payment of bills. They work to improve cash flow, reduce expenses, and negotiate with creditors and suppliers to stabilize the hotel's financial position.

- Practical Example: A hotel in Chicago had outstanding payments to multiple suppliers. The receiver negotiated extended payment terms, allowing the hotel to maintain operations while managing its cash flow more effectively.

3. Preparing for Sale or Transition:

- In many cases, the receiver's role is to prepare the hotel for sale or transition back to the owner. This involves enhancing the hotel's value, addressing operational inefficiencies, and ensuring compliance with all legal requirements.

- Practical Example: A hotel in Los Angeles, under receivership, underwent a series of renovations and operational improvements, which increased its market value and attracted a qualified buyer.

Actionable Steps:

- Work closely with the receiver to understand the measures being implemented to improve the hotel's financial and operational health.

- Ensure that all financial records, contracts, and operational data are readily available to facilitate the receiver's work.

- Maintain open lines of communication with the

receiver to stay informed about the hotel's progress.

Identifying When Receivership is Necessary

Determining when receivership is necessary is a critical decision that often involves input from creditors, lenders, and hotel owners. It is typically considered as a last resort when other financial remedies, such as restructuring, workouts, or bankruptcy, have failed or are not viable.

Signs That Receivership May Be Necessary:

- Severe Financial Distress: The hotel is unable to meet its debt obligations, has defaulted on loans, or is facing imminent foreclosure.

- Declining Operational Performance: Operational inefficiencies, declining occupancy rates, or deteriorating guest services are threatening the hotel's profitability.

- Legal or Regulatory Issues: The hotel faces legal challenges, regulatory violations, or compliance issues that could jeopardize its ability to operate.

- Lender Intervention: Lenders may seek receivership to protect their investment if they believe the hotel's management is incapable of turning around the business.

Practical Example: A 200-room hotel in Orlando was consistently operating at a loss, with occupancy rates below 40% and mounting debt. The hotel's lender initiated receivership proceedings to prevent further financial deterioration and protect the property's value.

Case Study: How a Hotel Benefited from Receivership

The Palm View Resort, a 150-room property in a tourist destination, faced financial distress due to mismanagement and declining revenues. The lender petitioned for receivership, and a receiver was appointed to take control of the hotel's operations.

Actions Taken by the Receiver:

- Operational Improvements: The receiver implemented new management practices, optimized staffing levels, and renegotiated vendor contracts, resulting in a 30% reduction in operational costs.

- Marketing and Revenue Management: A targeted marketing campaign was launched, focusing on off-peak travel periods and local events, which improved occupancy rates by 25% within six months.

- Asset Preservation: The receiver addressed deferred maintenance issues and made necessary repairs, enhancing the property's overall value.

Outcome: After 18 months in receivership, the Palm View Resort's financial performance had improved significantly, and it was sold to a new owner at a price that allowed the lender to recover the outstanding debt. The hotel continued to operate successfully under the new management.

Key Takeaway: Receivership, when managed effectively, can help a distressed hotel stabilize operations, improve financial performance, and ultimately achieve a more favorable outcome for creditors and owners.

The Legal Process of Appointing a Receiver

The appointment of a receiver is a legal process that involves several steps, typically initiated by a creditor or lender seeking to protect their investment.

1. Filing a Petition with the Court:

- The creditor or lender files a petition with the court requesting the appointment of a receiver. The petition outlines the financial distress faced by the hotel and the reasons why receivership is necessary.

- Practical Example: A lender with a $10 million loan secured by a hotel property in Dallas filed a petition for receivership after the hotel defaulted on loan payments for six consecutive months.

2. Court Review and Decision:

- The court reviews the petition, examines evidence of the hotel's financial condition, and assesses whether receivership is warranted. If approved, the court appoints a receiver, who must act in the best interests of all parties involved.

- Practical Example: A judge appointed a receiver for a hotel in Phoenix after determining that the hotel's declining revenue and inability to meet debt obligations justified the intervention.

3. Receiver Takes Control:

- Once appointed, the receiver takes control of the hotel's operations, finances, and assets. The receiver operates under court supervision and must provide regular reports detailing the hotel's financial performance and progress.

Actionable Steps:

- If you are a hotel owner facing the possibility of receivership, consult with legal professionals to understand your rights and responsibilities.

- Prepare all financial documents and records in case they are required for court review.

- Cooperate with the receiver to ensure a smooth transition and management process.

Working with Courts and Legal Professionals

Navigating the receivership process requires effective communication and collaboration with legal professionals and the court. Hotel owners, lenders, and other stakeholders must understand the legal requirements and expectations during this process.

1. Engage Experienced Legal Advisors:

- Engage attorneys with expertise in hospitality receivership to guide you through the legal process, ensure compliance with court orders, and protect your interests.

- Practical Example: A hotel in San Diego hired a legal team specializing in receivership to negotiate terms with the lender and ensure the hotel's rights were protected throughout the process.

2. Comply with Court Orders and Reporting Requirements:

- The receiver must submit regular reports to the court detailing the hotel's financial status, operational performance, and progress toward the objectives of the receivership. Ensure that all required documentation is accurate and submitted on time.

- Practical Example: A hotel receiver in Las Vegas submitted monthly financial reports to the court, demonstrating improved cash flow and operational efficiency, which contributed to the successful sale of the property.

Actionable Steps:

- Work with legal professionals who have experience in receivership to navigate the process.

- Ensure compliance with all court orders and reporting requirements.

- Maintain open communication with the receiver and legal advisors to address any challenges or concerns.

Understanding the receivership process is essential for hotel owners, lenders, and stakeholders dealing with financial distress. By comprehending the role of a receiver, the legal process of appointing one, and the benefits that receivership can bring, hotels can navigate this challenging situation more effectively. Through proactive collaboration with legal professionals, creditors, and the receiver, hotels in receivership can stabilize operations, improve financial performance, and ultimately achieve a more favorable outcome. The case of the Palm View Resort demonstrates that, when managed well, receivership can be a valuable tool for transforming a distressed hotel into a financially stable and profitable asset.

Operating a Hotel Under Receivership

Operating a hotel under receivership can be challenging but offers an opportunity to implement strategic changes that can stabilize the business and improve financial performance. The receiver's role is crucial, as they must maintain daily operations, address financial and operational challenges, implement turnaround strategies, and ensure compliance with court orders, all while communicating effectively with stakeholders. This section provides in-depth analysis, practical examples, a case study, and actionable steps for successfully operating a hotel under receivership.

Maintaining Day-to-Day Hotel Operations

Maintaining smooth day-to-day operations is essential for sustaining revenue and preserving the hotel's reputation during receivership. Despite financial challenges, the hotel must continue to provide a positive guest experience and ensure that core services remain consistent.

1. Prioritizing Guest Experience:

- Even under receivership, maintaining high service standards is critical for retaining guests and generating revenue. This means ensuring that housekeeping, front desk services, and food and beverage operations continue without interruption.

- Practical Example: A hotel in New Orleans placed under receivership experienced a 15% drop in occupancy initially. The receiver introduced service enhancements, such as complimentary breakfast and faster check-in/check-out processes, which led to positive guest reviews and a gradual recovery in occupancy rates.

2. Streamlining Operations:

- Receivers often need to implement cost-saving measures without compromising service quality. This could involve optimizing staff schedules, renegotiating vendor contracts, or consolidating services.

- Practical Example: A hotel in San Francisco under receivership reduced operating hours for its restaurant and bar to align with peak demand periods, lowering labor costs while still providing a high-quality guest experience.

Actionable Steps:

- Evaluate all aspects of hotel operations to identify areas where efficiencies can be achieved.

- Maintain open communication with staff to ensure they understand the importance of providing exceptional service during this period.

- Monitor guest feedback and make adjustments to maintain service quality.

Addressing Financial and Operational Challenges

One of the receiver's primary responsibilities is to address the financial and operational challenges that led to the hotel's distress. This involves conducting a thorough analysis of the hotel's finances, identifying areas of inefficiency, and implementing changes to improve profitability.

1. Financial Analysis and Budget Management:

- The receiver must assess the hotel's cash flow, expenses, and revenue streams to identify inefficiencies and opportunities for cost savings. This may include negotiating payment terms with creditors, identifying unnecessary expenses, or renegotiating contracts with suppliers.

- Practical Example: A receiver at a Chicago-based hotel renegotiated long-term supply contracts, resulting in a 20% reduction in costs for linens and cleaning supplies. These savings helped improve the hotel's cash flow and overall financial stability.

2. Operational Assessment:

- An operational assessment involves evaluating the hotel's staffing, marketing, maintenance, and guest services. The receiver identifies areas where operational adjustments can improve efficiency, such as cross-training staff or implementing energy-saving measures.

- Practical Example: A hotel in Los Angeles, under receivership, implemented an energy-saving program by upgrading to LED lighting and installing motion sensors in hallways. This initiative reduced utility expenses by 15% within six months.

Actionable Steps:

- Conduct a detailed financial analysis to identify inefficiencies and areas for improvement.

- Review all operational aspects of the hotel to implement cost-saving measures without compromising guest experience.

- Communicate with suppliers and vendors to negotiate more favorable terms.

Implementing Turnaround Strategies Under Receivership

Implementing effective turnaround strategies is critical for improving the hotel's financial health and operational performance. These strategies should focus on enhancing revenue, reducing costs, and optimizing efficiency.

1. Revenue Enhancement Strategies:

- The receiver may introduce initiatives to increase revenue, such as dynamic pricing strategies, targeted marketing campaigns, or offering value-added packages to attract guests.

- Practical Example: A hotel in Miami under receivership introduced a dynamic pricing model, adjusting room rates based on demand and market trends. This strategy resulted in a

10% increase in average daily rates (ADR) over six months.

2. Cost-Reduction Measures:

- Implementing cost-reduction measures, such as optimizing staffing levels, reducing waste, or consolidating services, is essential for improving profitability.

- Practical Example: A hotel in Austin, under receivership, identified that its laundry services were being outsourced at a high cost. The receiver invested in an in-house laundry facility, reducing expenses by 25% annually.

3. Marketing and Branding Efforts:

- Repositioning the hotel in the market through targeted marketing campaigns, partnerships with travel agencies, or digital marketing can help increase visibility and attract more guests.

- Practical Example: A hotel in Denver created a targeted social media campaign promoting weekend getaway packages, resulting in a 30% increase in weekend bookings.

Actionable Steps:

- Analyze market trends to implement dynamic pricing strategies.

- Identify opportunities for cost savings and operational efficiency improvements.

- Invest in marketing initiatives that highlight the hotel's unique selling points.

Case Study: How a Receiver Improved a Hotel's Performance

The Sunset Harbor Hotel, a 180-room property in a popular coastal destination, was placed under receivership due to financial difficulties, declining occupancy rates, and operational inefficiencies.

Actions Taken by the Receiver:

- Operational Restructuring: The receiver conducted a thorough operational assessment and introduced cross-training programs for staff, allowing the hotel to reduce labor costs by 20%.

- Financial Management: The receiver renegotiated contracts with suppliers, reducing expenses by 15%. Additionally, the hotel's marketing budget was reallocated to focus on digital advertising, which generated a higher return on investment.

- Revenue Enhancement: The receiver implemented a dynamic pricing strategy, introduced weekend stay packages, and partnered with local businesses to offer discounted tickets for nearby attractions.

Outcome: Within 12 months, the Sunset Harbor Hotel's occupancy rate increased from 40% to 70%, and revenue improved by 35%. The hotel's improved financial performance attracted the interest of potential buyers, leading to a successful sale that allowed creditors to recover their investments.

Key Takeaway: Effective operational restructuring, financial management, and revenue enhancement strategies can significantly improve a hotel's performance under receivership, making it more attractive to potential buyers.

Ensuring Compliance with Court Orders

Operating a hotel under receivership requires strict compliance with court orders, as the receiver is accountable to the court and must operate within the legal framework established by the receivership process.

1. Adhering to Reporting Requirements:

- The receiver must submit regular financial reports, operational updates, and progress reports to the court. These reports demonstrate how the hotel is performing under receivership and whether the turnaround strategies are effective.

- Practical Example: A hotel in Las Vegas, under receivership, submitted monthly financial reports to the court, detailing improvements in cash flow and occupancy rates. This transparency helped build trust with the court and creditors.

2. Following Legal Guidelines:

- The receiver must ensure that all actions taken during the receivership process comply with legal requirements. This includes adhering to labor laws, maintaining accurate financial records, and ensuring that all stakeholders' rights are protected.

- Practical Example: A hotel receiver in Atlanta worked closely with legal advisors to ensure that staffing changes and contract negotiations were compliant with employment laws and court orders.

Actionable Steps:

- Work closely with legal professionals to ensure compliance with court orders.

- Maintain accurate financial records and submit required reports on time.

- Communicate regularly with the court and stakeholders about the hotel's progress.

Communicating with Stakeholders During Receivership

Effective communication with stakeholders—such as creditors, employees, guests, vendors, and hotel owners—is crucial for maintaining trust and ensuring a smooth receivership process.

1. Transparent Communication with Employees:

- Employees may feel uncertain about their job security during receivership. It's essential to communicate openly about the situation, reassure staff, and keep them informed about changes in operations or management.

- Practical Example: The receiver at a hotel in Orlando held regular meetings with staff to provide updates on the receivership process, answer questions, and outline the plan for improving the hotel's performance. This transparency helped maintain employee morale and engagement.

2. Keeping Creditors Informed:

- Regularly updating creditors about the hotel's financial performance, progress, and turnaround strategies can build trust and demonstrate that the receivership process is moving in the right direction.

- Practical Example: A hotel in Seattle under receivership provided quarterly updates to creditors, showing how cost-saving measures and revenue enhancements were improving the hotel's financial health.

3. Engaging with Guests and Vendors:

- Continue to communicate with guests to reassure them that the hotel's service quality will not be compromised. Maintain open communication with vendors to negotiate payment terms and ensure the continued supply of essential goods and services.

- Practical Example: A hotel in Dallas maintained regular contact with its top suppliers during receivership, negotiating extended payment terms that allowed operations to continue uninterrupted.

Actionable Steps:

- Hold regular meetings with employees to provide updates on the receivership process.

- Communicate frequently with creditors, guests, and vendors to maintain trust and confidence.

- Be transparent and proactive in addressing concerns raised by stakeholders.

Operating a hotel under receivership requires effective management of day-to-day operations, addressing financial and operational challenges, implementing turnaround strategies, ensuring compliance with court orders, and maintaining clear communication with all stakeholders. The case of the Sunset Harbor Hotel demonstrates how a receiver can significantly improve a hotel's performance, turning a distressed asset into a valuable property. By focusing on operational efficiency, financial management, and stakeholder communication, hotels under receivership can achieve stability, improve profitability, and ultimately emerge stronger from the process.

Exit Strategies from Receivership

Exiting receivership represents a significant milestone for a distressed hotel, but it requires careful planning and execution to ensure long-term success. This process involves preparing the hotel for sale or transfer, completing legal and financial obligations, and transitioning back to ownership or new management. Properly implementing an exit strategy is crucial to ensure that the hotel emerges from receivership in a strong financial and operational position. In this section, we'll explore how to navigate this process effectively, illustrated with practical examples, a case study, and actionable steps.

Preparing the Hotel for Sale or Transfer

One of the most common exit strategies from receivership is to sell or transfer the hotel to new ownership. Proper preparation is essential to maximize the property's value and ensure a successful transaction.

1. Enhancing the Hotel's Marketability:

- To attract potential buyers, the hotel must be presented as an attractive investment opportunity. This may involve addressing deferred maintenance, upgrading guest rooms, enhancing common areas, and improving curb appeal.

- Practical Example: A hotel in Miami under receivership invested in renovating the lobby, updating outdated fixtures, and repainting the exterior. These enhancements increased the hotel's perceived value and attracted several interested buyers.

2. Conducting a Pre-Sale Audit:

- Before listing the hotel for sale, conduct a comprehensive audit of the property, including financial records, operational performance, and compliance with regulations. This audit ensures that any issues are identified and addressed before potential buyers conduct their due diligence.

- Practical Example: A hotel in Chicago conducted a pre-sale audit that revealed minor code violations related to fire safety. The receiver promptly addressed these issues, ensuring they did not become a stumbling block during the sale process.

3. Developing a Marketing Strategy:

- Create a targeted marketing strategy to promote the hotel to potential buyers. This may include listing the property with commercial real estate brokers, advertising through industry publications, and leveraging online platforms.

- Practical Example: A receiver in Los Angeles partnered with a commercial real estate broker specializing in hospitality properties, resulting in a well-targeted marketing campaign that reached a wide pool of potential investors.

Actionable Steps:

- Address deferred maintenance and make necessary improvements to enhance the hotel's marketability.

- Conduct a pre-sale audit to identify and resolve any issues that may affect the sale.

- Develop a targeted marketing strategy to promote the hotel to potential buyers.

Completing Legal and Financial Obligations

Successfully exiting receivership requires the completion of all legal and financial obligations. This ensures that the hotel's assets, debts, and liabilities are properly managed and transferred to the new owner or back to the original owner.

1. Settling Debts and Liabilities:

- Work closely with creditors and legal professionals to settle outstanding debts and liabilities. This may involve negotiating payment terms, restructuring debt, or settling claims. It's essential to ensure that all financial obligations are resolved before the transfer or sale.

- Practical Example: A hotel in Dallas, under receivership, negotiated with creditors to settle outstanding debts at a reduced rate, allowing the hotel to exit receivership with a manageable financial structure.

2. Finalizing Legal Documentation:

- Ensure that all legal documents, including contracts, leases, licenses, and permits, are up-to-date and accurately reflect the hotel's current status. This step is crucial to avoid legal complications during the sale or transfer.

- Practical Example: A hotel in New York faced delays in its sale process because its liquor license was expired. The receiver quickly renewed the license, allowing the transaction to proceed smoothly.

3. Preparing Financial Statements:

- Prepare comprehensive financial statements, including profit and loss statements, balance sheets, and cash flow projections. Accurate financial records provide transparency and build trust with potential buyers or investors.

- Practical Example: A hotel in Atlanta presented a detailed financial report that included projections of future revenue based on recent operational improvements. This transparency helped attract a qualified buyer willing to pay a premium price.

Actionable Steps:

- Work with legal and financial advisors to settle outstanding debts and liabilities.

- Ensure all legal documents are updated and

accurately reflect the hotel's current status.

- Prepare comprehensive financial statements to present to potential buyers or investors.

Transitioning Back to Ownership or New Management

Once the hotel exits receivership, it must transition back to ownership or transfer to new management. This process involves implementing a seamless handover of operations and ensuring continuity in service quality.

1. Establishing a Transition Plan:

- Develop a detailed transition plan that outlines the steps required to transfer control from the receiver to the owner or new management team. This plan should include timelines, responsibilities, and key tasks to ensure a smooth handover.

- Practical Example: A hotel in Seattle created a transition plan that included training sessions for the new management team, ensuring they understood the hotel's operational procedures and financial systems.

2. Communicating with Staff and Stakeholders:

- Communicate with employees, guests, vendors, and other stakeholders about the transition process. Reassure staff about job security and inform guests about the change in ownership or management to maintain trust and confidence.

- Practical Example: A hotel in Orlando held an all-staff meeting to introduce the new management team and outline the hotel's future plans. This transparency helped maintain employee morale during the transition.

3. Monitoring the Transition Process:

- Monitor the transition process closely to identify any issues or challenges that arise. This allows for quick adjustments and ensures that the hotel continues to operate smoothly during the changeover.

- Practical Example: A hotel in Houston conducted weekly meetings with the new management team during the first month of the transition, providing ongoing support and addressing any operational challenges that emerged.

Actionable Steps:

- Develop a comprehensive transition plan outlining responsibilities and timelines.

- Communicate with staff and stakeholders to ensure a smooth transition.

- Monitor the transition process closely and provide support as needed.

Case Study: A Successful Exit from Receivership

The Ocean Breeze Hotel, a 120-room property in a popular coastal destination, was placed under receivership due to declining revenue and mounting debt. After 18 months of operational improvements and financial restructuring under the receiver's guidance, the hotel was prepared for a successful exit from receivership.

Actions Taken:

Enhancing Marketability: The receiver invested in renovations, including upgrading guest rooms, modernizing the lobby, and enhancing landscaping. These improvements significantly increased the hotel's value and appeal to potential buyers.

- Completing Legal and Financial Obligations: The receiver negotiated with creditors to settle outstanding debts, ensuring that the hotel's financial obligations were fully resolved before the sale.

- Transitioning to New Ownership: The receiver worked with a commercial real estate broker to market the hotel, ultimately securing a buyer willing to pay a premium price. The new owner was provided with a detailed transition plan, ensuring a smooth handover.

Outcome: The Ocean Breeze Hotel was successfully sold at a price that allowed creditors to recover their investments, and the new owner continued to operate the hotel profitably, maintaining the improvements made during receivership.

Key Takeaway: By enhancing marketability, completing legal and financial obligations, and ensuring a smooth transition to new ownership, the Ocean Breeze Hotel achieved a successful exit from receivership.

Tips for a Smooth Transition

Exiting receivership can be a complex process, but following these tips can help ensure a smooth transition:

- Engage with Professionals: Work with legal, financial, and operational advisors who specialize in receivership exits to guide you through the process and ensure compliance with all requirements.

- Maintain Clear Communication: Keep all stakeholders, including employees, vendors, guests, and creditors, informed throughout the transition to build trust and minimize disruptions.

- Focus on Continuity: Ensure that operational systems, processes, and service standards are maintained during the transition to avoid any negative impact on guest experiences or hotel performance.

Actionable Steps:

- Engage experienced professionals to guide you through the exit process.

- Communicate regularly with all stakeholders to maintain trust and confidence.

- Focus on maintaining continuity in operations and service quality.

Preventing Future Financial Distress

Preventing future financial distress is essential to avoid re-entering receivership. Implementing proactive financial management strategies and maintaining operational efficiency are key to long-term stability.

1. Establishing Financial Controls:

- Implement robust financial controls, including regular financial monitoring, budgeting, and forecasting. This ensures that the hotel's financial health is closely monitored and potential issues are addressed early.

- Practical Example: A hotel in Denver established monthly financial reviews, allowing management to identify revenue shortfalls and implement corrective measures promptly.

2. Building Cash Reserves:

- Create a cash reserve fund to provide a

financial buffer during periods of low occupancy or unexpected expenses. Having cash reserves can help prevent future financial crises.

- Practical Example: A hotel in Las Vegas established a cash reserve fund by setting aside a portion of monthly profits, which helped the hotel navigate a temporary decline in bookings without financial distress.

3. Adopting Risk Management Practices:

- Regularly assess and mitigate risks, such as market fluctuations, operational inefficiencies, or changes in regulations. This proactive approach helps prevent future financial challenges.

- Practical Example: A hotel in Boston conducted an annual risk assessment, allowing management to identify potential threats and implement mitigation strategies.

Actionable Steps:

- Implement regular financial monitoring and establish robust financial controls.

- Build a cash reserve fund to provide a financial safety net.

- Conduct regular risk assessments to identify and address potential threats.

Exiting receivership requires a strategic and well-executed approach, involving careful preparation for sale or transfer, completion of legal and financial obligations, and a seamless transition back to ownership or new management. The journey of the Ocean Breeze Hotel demonstrates that with proper planning, communication, and execution, a hotel can successfully exit receivership and thrive in a competitive market. By focusing on proactive financial management and risk mitigation, hotels can avoid future financial distress and build a foundation for long-term stability and success.

Lessons Learned from Receivership

Receivership is often seen as a last resort for distressed hotels, but it can also be a pivotal turning point that leads to successful turnarounds and long-term stability. Understanding the lessons learned during this challenging process is crucial for avoiding future pitfalls, building resilience, and preparing for sustainable success. This section provides an in-depth analysis of common pitfalls, how receivership can facilitate a successful turnaround, strategies for building resilience, actionable steps for a post-receivership action plan, and a case study demonstrating how a hotel emerged stronger after receivership.

Common Pitfalls and Challenges

Operating a hotel under receivership is fraught with obstacles, but recognizing these challenges early can help avoid common pitfalls and set the stage for a successful recovery.

1. Inadequate Financial Oversight:

- One of the most frequent issues leading to receivership is poor financial management, including inadequate cash flow monitoring, unchecked expenses, or failure to address mounting debt. These issues often stem from a lack of financial discipline or insufficient expertise in managing complex hospitality finances.

- Practical Example: A hotel in Chicago failed to monitor its cash flow regularly, leading to unpaid vendor bills and missed loan payments. By the time the hotel entered receivership, it faced significant debt, making recovery more challenging.

2. Failure to Adapt to Market Trends:

- Many hotels that end up in receivership struggle to adapt to changing market demands, such as shifts in guest preferences, technological advancements, or evolving competitive landscapes. Ignoring these trends often results in declining occupancy rates and revenue.

- Practical Example: A hotel in Miami failed to upgrade its facilities or offer digital booking options, leading to a drop in bookings as competitors with modern amenities gained market share.

3. Communication Breakdowns:

- Ineffective communication with stakeholders, including staff, creditors, vendors, and guests, can exacerbate the challenges of receivership. This can result in lost trust, low employee morale, and operational inefficiencies.

- Practical Example: A hotel in Los Angeles failed to communicate its receivership status to employees, leading to rumors, uncertainty, and increased staff turnover, which hindered the turnaround process.

Actionable Steps:

- Implement regular financial monitoring and review processes to stay on top of cash flow and expenses.

- Stay informed about market trends and guest preferences to adapt service offerings accordingly.

- Maintain open and transparent communication with all stakeholders to build trust and minimize disruptions.

How Receivership Can Lead to Successful Turnarounds

Despite the challenges, receivership can be a catalyst for positive change, helping hotels restructure, improve operations, and emerge stronger.

1. Financial Restructuring:

- Receivership allows for financial restructuring, including negotiating with creditors to settle debts, renegotiating contracts, and implementing cost-saving measures. These steps can improve cash flow and stabilize the hotel's financial health.

- Practical Example: A hotel in Orlando under receivership reduced its debt burden by 30% through negotiations with creditors, allowing it to reinvest in marketing and guest services.

2. Operational Improvements:

- Receivers often bring a fresh perspective and expertise in hospitality management, enabling them to identify inefficiencies and implement operational changes that improve profitability.

- Practical Example: A receiver at a hotel in Denver streamlined housekeeping operations by introducing more efficient scheduling and cross-training staff, resulting in a 20% reduction in labor costs without compromising service quality.

3. Strategic Repositioning:

- Receivership can provide an opportunity for strategic repositioning, such as updating branding, renovating facilities, or targeting new market segments. This can help the hotel attract a broader customer base and increase revenue.

- Practical Example: A hotel in New York underwent a rebranding process during receivership, positioning itself as a boutique property catering to business travelers, which led to a 15% increase in occupancy rates.

Actionable Steps:

- Work with the receiver to identify opportunities for financial restructuring and cost savings.

- Implement operational improvements that enhance efficiency and guest experience.

- Consider repositioning the hotel to target new market segments or improve brand perception.

Building Resilience for Future Challenges

Emerging from receivership offers an opportunity to build resilience and prepare for future challenges. The lessons learned during this period can help hotels avoid similar financial distress in the future.

1. Establish Strong Financial Controls:

- Implement robust financial controls, such as regular cash flow monitoring, budgeting, and expense tracking, to prevent future financial mismanagement.

- Practical Example: A hotel in Atlanta

introduced monthly financial reviews and performance metrics, enabling management to identify potential issues early and take corrective action.

2. Develop a Culture of Adaptability:

- Encourage a culture of adaptability and innovation to ensure the hotel remains responsive to market trends, guest preferences, and industry changes.

- Practical Example: A hotel in Las Vegas formed an innovation team to explore new revenue streams, such as offering virtual event hosting during periods of low occupancy, which helped maintain profitability during off-peak seasons.

3. Build Cash Reserves and Contingency Plans:

- Establish a cash reserve fund and contingency plans to provide a financial buffer during periods of uncertainty or economic downturns.

- Practical Example: A hotel in Boston allocated a portion of monthly profits to a cash reserve fund, allowing it to weather unexpected challenges, such as a temporary drop in bookings due to a natural disaster.

Actionable Steps:

- Implement financial controls and regular performance reviews.

- Foster a culture of adaptability and innovation among staff.

- Build cash reserves to provide a financial safety net for future challenges.

Developing a Post-Receivership Action Plan

Creating a post-receivership action plan is essential for maintaining momentum and ensuring long-term stability. This plan should outline strategies for improving operations, financial management, and marketing efforts.

1. Reassess Financial Goals and Objectives:

- Reevaluate the hotel's financial goals and create a roadmap for achieving profitability and growth. Set realistic targets for revenue, expenses, and debt repayment.

- Practical Example: A hotel in San Francisco developed a five-year financial plan post-receivership that included targets for revenue growth, cost reduction, and capital improvements.

2. Focus on Guest Experience and Service Quality:

- Invest in training programs and initiatives that enhance the guest experience, as this is critical for building brand loyalty and attracting repeat business.

- Practical Example: A hotel in Dallas launched a

customer service training program for its staff, resulting in higher guest satisfaction scores and an increase in positive online reviews.

3. Strengthen Marketing and Branding Efforts:

- Develop a marketing strategy that highlights the hotel's unique selling points and improvements made during receivership. Leverage social media, email marketing, and partnerships with travel agencies to reach potential guests.

- Practical Example: A hotel in Miami re-engaged with past guests through an email marketing campaign, offering special discounts for returning customers, which led to a 20% increase in bookings.

Actionable Steps:

- Create a post-receivership financial plan with clear goals and objectives.

- Invest in staff training to improve guest service and experience.

- Develop a targeted marketing strategy to promote the hotel's revitalization.

Case Study: A Hotel's Journey After Receivership

The Palm Coast Inn, a 140-room hotel in a popular tourist destination, was placed under receivership due to declining revenue, high operating costs, and mounting debt. After 18 months of operational improvements and financial restructuring under receivership, the hotel emerged with a solid foundation for growth.

Actions Taken:

- Financial Restructuring: The receiver negotiated with creditors to reduce debt by 35% and implemented cost-saving measures, such as energy-efficient upgrades, reducing utility expenses by 20%.

- Operational Improvements: The receiver optimized staffing levels, introduced a dynamic pricing strategy, and invested in marketing campaigns targeting local and regional travelers.

- Repositioning and Rebranding: The hotel underwent a rebranding process, positioning itself as a family-friendly resort with new amenities, including a children's play area and family packages.

Outcome: Within two years of exiting receivership, the Palm Coast Inn's occupancy rate increased by 40%, and annual revenue grew by 30%. The hotel established a strong financial position and continued to thrive, even during off-peak seasons.

Key Takeaway: By addressing financial challenges, implementing operational improvements, and strategically repositioning itself, the Palm Coast Inn successfully transitioned from receivership to profitability and growth.

Preparing for Long-Term Success

Ensuring long-term success after receivership requires a commitment to ongoing financial discipline, operational excellence, and adaptability.

1. Continuously Monitor Financial Performance:

- Regularly review financial statements, track performance metrics, and adjust strategies as needed to maintain profitability and prevent future distress.

- Practical Example: A hotel in Phoenix held monthly financial review meetings, enabling the management team to make data-driven decisions and adapt to changing market conditions.

2. Invest in Staff Development and Training:

- Invest in ongoing staff training and development to ensure consistent service quality and maintain a competitive edge.

- Practical Example: A hotel in Seattle implemented a staff training program that focused on leadership development, resulting in higher employee engagement and improved guest experiences.

3. Stay Informed About Industry Trends:

- Keep abreast of industry trends, technological advancements, and consumer preferences to ensure the hotel remains competitive and responsive to market changes.

- Practical Example: A hotel in Los Angeles adopted contactless check-in technology, which enhanced the guest experience and set the property apart from competitors.

Actionable Steps:

- Implement regular financial monitoring and adjust strategies based on performance.

- Invest in ongoing staff training and development.

- Stay informed about industry trends and technological advancements.

Receivership can be a challenging experience, but it also offers valuable lessons that can pave the way for long-term success. By recognizing common pitfalls, leveraging the benefits of receivership, building resilience, and developing a robust post-receivership action plan, hotels can emerge stronger and better equipped to navigate future challenges. The journey of the Palm Coast Inn demonstrates that with strategic planning, operational improvements, and a commitment to financial discipline, hotels can successfully transition from receivership to profitability and long-term success.

Working with Professional Advisors

Engaging the right professional advisors can be a critical factor in successfully navigating receivership for distressed hotels. These experts provide the specialized knowledge and guidance needed to manage complex legal, financial, and operational challenges. This section explores the role of advisors in the receivership process, offers insights into building a team of experts, and provides practical tips for choosing, communicating with, and managing these relationships.

The Role of Legal, Financial, and Operational Advisors

Professional advisors play distinct yet interconnected roles during the receivership process, helping hotel owners and stakeholders make informed decisions that can lead to a successful turnaround.

1. Legal Advisors:

- Role: Legal advisors guide hotel owners through the legal complexities of receivership, ensuring compliance with court orders, protecting the hotel's assets, and navigating negotiations with creditors, lenders, and other stakeholders.

- Practical Example: A hotel in San Francisco, facing receivership, hired a legal advisor who specialized in hospitality law. The advisor helped the hotel owner understand the legal implications of receivership and facilitated negotiations with creditors, resulting in a more favorable debt restructuring agreement.

2. Financial Advisors:

- Role: Financial advisors assess the hotel's financial health, develop strategies to improve cash flow, and assist with financial restructuring. They also create financial forecasts and monitor performance throughout the receivership process.

- Practical Example: A distressed hotel in New York worked with a financial advisor who identified high labor costs as a significant issue. By implementing labor cost controls and optimizing scheduling, the hotel achieved a 15% reduction in expenses within six months.

3. Operational Advisors:

- Role: Operational advisors analyze the hotel's day-to-day operations, identify inefficiencies, and recommend strategies to improve productivity and profitability. They often focus on areas such as guest services, marketing, sales, and property management.

- Practical Example: An operational advisor helped a hotel in Miami implement a dynamic pricing strategy, which adjusted room rates based on demand. This resulted in a 20% increase in occupancy rates and significantly improved revenue.

Actionable Steps:

- Engage legal, financial, and operational advisors with experience in the hospitality industry and receivership cases.

- Clearly define the scope of each advisor's role to ensure that they work collaboratively and effectively.

Building a Team of Experts for Successful Receivership Management

Assembling a team of professional advisors who can work together is essential for a successful receivership process. Each expert brings unique skills and insights that can help address the hotel's specific challenges.

1. Identify the Areas of Expertise Needed:

- Assess the hotel's unique challenges to determine the areas where professional guidance is required. This could include legal compliance, financial restructuring, operational efficiency, marketing, or human resources.

- Practical Example: A hotel in Las Vegas identified legal, financial, and operational challenges, and therefore built a team consisting of a hospitality lawyer, a financial restructuring specialist, and an operational advisor with experience in hotel management.

2. Ensure Advisors Have Relevant Experience:

- Select advisors who have proven experience in the hospitality sector and have successfully managed receivership cases. This ensures they understand the nuances of the hotel industry and can provide tailored solutions.

- Practical Example: A hotel in Chicago hired an operational advisor who had previously managed turnarounds for several distressed hotels. This expertise allowed the advisor to quickly implement strategies that improved guest experience and operational efficiency.

3. Foster Collaboration Among Advisors:

- Encourage open communication and collaboration among advisors to ensure a cohesive approach to the receivership process. Regular meetings and updates can help keep everyone aligned on goals and strategies.

- Practical Example: A hotel in Denver held weekly meetings with its legal, financial, and operational advisors to discuss progress and challenges. This collaborative approach ensured that strategies were implemented effectively and that all aspects of the hotel's recovery were addressed.

Actionable Steps:

- Identify the key areas where expert guidance is needed and build a team accordingly.

- Select advisors with a proven track record in the hospitality industry.

- Facilitate regular communication and collaboration among the advisory team.

Case Study: How Advisors Helped Navigate Receivership

The Sunrise Bay Resort, a 200-room hotel in a popular tourist destination, faced financial distress due to declining revenue, high operational costs, and significant debt. The hotel entered receivership, and the receiver assembled a team of professional advisors to guide the turnaround process.

Actions Taken:

- Legal Advisor: The legal advisor facilitated negotiations with creditors, resulting in a debt restructuring plan that reduced monthly payments by 30%. This allowed the hotel to allocate more funds toward operational improvements.

- Financial Advisor: The financial advisor conducted a comprehensive analysis of the hotel's finances, identified areas of overspending, and implemented cost-saving measures. This included renegotiating supplier contracts and optimizing labor costs, which led to a 25% reduction in expenses.

- Operational Advisor: The operational advisor

introduced a revenue management strategy that included dynamic pricing, targeted marketing campaigns, and improved guest service training. These initiatives increased occupancy rates and guest satisfaction.

Outcome: Within 18 months, the Sunrise Bay Resort's revenue increased by 35%, and operational costs decreased by 20%. The hotel emerged from receivership with a stronger financial position and a more efficient operation.

Key Takeaway: The collaborative efforts of legal, financial, and operational advisors were instrumental in the successful turnaround of the Sunrise Bay Resort, demonstrating the importance of a coordinated approach to receivership management.

Tips for Choosing the Right Advisors

Selecting the right advisors is crucial for navigating the complexities of receivership. The following tips can help hotel owners choose the most suitable professionals for their situation:

1. Check Industry Experience:

- Look for advisors with experience in the hospitality sector and a track record of successful receivership cases. This ensures they understand the unique challenges of managing a hotel in financial distress.

- Practical Example: A hotel in Orlando chose a financial advisor who had previously worked with several large hotel chains, ensuring that the advisor understood the complexities of hospitality finances.

2. Assess Communication Skills:

- Choose advisors who communicate clearly and effectively. This is essential for ensuring that all stakeholders understand the strategies being implemented and the progress being made.

- Practical Example: An operational advisor working with a hotel in Seattle provided regular, easy-to-understand reports on the progress of implemented changes, which helped build trust with the hotel owner and other stakeholders.

3. Seek References and Recommendations:

- Ask for references from past clients or colleagues who can speak to the advisor's expertise, professionalism, and effectiveness.

- Practical Example: A hotel in Boston requested references from a potential legal advisor and received positive feedback about their experience managing complex receivership cases in the hospitality industry.

Actionable Steps:

- Ensure advisors have relevant hospitality experience and a successful track record.

- Choose advisors with strong communication skills.

- Request references and recommendations before making a final decision.

Effective Communication with Advisors

Clear and consistent communication is key to a successful relationship with advisors during receivership. It ensures that all parties remain informed, aligned, and focused on the hotel's goals.

1. Establish Regular Meetings:

- Schedule regular meetings with advisors to review progress, discuss challenges, and plan the next steps. This keeps everyone updated and allows for prompt adjustments to strategies as needed.

- Practical Example: A hotel in Los Angeles held bi-weekly meetings with its financial and operational advisors, allowing them to address challenges promptly and adjust their approach to improving the hotel's cash flow.

2. Provide Access to Key Information:

- Share relevant financial, operational, and market data with advisors to ensure they have the information needed to make informed recommendations.

- Practical Example: A hotel in Houston granted

its financial advisor access to its accounting software, enabling real-time monitoring of cash flow and expenses.

3. Encourage Open Feedback:

- Encourage advisors to provide honest feedback and suggestions, even if they involve difficult decisions. Open communication fosters a collaborative environment and leads to better outcomes.

- Practical Example: An operational advisor working with a hotel in Denver suggested closing an underperforming restaurant to reduce costs. Although it was a tough decision, the hotel's management appreciated the honest feedback and implemented the change, which improved profitability.

Actionable Steps:

- Schedule regular meetings with advisors to discuss progress and challenges.

- Provide advisors with access to key financial and operational data.

- Encourage open and honest feedback to foster a collaborative environment.

Strategies for Managing Advisor Relationships

Managing relationships with professional advisors effectively is essential for achieving the desired outcomes during receivership.

1. Set Clear Expectations and Goals:

- Define clear expectations, goals, and deliverables for each advisor. This helps keep everyone focused and ensures that all efforts are aligned with the hotel's objectives.

- Practical Example: A hotel in Phoenix developed a performance metrics system for its advisors, outlining specific targets such as reducing operating expenses by 20% and increasing occupancy rates by 15%.

2. Monitor Progress and Performance:

- Regularly monitor the progress and performance of advisors to ensure they are meeting their objectives and delivering value. Provide feedback and make adjustments if necessary.

- Practical Example: A hotel in New York conducted monthly performance reviews with its team of advisors, which helped identify areas for improvement and ensured that everyone stayed on track.

3. Maintain Professional Boundaries:

- While building a positive working relationship with advisors is important, maintain professional boundaries to ensure that the relationship remains focused on achieving results.

- **Practical Example:** A hotel in San Diego maintained a formal relationship with its financial advisor, ensuring that all communications and recommendations were documented and tied to specific goals.

Actionable Steps:

- Set clear expectations, goals, and deliverables for each advisor.

- Monitor progress regularly and provide constructive feedback.

- Maintain professional boundaries to ensure a results-oriented relationship.

Working with professional advisors during receivership is a critical component of achieving a successful turnaround for a distressed hotel. By understanding the roles of legal, financial, and operational advisors, building a cohesive team, and maintaining effective communication, hotel owners can navigate the complexities of receivership more effectively. The case of the Sunrise Bay Resort demonstrates that with the right advisors in place, even a hotel facing significant financial challenges can emerge stronger and more profitable. By carefully selecting advisors with relevant experience, setting clear expectations, and fostering open communication, hotel owners can leverage the expertise of their advisory team to achieve a successful receivership outcome.

In summary, professional advisors play a crucial role in guiding distressed hotels through the receivership process, from financial restructuring to operational improvements. By collaborating with advisors, hotel owners can develop and implement strategies that not only address immediate financial challenges but also set the stage for long-term success. Investing in the right team of experts, managing these relationships effectively, and learning from their insights can transform the receivership experience from a period of distress into a powerful catalyst for recovery and growth.

Rebuilding the Hotel's Brand and Reputation

Emerging from receivership is a crucial turning point for a distressed hotel, but it often comes with a tarnished brand and reputation. Restoring trust, confidence, and market presence requires a deliberate effort to re-engage guests, travel agents, and other stakeholders. This section provides in-depth analysis, practical examples, a case study, and actionable steps on how to rebuild the hotel's brand and reputation post-receivership.

Restoring Trust and Confidence with Guests

One of the most significant challenges after receivership is regaining the trust and confidence of past and potential guests. A hotel's reputation often takes a hit during financial distress, and rebuilding it requires a consistent and transparent approach.

1. Communicate the Changes:
   - Be transparent about the improvements made

during and after receivership. Share information about upgrades, enhanced services, and operational changes that have been implemented to ensure a better guest experience.

- Practical Example: A hotel in Miami created a detailed webpage titled "Our New Chapter" that highlighted renovations, upgraded amenities, and the new management team. This transparency reassured guests that the hotel had made positive changes.

2. Deliver Exceptional Guest Experiences:

- The best way to restore trust is by exceeding guest expectations. Train staff to deliver exceptional service, respond promptly to guest inquiries, and ensure that every interaction is positive.

- Practical Example: A hotel in Los Angeles focused on personalized service, such as greeting guests by name and providing customized welcome amenities. These small gestures led to an increase in positive online reviews and word-of-mouth referrals.

3. Address Past Issues Proactively:

- Identify common complaints from guests before and during receivership and take steps to address them. Communicate these improvements clearly to show that the hotel is actively responding to feedback.

- Practical Example: A hotel in New York, which faced criticism for outdated facilities, launched a social media campaign showcasing its newly renovated rooms and modern amenities, emphasizing the steps taken to improve guest experiences.

Actionable Steps:

- Create a communication plan to share improvements made post-receivership.

- Train staff to provide exceptional service and personalized experiences.

- Address past complaints publicly and highlight how they've been resolved.

Re-engaging with Travel Agents and Distribution Networks

Travel agents and distribution networks play a crucial role in driving bookings, especially for hotels that have recently emerged from receivership. Rebuilding relationships with these partners can help regain market share and boost occupancy rates.

1. Reach Out to Key Partners:

- Proactively contact travel agents, online travel agencies (OTAs), and distribution networks to inform them of the hotel's new direction, enhancements, and management team. Offer special rates or incentives to encourage them to feature your property.

- Practical Example: A hotel in Orlando contacted its top travel agent partners and offered them exclusive discounted rates for their clients. This gesture helped rekindle relationships and generated an immediate uptick in bookings.

2. Update Profiles and Listings:

- Ensure that all online profiles, including those on OTAs, travel agency platforms, and review sites, reflect the hotel's recent improvements, new amenities, and rebranding efforts.

- Practical Example: A hotel in Chicago updated its profile on major OTAs, adding new photos, an updated description of its services, and details about renovations. This led to a 15% increase in bookings from these platforms.

3. Attend Industry Events and Trade Shows:

- Participating in hospitality industry events, trade shows, and travel fairs provides an opportunity to network with travel agents and distribution partners, showcase the hotel's new brand, and build relationships.

- Practical Example: A hotel in Las Vegas attended a regional travel trade show and set up a booth showcasing its rebranding efforts. The hotel's representatives met with over 100 travel agents, resulting in new partnerships and increased visibility.

Actionable Steps:

- Reach out to travel agents and distribution networks with special offers.

- Update online profiles and listings to reflect the hotel's new brand and improvements.

- Participate in industry events to build relationships with travel partners.

Launching Marketing Campaigns Post-Receivership

A well-executed marketing campaign is essential for reintroducing the hotel to the market and attracting guests. The goal is to highlight the hotel's improvements, new offerings, and commitment to delivering an exceptional guest experience.

1. Create a Grand Reopening Campaign:

- Launch a "Grand Reopening" campaign to announce the hotel's emergence from receivership and highlight recent renovations, service enhancements, and special offers.

- Practical Example: A hotel in Houston hosted a grand reopening event, inviting local media, travel influencers, and loyal guests. The event was live-streamed on social media, generating buzz and attracting new bookings.

2. Utilize Social Media and Digital Marketing:

- Use social media platforms, email marketing, and online ads to reach your target audience. Share content that showcases the hotel's transformation, special promotions, and unique experiences.

- Practical Example: A hotel in Seattle launched a digital marketing campaign featuring before-and-after photos of its renovations, guest testimonials, and limited-time discount offers. The campaign led to a 30% increase in website traffic and bookings.

3. Partner with Influencers and Bloggers:

- Collaborate with travel influencers, bloggers, and local media to generate positive publicity and reach a wider audience.

- Practical Example: A hotel in Miami invited travel bloggers for a complimentary weekend stay, resulting in several blog posts and social media mentions that highlighted the hotel's new features and services.

Actionable Steps:

- Plan and execute a grand reopening event to generate excitement.

- Use social media and digital marketing to reach a broader audience.

- Partner with influencers to create authentic content about the hotel's improvements.

Case Study: A Rebranding Success Story

The Beachside Haven Hotel, a 150-room beachfront property, faced financial distress and entered receivership. After emerging from receivership, the hotel's management team embarked on a comprehensive rebranding and marketing campaign to rebuild its reputation.

Actions Taken:

- Renovations and Enhancements: The hotel invested in renovating guest rooms, upgrading common areas, and adding new amenities such as a rooftop bar and spa services.

- Marketing Campaign: The hotel launched a "New Beginnings" marketing campaign, which included a grand reopening event, targeted social media ads, email newsletters to past guests, and partnerships with travel influencers.

- Re-engaging Travel Partners: The hotel contacted travel agents and OTAs, offering exclusive promotions and showcasing the improvements made during and after receivership.

Outcome: Within 12 months, the Beachside Haven Hotel's occupancy rate increased by 40%, and average daily rates (ADR) improved by 25%. The hotel's reputation was restored, with positive reviews and media coverage helping to attract a steady stream of bookings.

Key Takeaway: A strategic rebranding and marketing campaign, combined with a focus on delivering exceptional guest experiences, can significantly improve a hotel's reputation and performance after receivership.

Tips for Leveraging Guest Feedback

Guest feedback is a valuable resource for understanding how well the hotel is meeting expectations and identifying areas for improvement.

1. Encourage Guest Reviews:

- Encourage guests to leave reviews on popular platforms such as TripAdvisor, Google, and OTAs. Positive reviews help build credibility and attract more guests.

- Practical Example: A hotel in San Diego offered a small discount on future bookings to guests who left a review, resulting in a significant increase in positive feedback online.

2. Respond to Reviews Professionally:

- Respond promptly and professionally to all reviews, both positive and negative. Address any concerns raised by guests and highlight the steps taken to resolve them.

- Practical Example: A hotel in New York responded to a negative review about slow check-in times by explaining that they had recently implemented a new express check-in system, which had since improved the experience for guests.

3. Use Feedback for Continuous Improvement:

- Analyze guest feedback to identify trends and areas for improvement. Use this information to refine services, amenities, and guest experiences.

- Practical Example: A hotel in Atlanta noticed several reviews mentioning outdated bathrooms. As a result, the hotel prioritized bathroom renovations, which led to improved guest satisfaction scores.

Actionable Steps:

- Encourage guests to leave reviews on popular platforms.

- Respond to guest feedback promptly and professionally.

- Use feedback to identify areas for continuous improvement.

Creating a Positive Brand Image

Creating a positive brand image involves consistently delivering high-quality experiences, maintaining a strong online presence, and building relationships with guests.

1. Develop a Unique Brand Identity:

- Establish a brand identity that reflects the hotel's values, mission, and unique offerings. This includes updating the logo, website, marketing materials, and guest communication to align with the brand message.

- Practical Example: A hotel in Boston rebranded itself as a luxury boutique property, incorporating elegant design elements and personalized services that reinforced its brand image.

2. Maintain Consistent Messaging:

- Ensure that all marketing materials, social media posts, website content, and guest communications reflect the hotel's brand identity and core values.

- Practical Example: A hotel in Chicago used consistent messaging in all its marketing campaigns, emphasizing themes of relaxation, comfort, and exceptional service.

3. Engage with the Local Community:

- Build a positive brand image by engaging with the local community through sponsorships, partnerships, or hosting events.

- Practical Example: A hotel in Dallas hosted charity events and supported local artists by displaying their work in the lobby, creating a positive connection with the community and enhancing its brand image.

Actionable Steps:

- Develop a unique and consistent brand identity.

- Ensure all communications reflect the hotel's core values and mission.

- Engage with the local community to build a positive brand reputation.

Rebuilding a hotel's brand and reputation after receivership requires strategic planning, effective marketing, and a commitment to delivering exceptional guest experiences. By focusing on restoring trust with guests, re-engaging travel agents and distribution networks, launching impactful marketing campaigns, leveraging guest feedback, and building a positive brand image, a hotel can transform its reputation and regain its competitive position in the market.

The case study of the Beachside Haven Hotel demonstrates that even after financial distress, a hotel can experience a successful turnaround by implementing strategic branding and marketing initiatives. Hotels that prioritize communication, consistently deliver quality service, and adapt to guest feedback will be well-positioned to rebuild their brand reputation and achieve long-term success.
In summary, rebuilding a hotel's brand and reputation is not an overnight process; it requires dedication, a willingness to adapt, and a focus on delivering memorable guest experiences. By embracing these strategies, hotel owners and

managers can turn the page on financial distress and write a new chapter of success, ensuring that their property not only recovers but thrives in the competitive hospitality landscape.

Chapter 10: Asset Management of Distressed Hotels

Asset management plays a pivotal role in the recovery and long-term success of distressed hotels, making it a vital component for maximizing value and ensuring sustainable profitability. This chapter delves into the key principles and strategies of hotel asset management, emphasizing its importance in turning around distressed properties and building a foundation for ongoing growth. Effective asset management goes beyond addressing immediate financial challenges; it involves a comprehensive approach that encompasses revenue management, cost control, capital improvement planning, and performance monitoring.

To start, we explore the fundamental concept of hotel asset management and the crucial role asset managers play in the recovery process. Asset managers act as strategic partners, overseeing the financial and operational aspects of a hotel to maximize its performance. Their responsibilities range from analyzing financial statements and negotiating vendor contracts to implementing strategies that enhance the property's overall value. By examining a case study of how asset management improved a distressed hotel's performance, we gain insights into the tangible impact a well-executed asset management plan can have on a struggling property.

One of the primary objectives of asset management is implementing effective revenue management strategies. This chapter outlines the importance of dynamic pricing, inventory management, and optimizing distribution channels to boost a hotel's revenue per available room (RevPAR). By leveraging technology and data analytics, hotels can make informed decisions that enhance profitability. We highlight a case study demonstrating how a distressed hotel increased its RevPAR through revenue management and provide actionable steps for implementing similar strategies.

Cost control and expense management are equally crucial in the asset management process, especially for distressed hotels. Identifying cost-saving opportunities, negotiating vendor contracts, and implementing energy-efficient practices can significantly reduce operational expenses without compromising guest experience. Through a real-world example, we illustrate how a hotel successfully reduced expenses and maintained quality, showcasing the benefits of diligent expense management. Practical tips for maintaining a lean operation and using technology to monitor expenses are also covered, providing readers with valuable tools to manage costs effectively.

Capital improvement planning is another essential aspect of asset management, as it ensures that hotels remain competitive and appealing to guests. This section addresses how to identify and prioritize capital projects, budget for renovations, and finance improvements while minimizing disruption to operations. By examining a case study of a hotel that implemented a successful capital improvement plan, we gain insights into the long-term benefits of investing in property upgrades and maintenance.

Monitoring and reporting performance is a critical component of asset management, enabling hotels to track key performance indicators (KPIs) and make data-driven decisions. Regular asset reviews and audits, combined with the use of technology, ensure that a hotel's performance is continuously assessed and optimized. We present a case study illustrating how performance monitoring improved a hotel's profitability and provide tips for engaging stakeholders in this process to maintain accountability and drive results.

Finally, the chapter explores strategies for building a sustainable future for distressed hotels, focusing on long-term growth, fostering a culture of continuous improvement, and implementing risk management practices. By learning from a hotel's journey to sustainable profitability, readers will understand how to navigate market changes, challenges, and uncertainties. This comprehensive approach to asset management not only helps distressed hotels regain stability but also sets the stage for achieving lasting success in an ever-evolving hospitality landscape.

Through in-depth analysis, real-world examples, and actionable strategies, this chapter offers a practical guide to hotel asset management, equipping readers with the knowledge and tools needed to transform distressed properties into profitable and thriving assets.

Understanding Hotel Asset Management

Hotel asset management is a strategic approach to maximizing the value, profitability, and performance of a hotel property. It involves a comprehensive analysis of the hotel's operations, financial performance, and market positioning to make informed decisions that enhance its long-term success. This process is particularly crucial for distressed hotels, as it helps identify opportunities for improvement, implement cost-saving measures, and develop revenue-generating strategies. In this section, we will explore the role of hotel asset managers in distressed hotel recovery, their key responsibilities, a case study demonstrating the impact of effective asset management, and actionable steps for building an asset management plan and selecting the right asset manager.

What is Hotel Asset Management?

Hotel asset management is the process of overseeing and optimizing a hotel's operations, financial performance, and overall value. It involves evaluating the property's strengths, weaknesses, opportunities, and threats (SWOT analysis) and implementing strategies to improve profitability, efficiency, and guest satisfaction. Asset management is more than just managing day-to-day operations; it requires a long-term vision and a strategic approach to ensure the hotel remains competitive in a dynamic market.

For distressed hotels, asset management is especially critical. It involves identifying areas where expenses can be reduced, revenue can be increased, and operational efficiencies can be implemented. By taking a proactive and data-driven approach, asset managers can help distressed properties recover from financial difficulties and achieve sustainable growth.

The Role of an Asset Manager in Distressed Hotel Recovery

An asset manager serves as a strategic partner who acts on behalf of the hotel's owner, overseeing the property's financial and operational performance to maximize its value. In the context of distressed hotels, the asset manager's role becomes even more vital, as they are responsible for turning around the hotel's fortunes and steering it toward profitability.

1. Analyzing Financial Performance:

- The asset manager conducts a thorough financial analysis to identify revenue shortfalls, high expenses, and cash flow challenges. By examining profit and loss statements, balance sheets, and key financial metrics, the asset manager can pinpoint areas that require immediate attention.

- Practical Example: An asset manager working with a distressed hotel in Miami identified that food and beverage costs were significantly higher than the industry average. By renegotiating supplier contracts and implementing portion control measures, the hotel reduced its costs by 15%.

2. Developing Revenue Management Strategies:

- The asset manager collaborates with the hotel's management team to implement revenue management strategies, such as dynamic pricing, optimizing distribution channels, and identifying new market segments. This approach helps increase occupancy rates, average daily rates (ADR), and revenue per available room (RevPAR).

- Practical Example: At a distressed hotel in Los Angeles, the asset manager introduced a dynamic pricing model that adjusted room rates based on demand, seasonality, and local events. This strategy resulted in a 20% increase in revenue over six months.

3. Enhancing Operational Efficiency:

- Asset managers identify operational inefficiencies and work with the hotel's management team to implement cost-saving measures. This may involve optimizing staffing levels, reducing waste, and improving inventory management.

- Practical Example: An asset manager at a hotel in Chicago implemented cross-training for staff members, allowing employees to perform multiple roles. This reduced labor costs by 10% without compromising service quality.

Key Responsibilities of Hotel Asset Managers

The responsibilities of a hotel asset manager are

multifaceted and require a deep understanding of the hospitality industry, financial management, and strategic planning. The following are some of the key responsibilities that asset managers undertake when managing distressed hotels:

1. Financial Analysis and Reporting:

- Conducting regular financial reviews and preparing reports that outline the hotel's financial performance, cash flow, profitability, and key performance indicators (KPIs). This helps owners make informed decisions about the property's future.

2. Strategic Planning and Implementation:

- Developing and implementing strategic plans to improve the hotel's financial health, operational efficiency, and market positioning. This may involve launching marketing campaigns, implementing revenue management strategies, or repositioning the hotel in the market.

3. Capital Improvement Planning:

- Identifying capital projects that will enhance the hotel's value, such as renovations, technology upgrades, or amenity enhancements. Asset managers are responsible for budgeting, prioritizing, and overseeing these projects to ensure they align with the hotel's long-term goals.

4. Contract Negotiations and Vendor Management:

- Negotiating contracts with suppliers, vendors, and service providers to ensure the hotel receives the best possible terms. This can lead to significant cost savings, especially for distressed hotels with tight budgets.

5. Monitoring and Reporting Performance:

- Regularly monitoring the hotel's performance and providing detailed reports to owners and stakeholders. This includes tracking KPIs such as RevPAR, ADR, occupancy rates, and profit margins to measure the hotel's progress.

Case Study: How Asset Management Improved a Distressed Hotel's Performance

The Sunset Bay Resort, a 180-room beachfront hotel, faced financial distress due to declining revenue, high operational costs, and poor market positioning. The hotel's owners hired an asset manager to turn around the property's performance and improve profitability.

Actions Taken by the Asset Manager:

- Financial Analysis: The asset manager conducted a comprehensive financial analysis, identifying that the hotel's food and beverage department was operating at a 25% loss due to high labor costs and inefficient inventory management.

- Revenue Management: The asset manager implemented a dynamic pricing strategy, optimized distribution channels, and introduced weekend getaway packages targeting local travelers. This resulted in a 15% increase in occupancy rates.

- Operational Efficiency: The asset manager worked with the hotel's management team to reduce labor costs by implementing flexible staffing schedules and cross-training employees. This approach led to a 20% reduction in payroll expenses.

Outcome: Within 12 months, the Sunset Bay Resort's revenue increased by 30%, and its operating expenses decreased by 25%. The hotel regained profitability and attracted interest from potential buyers, ultimately leading to a successful sale that exceeded the owners' expectations.

Key Takeaway: Effective asset management can significantly improve the financial performance of a distressed hotel, turning it into a valuable asset with long-term growth potential.

Building an Asset Management Plan

An asset management plan is a strategic roadmap that outlines how a hotel will achieve its financial and operational goals. It serves as a guide for asset managers to implement strategies that maximize the property's value and profitability.

1. Assess the Hotel's Current Performance:

- Conduct a comprehensive analysis of the hotel's financial health, operational efficiency, and market positioning. Identify areas of weakness and opportunities for improvement.

2. Develop a Strategic Vision:

- Define the hotel's long-term goals and objectives, including revenue targets, cost-saving initiatives, and capital improvement projects. This vision should align with the hotel's brand, market positioning, and owner expectations.

3. Implement Revenue Management Strategies:

- Create a revenue management plan that includes dynamic pricing, distribution channel optimization, and targeted marketing campaigns. Focus on maximizing RevPAR and occupancy rates.

4. Monitor and Adjust the Plan:

- Regularly monitor the hotel's performance against the asset management plan and make adjustments as needed. This ensures the plan remains relevant and effective in achieving the hotel's goals.

Actionable Steps:

- Conduct a SWOT analysis to identify strengths, weaknesses, opportunities, and threats.

- Develop a clear vision for the hotel's future and align it with financial and operational goals.

- Implement revenue management strategies that drive occupancy and profitability.

- Monitor progress regularly and adjust the plan as needed.

Tips for Selecting the Right Asset Manager

Choosing the right asset manager is crucial for the success of a distressed hotel. The right professional can transform a struggling property into a thriving asset, while the wrong choice can exacerbate existing challenges.

1. Look for Industry Experience:

- Select an asset manager with extensive experience in the hospitality industry, particularly in managing distressed hotels. An experienced professional will have the knowledge and skills to navigate the complexities of hotel operations and financial recovery.

2. Evaluate Their Track Record:

- Review the asset manager's past successes in turning around distressed properties. Ask for case studies or references from previous clients to assess their ability to deliver results.

3. Assess Their Strategic Approach:

- Ensure the asset manager has a clear and strategic approach to asset management. They should be able to articulate their plan for improving the hotel's financial performance, operational efficiency, and market positioning.

4. Consider Communication Skills:

- An effective asset manager should be an excellent communicator who can provide regular updates, reports, and insights to owners and stakeholders. Clear communication ensures that everyone is informed and aligned with the hotel's goals.

Actionable Steps:

- Interview multiple asset managers to evaluate their experience and track record.

- Request case studies or references to verify their success in managing distressed hotels.

- Choose an asset manager with strong communication skills and a strategic approach.

Hotel asset management is a critical component of the recovery process for distressed hotels. By understanding the role of an asset manager, their key responsibilities, and how they can implement strategies to improve financial performance and operational efficiency, hotel owners can effectively navigate the challenges of distress and achieve long-term success. Selecting the right asset manager and building a comprehensive asset management plan are essential steps in transforming a distressed property into a thriving, profitable asset that delivers value for owners, guests, and stakeholders alike.

Implementing Revenue Management Strategies

Revenue management is a critical element in the successful recovery of distressed hotels, helping to optimize profitability by effectively balancing room rates, inventory, and distribution channels. By implementing strategic revenue management techniques, hotels can enhance their revenue per available room (RevPAR), maximize occupancy rates, and improve overall financial performance. This section delves into dynamic pricing, optimizing distribution channels, the role of technology and data analytics, and provides actionable steps and tips for enhancing revenue management.

Dynamic Pricing and Inventory Management

Dynamic pricing is a core component of revenue management that involves adjusting room rates in real-time based on demand, market trends, competitor pricing, and other factors. By implementing a dynamic pricing strategy, hotels can respond to fluctuations in demand, ensuring they capture maximum revenue.

1. Understanding Dynamic Pricing:

- Dynamic pricing allows hotels to adjust room rates based on real-time data, such as occupancy levels, local events, seasonality, and market conditions. This approach ensures that room rates reflect current demand, optimizing revenue potential.

- Practical Example: A hotel in New Orleans adjusted its rates during the annual Mardi Gras festival, increasing prices as demand surged and lowering them afterward. This strategy maximized revenue during peak demand while maintaining occupancy during slower periods.

2. Inventory Management:

- Effective inventory management involves allocating room inventory to different market segments and distribution channels based on demand patterns. This approach helps prevent overbooking or underbooking while ensuring rooms are sold at optimal rates.

- Practical Example: A hotel in Miami segmented its room inventory for corporate travelers during weekdays and leisure guests on weekends. By adjusting inventory allocation based on demand, the hotel maintained high occupancy rates throughout the week.

Actionable Steps for Dynamic Pricing and Inventory Management:

- Monitor market trends, competitor pricing, and local events to adjust room rates in real time.

- Segment your inventory based on demand patterns and allocate rooms to the most profitable market segments.

- Implement a revenue management system (RMS) to automate dynamic pricing and inventory management processes.

Optimizing Distribution Channels

Optimizing distribution channels is essential for ensuring that your hotel reaches the right customers at the right time. Distribution channels include direct bookings through your website, online travel agencies (OTAs), global distribution systems (GDS), and traditional travel agents.

1. Diversifying Distribution Channels:

- A well-diversified distribution strategy ensures that your hotel reaches a broad audience. This includes leveraging OTAs, travel agents, corporate booking platforms, and your direct website.

- Practical Example: A hotel in Las Vegas increased its bookings by expanding its presence on multiple OTAs while also offering exclusive promotions for guests who booked directly through the hotel's website.

2. Managing Channel Costs and Commissions:

- OTAs can be an effective way to reach a wider audience but often come with high commission fees. Balancing OTA bookings with direct bookings can help reduce distribution costs and improve profitability.

- Practical Example: A hotel in New York implemented a loyalty program for guests who booked directly, offering discounts and perks for repeat bookings. This strategy reduced the reliance on OTAs and increased direct bookings by 25%.

Actionable Steps for Optimizing Distribution Channels:

- Analyze the performance of each distribution channel and identify the most profitable ones.

- Negotiate favorable commission rates with OTAs and encourage direct bookings through incentives and promotions.

- Use a channel manager to streamline inventory management across multiple distribution channels, ensuring accurate availability and pricing.

Case Study: A Hotel That Increased RevPAR Through Revenue Management

The Sunset Plaza Hotel, a 200-room property in a popular tourist destination, struggled with low occupancy rates and declining revenue. The hotel's management team hired a revenue manager to implement a comprehensive revenue management strategy, focusing on dynamic pricing, optimizing distribution channels, and using data analytics.

Actions Taken:

- Dynamic Pricing: The revenue manager introduced a dynamic pricing model that adjusted room rates based on demand, seasonality, competitor rates, and local events. This strategy ensured that the hotel's rates were always competitive and aligned with market conditions.

- Optimizing Distribution Channels: The hotel expanded its presence on OTAs, travel websites, and direct booking platforms. The revenue manager also implemented a loyalty program for direct bookings, offering discounts and perks to repeat guests.

- Data Analytics: The hotel utilized data analytics tools to monitor booking patterns, market trends, and competitor pricing. This data-driven approach allowed the revenue manager to make informed decisions about pricing and inventory allocation.

Outcome: Within 12 months, the Sunset Plaza Hotel's RevPAR increased by 35%, and occupancy rates improved by 20%. The hotel's profitability increased significantly, and it became one of the top-performing properties in its market.

Key Takeaway: Implementing a data-driven revenue management strategy that includes dynamic pricing, optimized distribution channels, and data analytics can have a transformative impact on a hotel's financial performance.

Using Technology and Data Analytics

Technology and data analytics play a vital role in modern revenue management, providing valuable insights that inform pricing, inventory management, and distribution strategies.

1. Revenue Management Systems (RMS):

- An RMS automates the process of dynamic pricing, inventory allocation, and data analysis, enabling hotels to adjust room rates and distribution strategies in real time. This technology allows hotels to respond quickly to market changes and maximize revenue.

- Practical Example: A hotel in Chicago implemented an RMS that analyzed booking trends, competitor rates, and market demand. This system allowed the hotel to adjust its pricing strategy daily, resulting in a 15% increase in RevPAR.

2. Data Analytics Tools:

- Data analytics tools provide insights into guest booking patterns, market trends, and competitor pricing. This information helps hotels make informed decisions about pricing, marketing, and inventory allocation.

- Practical Example: A hotel in San Francisco used data analytics to identify that bookings from a particular OTA had lower average daily rates (ADR) than other channels. By adjusting its distribution strategy, the hotel increased its ADR and overall revenue.

3. Integrating Technology Across Operations:

- Integrating technology across various hotel operations, such as property management systems (PMS), customer relationship management (CRM) systems, and channel managers, ensures a seamless flow of data and enhances decision-making.

- Practical Example: A hotel in Dallas integrated its PMS, CRM, and RMS, allowing for real-time data sharing and more accurate revenue management decisions.

Actionable Steps for Using Technology and Data Analytics:

- Invest in an RMS that provides real-time pricing and inventory recommendations.

- Utilize data analytics tools to monitor market trends, competitor pricing, and booking patterns.

- Integrate your PMS, CRM, and RMS to ensure seamless data flow and informed decision-making.

Actionable Steps for Enhancing Revenue Management

- Conduct a Market Analysis: Regularly analyze your hotel's competitive set, local market trends, and demand patterns to make informed pricing decisions.

- Implement a Dynamic Pricing Strategy: Use a revenue management system to adjust room rates based on real-time demand, competitor pricing, and local events.

- Optimize Distribution Channels: Identify the most profitable distribution channels and ensure your hotel has a strong presence on those platforms. Encourage direct bookings through exclusive promotions and loyalty programs.

- Leverage Data Analytics: Use data analytics to gain insights into guest behavior, booking patterns, and market trends. Adjust your pricing and inventory strategies based on these insights.

- Train Staff on Revenue Management

Principles: Ensure that your team understands the importance of revenue management and how their roles contribute to the hotel's financial success.

Tips for Maximizing Profitability

- Monitor and Adjust Pricing Regularly: Regularly monitor competitor rates, market demand, and occupancy levels to adjust pricing strategies in real time.

- Focus on Ancillary Revenue: Look for opportunities to generate additional revenue through upselling, cross-selling, and offering value-added services (e.g., breakfast packages, spa services, or guided tours).

- Utilize Promotions During Low Demand Periods: Offer special promotions, discounts, or packages during periods of low demand to attract guests and maintain occupancy.

- Minimize OTA Commission Fees: Encourage direct bookings through incentives, such as exclusive discounts or loyalty program benefits, to reduce OTA commission expenses.

- Track Key Performance Indicators (KPIs): Regularly track KPIs such as RevPAR, ADR, occupancy rate, and gross operating profit per available room (GOPPAR) to assess the effectiveness of your revenue management strategies.

Implementing effective revenue management strategies is crucial for distressed hotels aiming to improve profitability and regain financial stability. By leveraging dynamic pricing, optimizing distribution channels, utilizing technology and data analytics, and implementing actionable revenue management practices, hotels can significantly increase RevPAR and overall profitability. The case study of the Sunset Plaza Hotel demonstrates the transformative impact that a well-executed revenue management strategy can have on a distressed property's performance. By following the actionable steps and tips provided, hotel owners and managers can maximize profitability, enhance guest experiences, and achieve long-term success in a competitive market.

Cost Control and Expense Management

Effective cost control and expense management are essential for distressed hotels aiming to regain financial stability and improve profitability. By identifying cost-saving opportunities, implementing energy-efficient practices, negotiating favorable vendor contracts, and leveraging technology, hotels can reduce expenses without compromising quality. This section provides an in-depth analysis of cost control strategies, real-world examples, a case study, and actionable steps to help hotels maintain a lean operation.

Identifying Cost-Saving Opportunities

The first step in expense management is identifying areas where costs can be reduced without negatively impacting guest experience or service quality. This requires a thorough analysis of the hotel's operations, expenses, and processes.

1. Analyzing Operational Expenses:

- Conduct a detailed review of operational expenses, including labor costs, utilities, supplies, and maintenance. Look for inefficiencies, redundancies, or areas where expenses are higher than industry benchmarks.

- Practical Example: A hotel in San Francisco discovered that its housekeeping department had excessive overtime expenses. By optimizing staff schedules and implementing more efficient cleaning processes, the hotel reduced labor costs by 15%.

2. Evaluating Food and Beverage Costs:

- Food and beverage (F&B) operations often have significant cost-saving potential. Evaluate portion sizes, inventory management, and waste levels to identify areas for improvement.

- Practical Example: A hotel in Miami reduced F&B costs by implementing portion control measures and negotiating better pricing with suppliers, resulting in a 20% decrease in food expenses.

3. Reviewing Contract Services:

- Many hotels outsource services such as laundry, security, and landscaping. Reviewing these contracts and exploring alternatives can lead to significant savings.

- Practical Example: A hotel in Chicago switched from an outsourced laundry service to an in-house laundry operation, reducing laundry expenses by 30%.

Actionable Steps:

- Conduct a comprehensive review of all operational expenses and identify areas where costs exceed industry benchmarks.

- Explore opportunities to optimize labor costs, reduce F&B expenses, and renegotiate service contracts.

- Implement regular expense reviews to identify and address cost-saving opportunities.

Implementing Energy-Efficient Practices

Energy costs are a major expense for hotels, but implementing energy-efficient practices can significantly reduce utility bills while also contributing to sustainability efforts.

1. Installing Energy-Efficient Lighting:

- Replacing traditional incandescent bulbs with LED or compact fluorescent lighting (CFL) can reduce energy consumption by up to 75%.

- Practical Example: A hotel in Dallas replaced

all incandescent bulbs with LED lighting, resulting in a 20% reduction in electricity costs.

2. Implementing Smart Thermostats:

- Smart thermostats and energy management systems allow hotels to monitor and control heating, ventilation, and air conditioning (HVAC) systems, reducing energy waste.

- Practical Example: A hotel in New York installed smart thermostats in guest rooms, allowing the HVAC system to adjust temperatures based on occupancy. This led to a 15% reduction in heating and cooling costs.

3. Adopting Water-Saving Practices:

- Installing low-flow faucets, showerheads, and toilets can significantly reduce water consumption and costs. Additionally, implementing towel and linen reuse programs encourages guests to conserve water.

- Practical Example: A hotel in Los Angeles implemented a towel and linen reuse program, which saved over 100,000 gallons of water annually and reduced laundry expenses by 10%.

Actionable Steps:

- Conduct an energy audit to identify areas where energy consumption can be reduced.

- Invest in energy-efficient lighting, smart thermostats, and water-saving fixtures.

- Educate staff and guests about energy conservation practices to encourage sustainable behavior.

Case Study: How a Hotel Reduced Expenses Without Compromising Quality

The Sunrise Beach Resort, a 250-room hotel, faced financial distress due to high operational expenses and declining revenue. To improve profitability, the hotel's management team implemented a cost control and expense management program.

Actions Taken:

- Labor Cost Optimization: The hotel cross-trained employees, allowing staff to perform multiple roles and reducing the need for additional hires during peak periods. This resulted in a 15% reduction in labor costs.

- Energy Efficiency Initiatives: The hotel conducted an energy audit and installed LED lighting, smart thermostats, and low-flow water fixtures. These measures reduced energy and water expenses by 20%.

- Vendor Contract Negotiations: The hotel's management team renegotiated contracts with key suppliers, achieving better pricing and payment terms. As a result, the hotel saved 10% on F&B and maintenance supplies.

Outcome: Within 12 months, the Sunrise Beach Resort reduced overall expenses by 25% without compromising service quality. The hotel's improved financial position enabled it to reinvest in marketing and guest experience initiatives, which contributed to a 30% increase in occupancy rates.

Key Takeaway: Implementing cost control strategies, energy-efficient practices, and effective vendor negotiations can significantly reduce expenses, improve profitability, and support a hotel's recovery. Negotiating Vendor Contracts and Agreements

Vendor contracts represent a significant portion of a hotel's expenses, so negotiating favorable terms can lead to substantial cost savings.

1. Conduct a Vendor Audit:

- Review all existing vendor contracts and agreements to identify opportunities for cost savings, such as renegotiating pricing, payment terms, or service levels.

- Practical Example: A hotel in Orlando conducted a vendor audit and discovered that its linen supplier was charging above-market rates. By negotiating a new contract with competitive pricing, the hotel reduced linen expenses by 20%.

2. Consolidate Purchases:

- Consolidating purchases with a single supplier

can often lead to volume discounts, reducing overall costs.

- Practical Example: A hotel chain with multiple properties consolidated its cleaning supply orders with one supplier, resulting in bulk purchase discounts and savings of 15% across all properties.

3. Explore Alternative Suppliers:

- Research alternative suppliers to ensure you are receiving competitive pricing. Use this information as leverage when negotiating with existing vendors.

- Practical Example: A hotel in San Diego switched to a local produce supplier that offered lower prices and fresher ingredients, reducing F&B costs by 10%.

Actionable Steps:

- Conduct a vendor audit to identify opportunities for renegotiating contracts.

- Consider consolidating purchases with a single supplier to access volume discounts.

- Research alternative suppliers to ensure competitive pricing.

Using Technology to Monitor Expenses

Leveraging technology is a powerful way to monitor

expenses, identify inefficiencies, and implement cost-saving measures.

1. Implementing Expense Management Software:

- Expense management software allows hotels to track expenses in real time, monitor spending patterns, and identify areas where costs can be reduced.

- Practical Example: A hotel in Boston implemented an expense management system that provided real-time data on spending across departments. This visibility allowed management to identify excessive spending in F&B operations, leading to a 10% reduction in costs.

2. Using Property Management Systems (PMS):

- PMS platforms offer insights into labor costs, occupancy rates, and room inventory, helping hotels make informed decisions about staffing and resource allocation.

- Practical Example: A hotel in Atlanta used its PMS to identify low-occupancy periods and adjusted staff schedules accordingly, reducing labor expenses by 12%.

3. Monitoring Utility Usage with Smart Technology:

- Smart meters and energy management systems provide detailed information on energy and water consumption, allowing hotels to identify inefficiencies and reduce utility expenses.

- Practical Example: A hotel in Houston installed smart water meters to monitor usage patterns, which helped identify a leak in the irrigation system. By addressing the issue promptly, the hotel reduced water expenses by 15%.

Actionable Steps:

- Invest in expense management software to monitor spending and identify cost-saving opportunities.

- Use PMS data to optimize staffing and resource allocation.

- Install smart technology to monitor utility usage and reduce expenses.

Tips for Maintaining a Lean Operation

Maintaining a lean operation is essential for ensuring long-term profitability and sustainability. Here are some tips to help hotels stay efficient while delivering quality service:

1. Regularly Review Operational Processes:

- Continuously review operational processes to identify inefficiencies and opportunities for improvement. This can involve streamlining workflows, reducing waste, or automating repetitive tasks.

- Practical Example: A hotel in Las Vegas conducted a monthly review of housekeeping processes, leading to the discovery of time-saving techniques that increased productivity by 20%.

2. Train and Empower Staff:

- Invest in training programs that empower staff to identify and implement cost-saving measures. Encourage a culture of cost-consciousness throughout the organization.

- Practical Example: A hotel in Chicago implemented a staff training program that encouraged employees to suggest cost-saving ideas. One suggestion—using reusable cleaning cloths instead of disposable paper towels—saved the hotel $2,000 annually.

3. Monitor Key Performance Indicators (KPIs):

- Regularly track KPIs such as labor costs, utility expenses, and F&B costs to ensure the hotel remains on track with its cost control goals.

- Practical Example: A hotel in Seattle monitored its KPIs monthly and noticed a spike in energy costs. This prompted an investigation that led to repairing a malfunctioning HVAC system, resulting in energy savings.

Actionable Steps:

- Conduct regular reviews of operational

processes to identify areas for improvement.

- Invest in staff training to create a cost-conscious culture.

- Monitor KPIs regularly to track progress and identify cost-saving opportunities.

Effective cost control and expense management are fundamental to the successful recovery of distressed hotels. By identifying cost-saving opportunities, implementing energy-efficient practices, negotiating favorable vendor contracts, and leveraging technology, hotels can significantly reduce expenses and improve profitability. The case study of the Sunrise Beach Resort demonstrates that a strategic approach to expense management can lead to substantial financial improvements without compromising quality. By following the actionable steps and tips provided, hotel owners and managers can maintain a lean operation, achieve long-term financial stability, and position their property for future success in a competitive market. Maintaining a disciplined approach to expense management not only helps distressed hotels recover but also ensures they remain resilient and adaptable in the face of future challenges. By fostering a culture of cost-awareness, leveraging technology, and continuously monitoring financial performance, hotels can optimize their operations, deliver quality guest experiences, and sustain profitability in the long term. As the hospitality industry continues to evolve, mastering cost control and expense management will be a critical factor in achieving ongoing success and competitiveness.

Capital Improvement Planning

Capital improvement planning is a critical component of managing a distressed hotel, as it involves identifying, budgeting for, and implementing upgrades that can significantly enhance the property's value, guest experience, and long-term profitability. Effective planning ensures that capital projects are prioritized based on their potential return on investment (ROI), while also minimizing disruption to ongoing operations. This section explores how to identify and prioritize capital projects, budget for renovations, finance improvements, and develop a long-term asset maintenance plan, supported by real-world examples and actionable steps.

Identifying and Prioritizing Capital Projects

Identifying and prioritizing capital projects is the first step in developing an effective improvement plan. This process involves assessing the hotel's current condition, identifying areas that require immediate attention, and prioritizing projects that will have the most significant impact on the property's value and guest experience.

1. Conduct a Property Condition Assessment (PCA):

- A comprehensive PCA provides a detailed analysis of the hotel's physical condition, identifying areas that need repairs, upgrades, or replacements. This assessment covers key areas such as guest rooms, public spaces, building infrastructure, mechanical systems, and amenities.

- Practical Example: A hotel in Los Angeles conducted a PCA and discovered that its HVAC system was outdated and inefficient. Upgrading this system became a priority, as it would not only improve guest comfort but also reduce energy costs.

2. Prioritize Projects Based on ROI and Guest Experience:

- Projects that have a direct impact on guest satisfaction and can generate the highest ROI should be prioritized. These often include guest room renovations, lobby upgrades, and improvements to amenities such as fitness centers or spas.

- Practical Example: A hotel in Miami decided to renovate its pool area, which was a key attraction for guests. This investment led to a 20% increase in bookings and a boost in average daily rates (ADR) during peak seasons.

3. Consider Regulatory and Safety Requirements:

- Capital projects that address regulatory compliance, safety concerns, or code violations should take precedence. Ensuring that the property meets safety standards is crucial for avoiding potential legal and financial risks.

- Practical Example: A hotel in Chicago identified fire safety violations during an inspection and prioritized installing a new fire sprinkler system to comply with local regulations.

Actionable Steps:

- Conduct a thorough PCA to identify areas needing improvement.

- Rank projects based on their potential ROI, impact on guest experience, and regulatory requirements.

- Create a project timeline that outlines the priority and expected completion dates for each capital improvement.

Budgeting for Renovations and Upgrades

Creating a realistic budget for renovations and upgrades is essential for ensuring that capital projects are completed without exceeding financial constraints. A well-prepared budget considers all associated costs, including materials, labor, permits, and contingency funds.

1. Establish a Detailed Project Scope:

- Define the scope of each capital project, including the specific renovations or upgrades needed, estimated costs, and potential impact on operations. This helps in developing an accurate budget and avoiding unexpected expenses.

- Practical Example: A hotel in New York developed a detailed scope for a guest room renovation project, which included upgrading furnishings, lighting, and bathroom fixtures. By clearly defining the project's requirements, the hotel managed to stay within budget.

2. Include Contingency Funds:

- Allocate contingency funds (typically 10-15% of the total budget) to cover unexpected expenses that may arise during the renovation process.

- Practical Example: A hotel in Atlanta allocated a 15% contingency fund for its lobby renovation project, which proved crucial when unexpected plumbing issues were discovered, allowing the project to continue without financial setbacks.

3. Monitor Expenses Throughout the Project:

- Regularly track expenses against the budget to identify any deviations and make adjustments as needed. This helps prevent overspending and ensures that the project stays on track.

- Practical Example: A hotel in Seattle used expense tracking software to monitor renovation costs in real time, enabling the management team to make cost-saving adjustments and stay within the allocated budget.

Actionable Steps:

- Develop a detailed project scope and estimate costs for each renovation or upgrade.

- Include a contingency fund to account for unexpected expenses.

- Use expense tracking tools to monitor spending and stay within budget.

Case Study: A Hotel's Successful Capital Improvement Plan

The Harbor View Hotel, a 150-room property in a popular coastal destination, struggled with declining occupancy rates and guest satisfaction due to outdated facilities. The hotel's management decided to implement a comprehensive capital improvement plan to revitalize the property and enhance its competitive position.

Actions Taken:

- Identifying Priorities: The management team conducted a PCA and identified the need to renovate guest rooms, upgrade the HVAC system, and enhance the outdoor pool area.

- Budgeting and Financing: The hotel secured financing for the project through a combination of a traditional bank loan and owner equity. A detailed budget was established, with a 10% contingency fund for unexpected expenses.

- Implementing Improvements: The hotel implemented the renovations in phases to minimize disruption to guests, starting with the HVAC upgrade, followed by guest room renovations, and finally, the pool area.

Outcome: Within 18 months, the Harbor View Hotel saw a 30% increase in occupancy rates, and guest satisfaction scores improved by 40%. The property's ADR increased, leading to a significant boost in revenue and profitability.

Key Takeaway: A well-planned and executed capital improvement plan can transform a distressed hotel, leading to increased occupancy, revenue, and guest satisfaction.

Financing Capital Improvements

Securing financing for capital improvements can be challenging, especially for distressed hotels. However, there are several financing options available, including traditional bank loans, government-backed loans, private equity investment, and crowdfunding.

1. Traditional Bank Loans:

- Banks may offer loans for capital improvement projects based on the hotel's creditworthiness, financial performance, and the projected ROI of the improvements.

- Practical Example: A hotel in Chicago obtained a bank loan with a competitive interest rate to finance a lobby renovation, which increased the hotel's ADR by 15%.

2. Government-Backed Loans:

- Programs such as SBA 504 loans offer long-term, fixed-rate financing for major capital improvements, making them an attractive option for hotels that qualify.

- Practical Example: A hotel in Orlando used an SBA 504 loan to finance energy-efficient upgrades, including a new HVAC system and LED lighting, resulting in substantial energy savings.

3. Private Equity Investment:

- Private equity investors may be willing to finance capital improvements in exchange for an equity stake in the hotel. This option can provide access to substantial funding but may require giving up partial ownership.

- Practical Example: A distressed hotel in Los Angeles secured private equity investment to fund a complete renovation, resulting in a successful turnaround and increased profitability.

Actionable Steps:

- Evaluate financing options based on the hotel's financial position and the potential ROI of the capital improvements.

- Prepare a detailed business plan that outlines the expected benefits and financial projections of the capital projects.

- Explore government-backed loan programs and private equity investment opportunities.

Minimizing Disruption to Operations

Renovations can disrupt hotel operations, leading to potential revenue loss and guest dissatisfaction. It's essential to implement strategies that minimize disruption during capital improvement projects.

1. Phased Renovations:

- Implement renovations in phases, focusing on one area at a time to minimize disruption to guests and operations.

- Practical Example: A hotel in Las Vegas renovated its guest rooms floor by floor, allowing the hotel to continue operating at reduced capacity while minimizing the impact on guests.

2. Schedule Work During Low-Occupancy Periods:

- Schedule renovations during off-peak seasons or periods of low occupancy to minimize the impact on revenue and guest experience.

- Practical Example: A hotel in Miami scheduled pool renovations during the winter months when occupancy rates were lower, ensuring minimal disruption to guests.

3. Communicate with Guests:

- Inform guests about ongoing renovations and provide regular updates. Offer alternative amenities or services to compensate for any inconvenience.

- Practical Example: A hotel in San Francisco offered complimentary breakfast vouchers to guests during a lobby renovation, resulting in positive feedback despite the temporary inconvenience.

Actionable Steps:

- Plan renovations in phases to reduce disruption.
- Schedule work during periods of low occupancy.

- Communicate with guests and offer compensatory benefits.

Long-Term Planning for Asset Maintenance

Capital improvements require ongoing maintenance to protect the investment and ensure the property's long-term value. Developing a preventive maintenance plan helps extend the lifespan of renovations and minimizes future expenses.

1. Create a Preventive Maintenance Schedule:

- Develop a maintenance schedule that outlines regular inspections, cleaning, and repairs for key assets, such as HVAC systems, plumbing, and electrical equipment.

- Practical Example: A hotel in New York implemented a preventive maintenance program that reduced unexpected repair costs by 25%.

2. Budget for Future Maintenance:

- Allocate funds for ongoing maintenance in the annual budget to avoid deferred maintenance and costly repairs.

- Practical Example: A hotel in Dallas set aside 3% of annual revenue for maintenance, ensuring that the property remained in excellent condition.

3. Monitor Asset Performance:

- Regularly monitor the performance and condition of key assets to identify potential issues before they become costly problems.

- Practical Example: A hotel in Los Angeles used a computerized maintenance management system (CMMS) to track maintenance tasks, leading to a 15% reduction in equipment downtime.

Actionable Steps:

- Develop a preventive maintenance schedule for key assets.

- Allocate funds for ongoing maintenance in the annual budget.
- Use technology to monitor asset performance and manage maintenance tasks.

Capital improvement planning is a vital aspect of managing distressed hotels, helping to enhance guest experience, increase property value, and drive profitability. By identifying and prioritizing capital projects, budgeting effectively, securing financing, minimizing disruption, and implementing a long-term maintenance plan, hotels can ensure that their investments yield sustainable results. The case study of the Harbor View Hotel demonstrates how a well-executed capital improvement plan can transform a distressed property, leading to increased occupancy, guest satisfaction, and profitability.

By taking a strategic approach to capital improvement planning, hotel owners and managers can revitalize their properties, create a competitive edge in the market, and set the foundation for long-term success. Focusing on high-impact projects, securing the necessary financing, and maintaining the renovated assets ensures that the benefits of capital improvements are realized for years to come. As the hospitality industry continues to evolve, effective capital improvement planning will remain a key driver in maximizing the value and potential of distressed hotel assets.

Monitoring and Reporting Performance

Monitoring and reporting performance are essential practices for managing distressed hotels, ensuring that strategies and initiatives lead to measurable improvements in profitability and operational efficiency. Regularly tracking performance helps identify areas for improvement, maintain accountability, and make data-driven decisions that enhance a hotel's recovery process. In this section, we explore how to track key performance indicators (KPIs), conduct asset reviews and audits, use technology for reporting, engage stakeholders, and maintain accountability.

Tracking Key Performance Indicators (KPIs)

Key Performance Indicators (KPIs) are vital metrics that provide insights into a hotel's financial health, operational efficiency, and overall performance. By regularly tracking KPIs, hotel owners and managers can identify trends, measure progress, and make informed decisions to improve profitability.

1. Financial KPIs:

- Revenue per Available Room (RevPAR): Measures the hotel's ability to generate revenue from its available rooms. RevPAR is calculated by multiplying the average daily rate (ADR) by the occupancy rate. Monitoring RevPAR helps assess the effectiveness of pricing strategies and revenue management.

- Gross Operating Profit per Available Room (GOPPAR): Provides a comprehensive view of a hotel's profitability by considering both revenue and operating expenses. GOPPAR helps identify areas where costs can be reduced or revenue can be increased.

- Practical Example: A hotel in Chicago monitored its RevPAR and identified a trend of lower occupancy rates during weekdays. By offering special mid-week packages for business travelers, the hotel increased its RevPAR by 10%.

2. Operational KPIs:

- Occupancy Rate: Indicates the percentage of available rooms occupied over a specific period. Tracking occupancy rates helps identify trends in guest demand and informs pricing and marketing strategies.

- Labor Cost Percentage: Measures labor costs as a percentage of total revenue, helping hotels identify inefficiencies in staffing and manage labor expenses.

- Practical Example: A hotel in Miami reduced its labor cost percentage by optimizing staff schedules based on occupancy trends, resulting in a 15% reduction in labor expenses.

3. Guest Satisfaction KPIs:

- Guest Satisfaction Score (GSS): Measures guest

satisfaction based on feedback collected through surveys, reviews, or ratings. Monitoring GSS helps identify areas where the guest experience can be improved.

- Net Promoter Score (NPS): Assesses guest loyalty by asking how likely they are to recommend the hotel to others. A high NPS indicates strong guest loyalty, while a low score highlights areas for improvement.

- Practical Example: A hotel in New York monitored its GSS and identified that guests were dissatisfied with slow check-in times. By implementing a mobile check-in system, guest satisfaction improved by 25%.

Actionable Steps:

- Identify the most relevant financial, operational, and guest satisfaction KPIs for your hotel.

- Establish regular intervals for tracking KPIs, such as weekly, monthly, or quarterly.

- Use KPI data to identify trends and inform decision-making.

Conducting Regular Asset Reviews and Audits

Regular asset reviews and audits are crucial for assessing the condition and performance of a hotel's assets, ensuring they contribute to the property's overall success. These reviews help identify areas that require maintenance, upgrades, or cost-saving opportunities.

1. Performing Physical Asset Audits:

- Conduct regular inspections of the hotel's physical assets, such as guest rooms, public areas, HVAC systems, and kitchen equipment, to assess their condition and identify necessary repairs or replacements.

- Practical Example: A hotel in Orlando conducted a quarterly asset audit and discovered that its kitchen equipment was outdated and inefficient. Upgrading the equipment resulted in energy savings and improved kitchen operations.

2. Financial Audits:

- Regular financial audits involve reviewing the hotel's financial statements, expenses, and revenue streams to identify discrepancies, inefficiencies, or opportunities for cost savings.

- Practical Example: A hotel in Los Angeles conducted a financial audit and discovered that it was overpaying for linen services. By renegotiating the contract with the supplier, the hotel reduced linen costs by 20%.

3. Operational Reviews:

- Evaluate operational processes, such as housekeeping, front desk operations, and food and beverage services, to identify inefficiencies and implement improvements.

- Practical Example: A hotel in Dallas conducted an operational review and identified that its housekeeping team could be more efficient by implementing a new cleaning schedule. This change reduced labor costs and improved room turnover times.

Actionable Steps:

- Schedule regular physical, financial, and operational audits to assess asset performance.

- Document findings and develop action plans to address identified issues.

- Monitor the progress of corrective actions to ensure improvements are implemented.

Case Study: How Monitoring Improved a Hotel's Profitability

The Riverside Hotel, a 200-room property, faced declining profitability due to rising expenses and inefficient operations. To address these challenges, the hotel implemented a comprehensive performance monitoring program that tracked KPIs, conducted regular audits, and engaged stakeholders in the process.

Actions Taken:

- Tracking KPIs: The hotel tracked key financial

and operational KPIs, such as RevPAR, labor cost percentage, and guest satisfaction scores. This data revealed that the hotel's labor costs were higher than the industry average.

- Asset Audits: The hotel conducted physical audits that identified outdated equipment in the kitchen, leading to inefficiencies and higher energy costs.

- Implementing Improvements: Based on audit findings, the hotel invested in energy-efficient kitchen equipment, optimized staffing schedules, and introduced a guest feedback program.

Outcome: Within 12 months, the Riverside Hotel's profitability improved by 30%, and guest satisfaction scores increased by 20%. The hotel's RevPAR also increased by 15%, demonstrating the effectiveness of the performance monitoring program.

Key Takeaway: Regularly monitoring performance, conducting audits, and taking corrective actions can significantly improve a hotel's financial performance and guest satisfaction.

Using Technology for Performance Reporting

Technology plays a crucial role in monitoring and reporting performance, providing real-time data and insights that help hotels make informed decisions.

1. Implementing Property Management Systems (PMS):

- A PMS offers a centralized platform for tracking key data, such as occupancy rates, ADR, and revenue. It provides real-time insights into a hotel's performance and enables data-driven decision-making.

- Practical Example: A hotel in Boston used a PMS to track occupancy rates and identified periods of low demand. This data helped the hotel implement targeted marketing campaigns to boost bookings.

2. Using Business Intelligence Tools:

- Business intelligence (BI) tools aggregate data from various sources, such as the PMS, point-of-sale (POS) systems, and guest feedback platforms. These tools generate reports and visualizations that highlight performance trends.

- Practical Example: A hotel in Seattle used a BI tool to analyze its guest feedback and identified that many guests were unhappy with the breakfast offerings. By adjusting the menu based on guest preferences, the hotel improved guest satisfaction scores.

3. Mobile Reporting and Dashboards:

- Mobile reporting and dashboards allow hotel managers to access performance data on the go, enabling quick decision-making and timely responses to issues.

- Practical Example: A hotel in San Francisco implemented mobile dashboards that allowed managers to monitor KPIs in real-time, leading to faster responses to operational challenges and improved efficiency.

Actionable Steps:

- Invest in a PMS and BI tools to track performance data in real time.

- Use technology to generate performance reports and visualizations.

- Implement mobile reporting solutions for easy access to performance data.

Engaging Stakeholders in Performance Monitoring

Engaging stakeholders, including owners, investors, managers, and staff, in performance monitoring ensures accountability and fosters a culture of continuous improvement.

1. Sharing Performance Reports:

- Regularly share performance reports with stakeholders to keep them informed about the hotel's progress and challenges. This transparency helps build trust and encourages collaborative problem-solving.

- Practical Example: A hotel in Las Vegas held

monthly meetings with its management team and owners to review performance reports, discuss challenges, and identify improvement opportunities.

2. Involving Staff in Monitoring Efforts:

- Involve staff in monitoring performance by encouraging them to track KPIs relevant to their roles.

This approach fosters a sense of ownership and accountability.

- Practical Example: A hotel in Chicago empowered its housekeeping team to track room turnover times, leading to increased efficiency and reduced labor costs.

3. Engaging Guests for Feedback:

- Encourage guests to provide feedback through surveys, online reviews, and comment cards. Use this feedback to identify areas for improvement and enhance the guest experience.

- Practical Example: A hotel in Orlando used guest feedback to improve its breakfast service, resulting in higher guest satisfaction scores.

Actionable Steps:

- Share performance reports with stakeholders

regularly.

- Involve staff in tracking KPIs and encourage them to contribute to improvement efforts.

- Collect and analyze guest feedback to identify opportunities for enhancement.

Tips for Maintaining Accountability

Maintaining accountability is crucial for ensuring that performance monitoring leads to meaningful improvements.

1. Set Clear Goals and Objectives:

- Establish clear goals and objectives for each KPI and ensure that all team members understand their role in achieving these targets.

- Practical Example: A hotel in Denver set a goal to reduce labor costs by 10% within six months. By regularly tracking progress and involving staff in the process, the hotel achieved this target.

2. Regularly Review Progress:

- Conduct regular performance reviews to assess progress toward goals, identify challenges, and adjust strategies as needed.

- Practical Example: A hotel in Houston held weekly performance review meetings, which helped the team stay focused and address issues promptly.

3. Recognize and Reward Achievements:

- Recognize and reward team members who contribute to achieving performance goals. This recognition motivates staff and reinforces a culture of accountability.

- Practical Example: A hotel in Atlanta implemented an employee recognition program that rewarded staff for achieving KPI targets, resulting in improved performance across departments.

Actionable Steps:

- Set clear, measurable goals for each KPI and communicate them to your team.

- Conduct regular performance reviews to track progress and make adjustments.

- Implement a recognition and rewards program to celebrate achievements and maintain motivation.

Monitoring and reporting performance are fundamental to the successful recovery and management of distressed hotels. By tracking key performance indicators (KPIs), conducting regular asset reviews, engaging stakeholders, and leveraging technology, hotel owners and managers can gain valuable insights into their property's performance and identify opportunities for improvement. The case study of the Riverside Hotel demonstrates how a comprehensive monitoring program can lead to significant gains in profitability and guest satisfaction.

Engaging staff, owners, and other stakeholders in the monitoring process ensures a shared commitment to achieving performance goals. Regularly reviewing progress, maintaining transparency, and recognizing achievements fosters a culture of accountability and continuous improvement. With the right tools, processes, and strategies in place, hotels can effectively monitor their performance, make data-driven decisions, and ultimately enhance their financial stability and long-term success.

Building a Sustainable Future for Distressed Hotels

Creating a sustainable future for distressed hotels is an ongoing process that requires strategic planning, a commitment to continuous improvement, and proactive measures to adapt to changing market conditions. By developing long-term growth strategies, fostering a culture of improvement, preparing for challenges, and implementing risk management practices, distressed hotels can achieve profitability and stability. This section explores how hotels can build a sustainable future, supported by real-world examples, case studies, and actionable steps.

Developing Long-Term Growth Strategies

Long-term growth strategies are essential for transforming a distressed hotel into a profitable and competitive property. These strategies should focus on increasing revenue, enhancing the guest experience, and differentiating the hotel from its competitors.

1. Diversifying Revenue Streams:

- Relying solely on room revenue can be risky, especially during periods of low occupancy. By diversifying revenue streams through F&B outlets, events, spa services, and ancillary offerings, hotels can create additional sources of income.

- Practical Example: A hotel in Las Vegas expanded its revenue streams by offering event hosting, catering services, and guided tours, resulting in a 20% increase in total revenue.

2. Investing in Technology and Innovation:

- Implementing technology solutions, such as online booking platforms, mobile check-in/check-out, and property management systems (PMS), can enhance the guest experience and streamline operations.

Hotels should also consider investing in data analytics to monitor guest preferences and tailor their offerings.

- Practical Example: A hotel in Miami introduced a mobile app that allowed guests to book services, access room keys, and communicate with staff. This innovation improved guest satisfaction and led to a 15%

increase in repeat bookings.

3. Expanding into New Market Segments:

Targeting new market segments, such as business travelers, families, or eco-conscious guests, can help expand the hotel's customer base and increase occupancy rates. Hotels can create specialized packages or services to attract these segments.

- Practical Example: A hotel in New York identified a growing market for eco-friendly accommodations and implemented sustainability initiatives, such as using energy-efficient lighting and offering locally sourced products. This repositioning attracted environmentally conscious travelers and boosted occupancy by 10%.

Actionable Steps:

- Identify opportunities to diversify revenue streams by offering additional services or amenities.

- Invest in technology solutions that improve guest experience and operational efficiency.

- Research and target new market segments to expand the hotel's customer base.

Fostering a Culture of Continuous Improvement

A culture of continuous improvement is vital for

sustaining long-term success. By encouraging staff to seek opportunities for enhancement, hotels can remain competitive, improve guest experiences, and adapt to changing market demands.

1. Encouraging Employee Feedback:

- Employees are often the best source of ideas for improving operations, as they interact with guests daily. Encourage staff to share their insights, suggestions, and feedback for enhancing the guest experience.

- Practical Example: A hotel in Chicago implemented a monthly "idea-sharing" meeting, where employees could present suggestions for improving operations. This initiative led to numerous cost-saving measures and improved guest satisfaction scores.

2. Regular Training and Development:

- Investing in staff training ensures that employees are equipped with the skills needed to deliver exceptional service. Regular training also helps employees adapt to new technologies, processes, and industry trends.

- Practical Example: A hotel in Los Angeles provided its staff with ongoing customer service training, which resulted in higher guest satisfaction scores and more positive online reviews.

3. Implementing a Continuous Improvement Program:

- Establish a formal program that tracks and implements improvements across various departments. Set specific goals, monitor progress, and recognize employees who contribute to the hotel's success.

- Practical Example: A hotel in Orlando implemented a continuous improvement program that focused on reducing waste, improving energy efficiency, and enhancing guest services. This program resulted in a 15% reduction in operating expenses.

Actionable Steps:

- Create channels for employees to share feedback and suggestions for improvement.

- Offer regular training and development opportunities for staff.

- Implement a formal continuous improvement program with clear goals and metrics.

Case Study: A Hotel's Journey to Sustainable Profitability

The Ocean View Resort, a 180-room beachfront property, struggled with declining revenue, rising expenses, and low occupancy rates. To achieve sustainable profitability, the hotel's management team developed a comprehensive strategy that focused on long-term growth, continuous improvement, and risk management.

Actions Taken:

- Diversifying Revenue Streams: The hotel expanded its offerings by adding a beachfront restaurant, spa services, and water sports rentals. These new services contributed to 30% of the hotel's total revenue within the first year.

- Investing in Technology: The hotel introduced a mobile app that allowed guests to check in, order room service, and book activities. This technology improved operational efficiency and enhanced the guest experience.

- Fostering a Culture of Improvement: The management team implemented a staff recognition program that rewarded employees for suggesting improvements. This program resulted in numerous cost-saving initiatives, such as energy-efficient lighting and reduced food waste.

Outcome: Within two years, the Ocean View Resort increased its RevPAR by 40%, improved guest satisfaction scores by 35%, and achieved sustainable profitability. The hotel's success demonstrated the power of a strategic approach to building a sustainable future.

Key Takeaway: A comprehensive strategy that includes diversifying revenue streams, investing in technology, and fostering a culture of improvement can lead to sustainable profitability and long-term success.

Preparing for Market Changes and Challenges

The hospitality industry is constantly evolving, and hotels must be prepared to adapt to market changes and challenges. Being proactive and flexible is essential for navigating economic downturns, shifts in consumer preferences, and emerging trends.

1. Monitoring Market Trends:

- Stay informed about industry trends, competitor strategies, and consumer behavior by regularly conducting market research. This information can help hotels adapt to changing market conditions and make informed decisions.

- Practical Example: A hotel in Dallas identified an emerging trend of wellness tourism and introduced wellness packages, including yoga classes and healthy dining options. This move attracted a new segment of travelers and increased bookings.

2. Developing Contingency Plans:

- Create contingency plans for potential challenges, such as economic downturns, natural disasters, or pandemics. These plans should include strategies for maintaining operations, preserving cash flow, and minimizing losses during challenging times.

- Practical Example: A hotel in New Orleans developed a contingency plan for hurricane season, which included securing emergency supplies, training staff for evacuation procedures, and implementing flexible booking policies. This preparation minimized disruptions during a major storm.

3. Adapting to Technological Advancements:

- Embrace technological advancements that can improve operational efficiency, guest experience, and marketing efforts. This includes adopting contactless check-in, mobile payment solutions, and data analytics for personalized marketing.

- Practical Example: A hotel in San Francisco implemented contactless check-in technology, which improved guest safety and convenience during the COVID-19 pandemic, resulting in increased guest confidence and bookings.

Actionable Steps:

- Regularly conduct market research to stay informed about industry trends.

- Develop contingency plans for potential challenges and disruptions.

- Embrace technological advancements that enhance efficiency and guest experience.

Implementing Risk Management Practices

Risk management is crucial for ensuring a hotel's long-term stability and success. By identifying potential risks and implementing strategies to mitigate them, hotels can protect their assets and maintain profitability.

1. Conducting a Risk Assessment:

- Identify potential risks, such as financial, operational, legal, and environmental risks, that could impact the hotel's operations. Assess the likelihood and impact of each risk to prioritize mitigation efforts.

- Practical Example: A hotel in Atlanta conducted a risk assessment and identified that its outdated fire safety system posed a significant risk. The hotel invested in an upgraded fire suppression system to mitigate this risk.

2. Implementing Insurance Coverage:

- Ensure the hotel has adequate insurance coverage to protect against potential risks, such as property damage, liability claims, and business interruption.

- Practical Example: A hotel in Boston invested in business interruption insurance, which provided financial support during a temporary closure due to a natural disaster, helping the hotel recover quickly.

3. Establishing Safety Protocols:

- Develop and implement safety protocols to protect guests, employees, and assets. Regularly train staff on safety procedures and conduct drills to ensure preparedness.
- Practical Example: A hotel in Chicago implemented comprehensive safety protocols during the COVID-19 pandemic, including enhanced cleaning procedures and social distancing measures, which contributed to a safe and secure environment for guests.

Actionable Steps:

- Conduct a risk assessment to identify potential risks and prioritize mitigation efforts.

- Ensure the hotel has adequate insurance coverage for various risks.

- Develop and implement safety protocols to protect guests, employees, and assets.

Achieving Long-Term Success and Stability

Achieving long-term success and stability requires a commitment to continuous improvement, adaptability, and proactive planning. By implementing sustainable practices, engaging with guests and employees, and remaining responsive to market changes, hotels can thrive in a competitive industry.

1. Focusing on Guest Experience:

- Continuously seek ways to improve the guest experience, as satisfied guests are more likely to return and recommend the hotel to others.

- Practical Example: A hotel in Seattle regularly surveyed guests to gather feedback on their experience, using this information to make improvements that resulted in a 20% increase in repeat bookings.

2. Maintaining Financial Discipline:

- Monitor financial performance regularly and implement cost-saving measures to ensure long-term profitability.

- Practical Example: A hotel in Denver maintained a strict budget and reinvested profits into capital improvements, which enhanced the property's value and competitiveness.

3. Engaging with the Local Community:

- Build relationships with the local community through partnerships, sponsorships, and events. This engagement enhances the hotel's reputation and attracts local guests.

- Practical Example: A hotel in Austin partnered with
- local businesses and artists to host community events, such as art exhibitions and live music

nights. This initiative not only attracted local residents but also created a sense of community around the hotel, resulting in increased bookings and positive word-of-mouth.

Actionable Steps:

- Prioritize enhancing the guest experience through regular feedback and continuous improvements.

- Maintain financial discipline by regularly monitoring expenses, revenue, and profitability.

- Engage with the local community through partnerships, events, and sponsorships to strengthen the hotel's brand and reputation.

Building a sustainable future for distressed hotels requires a multifaceted approach that focuses on long-term growth strategies, a culture of continuous improvement, adaptability to market changes, and effective risk management practices. As demonstrated by the Ocean View Resort case study, implementing these strategies can transform a distressed property into a thriving and profitable asset.

By diversifying revenue streams, investing in technology, fostering employee engagement, preparing for market challenges, and maintaining financial discipline, hotels can achieve long-term stability and success. Additionally, engaging with stakeholders, prioritizing guest experiences, and building relationships with the local community contribute to a sustainable and competitive business model.

Ultimately, the path to a sustainable future involves being proactive, adaptable, and committed to continuous improvement. By embracing these principles, distressed hotels can overcome challenges, capitalize on opportunities, and position themselves for lasting success in an ever-evolving hospitality industry.

Chapter 11: Conclusion

"The Distressed Hotel Blueprint: A Comprehensive Guide to Navigating Distressed Hotel Assets" has provided an in-depth exploration of the challenges, strategies, and opportunities involved in managing distressed hotels. This journey began with understanding what constitutes a distressed hotel, delving into the root causes of distress, and identifying opportunities for revitalization. As we conclude, it's essential to revisit the key insights from each chapter, which offer a clear path forward for hotel owners, investors, and managers seeking to transform distressed assets into profitable ventures.

Chapter 1: Understanding Distressed Hotels

The foundation of this book lies in defining and understanding what makes a hotel distressed. We explored the signs and symptoms of distress, the impact of economic downturns, mismanagement, and market shifts on a hotel's performance. Real-life examples illustrated how poor financial management or operational inefficiencies can lead to distress, while detailed analysis of the effects on stakeholders provided a broader perspective on the ripple effects caused by distressed hotels in the market. This chapter highlighted that while distress can be daunting, it also presents opportunities for savvy investors and operators to acquire assets at a discount and turn them into successful enterprises.

Chapter 2: Analyzing Distressed Hotels

Analyzing distressed hotels is a crucial step in developing a turnaround strategy. Through comprehensive operational, financial, and market audits, we examined how to assess the financial health, operational efficiency, and competitive positioning of a hotel. This chapter emphasized the importance of identifying the root causes of distress, whether they stem from operational inefficiencies, financial mismanagement, or inadequate marketing strategies. Understanding these root causes enabled investors and hotel operators to create targeted strategies for revitalization. We also discussed the importance of stakeholder interests, risk assessment, and mitigation strategies, highlighting that a thorough analysis is the bedrock of any successful turnaround plan.

Chapter 3: Creating a Turnaround Plan for Distressed Hotels

A well-crafted turnaround plan is the roadmap to recovery for any distressed hotel. This chapter guided readers through establishing goals and objectives, developing a financial restructuring plan, and implementing operational improvements. Through real-life case studies, we saw how clear goal-setting and financial restructuring could lead to successful turnarounds, even in seemingly insurmountable situations. We covered the importance of engaging and training staff, as they are the driving force behind the implementation of any turnaround plan. Finally, we underscored the need for regular monitoring and adjusting the plan to ensure that the hotel stays on track toward recovery.

Chapter 4: Repositioning Distressed Hotels

Repositioning is a powerful tool for transforming a distressed hotel into a competitive asset. This chapter offered insights into identifying repositioning opportunities, developing a new brand identity, and implementing renovations and design elements that reflect the desired image. By focusing on case studies, such as the successful repositioning of a boutique hotel, we demonstrated how a strategic vision and well-executed plan could breathe new life into a property. We also addressed the challenges that arise during repositioning and the importance of evaluating the success of these efforts to ensure long-term sustainability.

Chapter 5: Bank Workouts for Distressed Hotels

Financial distress often necessitates working closely with lenders to navigate bank workouts. This chapter explored the different types of bank workouts, such as forbearance and loan modification, and offered practical steps for preparing and initiating the workout process. We examined negotiation strategies and the role of professional advisors in achieving successful outcomes. The real-world examples demonstrated how hotels could emerge from financial distress through effective communication and collaboration with lenders, proving that bank workouts can be a viable path to recovery when handled with expertise and strategic planning.

Chapter 6: Financing Options for Distressed Hotels

Securing financing is often a critical step in the turnaround process. This chapter examined the various financing options available, including traditional bank loans, government-backed loans, private equity, mezzanine financing, and crowdfunding. Each financing method was analyzed for its pros and cons, providing actionable guidance on how to choose the right option based on the hotel's needs. Case studies illustrated how creative financing solutions helped distressed hotels secure the capital necessary for renovations and repositioning, ultimately setting the stage for successful turnarounds.

Chapter 7: Disposition and Sale of Distressed Hotels

For some distressed hotels, the best option is disposition or sale. This chapter provided a comprehensive guide on how to prepare a hotel for sale, market the asset, negotiate offers, and close the sale. We discussed strategies for maximizing value, handling negotiations, and ensuring a smooth transition of ownership. The chapter also highlighted lessons learned from successful hotel dispositions, offering valuable insights into how to navigate the complexities of selling a distressed asset.

Chapter 8: Bankruptcy for Distressed Hotels

Bankruptcy can be a challenging but sometimes necessary step for distressed hotels. This chapter demystified the bankruptcy process, explaining the differences between Chapter 11 and Chapter 7 proceedings and how to operate a hotel during bankruptcy. Through case studies, we saw how hotels could emerge from bankruptcy stronger and more financially stable. By exploring strategies for developing a reorganization plan and rebuilding after bankruptcy, this chapter provided a roadmap for hotels facing the most severe financial challenges.

Chapter 9: Receivership for Distressed Hotels

Receivership is another pathway for distressed hotels, particularly when court-appointed receivers are involved. This chapter explained the receivership process, how to operate a hotel under receivership, and strategies for exiting the process. We discussed the role of professional advisors in navigating receivership and how to rebuild the hotel's brand and reputation post-receivership. The lessons learned from this chapter underscored that receivership, while complex, can lead to successful turnarounds when managed effectively.

Chapter 10: Asset Management of Distressed Hotels

The final chapter emphasized the importance of asset management in ensuring the long-term success and profitability of distressed hotels. By implementing revenue management strategies, controlling costs, planning capital improvements, and monitoring performance, hotel owners and managers can maximize value and maintain operational efficiency. Building a sustainable future requires a commitment to continuous improvement, proactive planning, and effective risk management practices. The case studies in this chapter demonstrated how asset management practices have transformed distressed properties into thriving, profitable assets.

Final Thoughts

"The Distressed Hotel Blueprint" has provided a comprehensive guide for navigating the complexities of distressed hotel assets, from identifying distress to executing successful turnaround strategies and achieving long-term profitability. The journey of revitalizing a distressed hotel is not without its challenges, but with a clear understanding of the root causes, a strategic turnaround plan, and a commitment to continuous improvement, it is possible to transform a distressed property into a profitable, sustainable, and competitive asset.

Whether you are an investor, hotel owner, manager, or industry professional, the insights, case studies, and actionable steps shared in this book serve as a valuable resource for tackling the challenges of distressed hotel management. By applying the principles and strategies outlined in each chapter, you are equipped to navigate the complex journey of revitalizing distressed hotels and ultimately build a brighter, more sustainable future in the hospitality industry.

* 9 7 9 8 3 3 0 4 5 6 7 1 0 *